THE TWENTIES

Poetry and Prose

20 Critical Essays

Edited by

RICHARD E. LANGFORD and

WILLIAM E. TAYLOR

COPYRIGHT © 1966
EVERETT EDWARDS PRESS, INC.
133 SOUTH PECAN AVENUE
DELAND, FLORIDA

Library of Congress Card Catalog No. 65-12104

COVER DESIGN BY LANIER C. DENSMORE

Printed in the United States of America
by Convention Press, Jacksonville, Fla.
First Printing January, 1966

The editors are grateful to the following publishers, authors, and author's representatives for permission to quote from the works named below:

Anderson, Sherwood, *Winesburg, Ohio.* Copyright 1919, Modern Library; 1919, B. W. Huebsch; 1919, 1956, New American Library; 1958, 1960, Viking. By permission of Viking Press, Inc.

Cather, Willa, *Death Comes for the Archbishop.* Copyright 1927, 1929, 1945, Knopf; 1931, Modern Library. By permission of Alfred A. Knopf, Inc.

Cather, Willa, *One of Ours.* Copyright 1922, 1926, Knopf. By permission of Alfred A. Knopf, Inc.

Cather, Willa, *O, Pioneers.* Copyright 1913, 1933, Houghton, Mifflin Co. By permission of Houghton, Mifflin Co.

Cather, Willa, *The Professor's House.* Copyright 1925, Knopf. By permission of Alfred A. Knopf, Inc.

Crane, Hart, *The Collected Poems of Hart Crane.* Copyright 1933, Liveright. By permission of Liveright Publishing Corporation.

Crosby, Harry, *Collected Poems.* (4 vols.) Edited by Caresse Crosby, Copyright 1931, The Black Sun Press. By permission of The Black Sun Press.

Dreiser, Theodore, *An American Tragedy.* Copyright 1925, Boni & Liveright; 1925, 1929, H. Liveright; 1934, Garden City Publishing Co.; 1949, New American Library; 1946, 1948, 1956, 1962, World Publishing Co.; 1953, 1956, Modern Library. By permission of World Publishing Co.

Fitzgerald, F. Scott, *The Great Gatsby.* Copyright 1925, Charles Scribner's Sons; renewal copyright 1961, 1962, Frances Scott Fitzgerald Lanahan.

Fitzgerald, F. Scott, *Tender Is the Night.* Copyright 1933, 1934, Charles Scribner's Sons; renewal copyright 1961, 1962, Frances Scott Fitzegerald Lanahan.

Hemingway, Ernest, *In Our Time.* Copyright 1930, 1955, 1958, Charles Scribner's Sons; 1925, Boni & Liveright. By permission of Chas. Scribner's Sons.

Hemingway, Ernest, *The Sun Also Rises.* Copyright 1926, Chas. Scribner's Sons; renewal copyright 1954, Ernest Hemingway.

Jeffers, Robinson, *The Selected Poetry of Robinson Jeffers.* Copyright 1938, Random House, Inc. By permission of Random House, Inc.

Pound, Ezra, *The Cantos of Ezra Pound.* Copyright 1935, 1937, 1940, 1948, Ezra Pound. By permission of New Directions.

Ransom John Crowe, *Poems About God.* Copyright 1919 by Holt, Rinehart, and Winston, Inc.; 1947, John Crowe Ransom. Reprinted by permission of Holt, Rinehart, and Winston, Inc.

Stevens, Wallace, *The Collected Poems of Wallace Stevens.* Copyright 1954, 1957, Knopf. By permission of Alfred A. Knopf, Inc.

Williams, William Carlos, *The Collected Earlier Poems.* Copyright 1938, 1951, Wm. Carlos Williams. By permission of New Directions.

Williams, William Carlos, *Selected Essays of William Carlos Williams.* Copyright 1934, 1936, William Carlos Williams. By permission of New Directions.

The poetry of T. S. Eliot and e. e. cummings, and the novels of Sinclair Lewis, by permission of Harcourt, Brace and World, Inc. e. e. cummings' poem "all world's have half-right," copyright 1958 by e. e. cummings; reprinted from his volume, *73 Poems,* by permission of Harcourt, Brace and World, Inc.

Contents

PREFACE

This collection is the beginning of a continuing "bookazine" or "magabook" series which will go on to the Thirties, the Forties, or perhaps back to the Eighties or Nineties, or to any ten-year period in our literary history that seems to have coherence and significance.

These essays are new, previously unpublished commentaries by teachers of American literature; some are more formal than others, but all of them are personal statements about major literary figures of the Twenties. They do not, of course, comprise a definitive treatment of the decade; there are other significant writers of the time than those treated in this volume.

The editors have thought that this kind of informal collection might prove appealing to students, teachers, and interested lay readers of American literature. Much entertaining and informative criticism is offered in college classrooms, every day, and it has been the editors' intention to present some of the best to a wider audience than that of the campus.

Richard E. Langford
William E. Taylor
DeLand, Florida, 1966

INTRODUCTION

In a recent letter to the editors, William Van O'Connor observed that American literature is the most religious literature in the world, but has seldom been examined from that viewpoint. On the other hand, the essays in this volume indicate that, if not religious in a limited sense, the typical American scholar certainly takes a moral approach to literature. Furthermore, it is apparent that these essayists are not only probing their subjects from a moral viewpoint, but find in the literature positive attempts to discover validity for man's existence.

At the center of the discussion, of course, is Eliot's Waste Land, but these Twenties writers refuse to accept the Waste Land as the only reality. The truth is, they actually begin to define the existential position that is the *zeitgeist* of the twentieth century, They see the Twenties as materialistic, shallow, secular. Much of their literature voices despair, but a despair not merely for themselves.

Starting with Dreiser, we have, indeed, a nineteenth century man crying out against an *a priori* Injustice. With Willa Cather, we see what the First World War did: it invalidated her world, eliminating the possibility of her writing about the contemporary scene. For Hemingway, however, the past never even existed, so far as its providing him with a system of moral values is concerned; and Fitzgerald knew that Gatsby's attempt to invoke the past was an error. A *priori* Justice had become an archaism, and the twentieth century was born. There was nothing to object to. Only the Waste Land remained, and the slim possibility that, if a man persisted, he might learn "how to live in it."

The key to learning how to do this was in a new kind of individualism; new, because, as opposed to the individualism of the 1830's, it no longer meant social involvement. Rather, it meant personal integrity, turning inward to a close examination of individual man to find a means to endure. Further, the first compromise with the Waste Land became the beginning of tragedy. Crane, Pound, cummings, Jeffers, Williams, Stevens, even Harry Crosby, sensed this truth and turned to developing a new system of literary symbols and techniques, almost a new language, through which to express their loneliness in a world, which, they discovered, they had not made, but which they loved. If meaning was to be found, it was to be found within, and alone.

Looking back from the second half of the century, understanding what has come to be called the self-fulfilling prophecy, we are no longer surprised at the virtuosity and uniqueness of the writers of the Twenties. We see them now as the creators of the language and symbols with which to fill the Waste Land of the existentialist world. In a very real sense, they created our twentieth century. As Edward Wagenknecht points out, even the most widely read biographer of the Twenties developed a new and personal method.

Of course, not all the writers discussed in these essays, as creative as they are, could discover an entirely viable solution. Hemingway, almost alone, worked his way through to a code, which is expressed not only in his "code heroes," but in their language and the form in which they and his protagonists live. No other writer of this decade sensed so acutely nor delineated so clearly the loneliness, the anguish, and the poignancy of the existential dilemma. As Mr. O'Connor shows in his essay, the other great writer of the first half of this century, William Faulkner, is essentially a writer of later decades, extending Hemingway's code to social relevance, after a soul-searching dialogue with him. It is a long way from Hemingway's "enduring" to Faulkner's "prevailing," but the latter would have been impossible without the former. Personal integrity precedes social responsibility.

There was nothing "lost" about a generation of writers such as these. They gave America—indeed, the world—much of the best and most vigorous literature it has had. The significance of the decade lies not in the gin mills and raccoon coats, but in the hard, anguished, sometimes violent (but always compassionate) prose and poetry these writers produced. Today, still trying to shape a private and public world that is rational, inheriting as he does the social consciousness of the Thirties, contemporary man might do well to read again the literature of the American Twenties. Behind the despair, beneath the whimper, lies the search for personal meaning.

REL
WET

THE TWENTIES

The Slender Fire of Harry Crosby

by SY KAHN

were it not for the abyss
there would be no need for bridges
no need
for sun-triumphant
arches of the soul

HARRY CROSBY

Harry Crosby was a dramatic, spectacular person. In his insistent, sometimes bizarre, individuality, in the general contours of his life, he symbolizes the various moods and the expatriate temper of the American writers of the 1920s. His suicide on December 9, 1929 is an exclamation mark that punctuates the end of an era. Often Crosby seems like a character F. Scott Fitzgerald might have created to symbolize the myths of the twenties. Compared to the glitter of Crosby himself, the romantic extravagance of Gatsby is less luminous, and the dozen suns reflected in Gatsby's golden car less bright than the real sun that Crosby worshipped in his private religion and that flashes in the patterns of sun imagery and symbolism that illuminate his prose and poetry.

When Crosby killed himself he was thirty-one years old, an expatriate editor, publisher, diarist and poet. He and Caresse Crosby, his wife, had founded The Black Press in Paris in 1927 through which they published in limited, attractive editions, most of Crosby's work as well as the work of some of the most exciting and sophisticated writers of the decade: Hart Crane, Ezra Pound, Kay Boyle, Archibald MacLeish, D. H. Lawrence and James Joyce. Through his activities as writer, traveller and publisher, he encountered many artists and richly participated in the life of the American expatriates in France.

Although Crosby's poetry is not unknown in America, his short life, his foreign residence and his small editions of his own work have limited his reputation. However, his work has been appreciated by the special audience his limited editions reached. Shortly after his death the avant-garde *Transition*, a magazine he helped support and edit, devoted part of its June, 1930 issue to memorial essays and poems to Crosby from Hart Crane, Stuart Gilbert, Eugene Jolas (chief editor), Archibald Mac-Leish and Kay Boyle. As further evidence of his impact, T. S. Eliot, Ezra Pound, Stuart Gilbert and D. H. Lawrence wrote introductory essays for the four volumes of Crosby's collected poems published by The Black Sun Press in 1931. The man and his work had caught their interest and imagination and

prompted their serious criticism. Later, Malcolm Cowley *(Exile's Return,* 1951) and Frederick J. Hoffman *(The Twenties,* 1955) discovered in Crosby himself a precise emblem for some of the important themes of the twenties.

Along with other young Americans who served in World War I and who were to become writers, Crosby, as a volunteer ambulance driver, knew violence and death. Death haunted, they wrote poems and novels that reverberated to those dark themes and that sometimes revealed a personal compulsion toward death itself. In this sense Crosby was a war casualty although the rendezvous occurred eleven years after the armistice. Crosby's tense response to the twenties seems to anticipate Fitzgerald's crack-up; his suicide points a shadowy finger at Hart Crane and Ernest Hemingway.

Crosby's *War Letters* to his family reveals his frequent exposure to death, though not yet an obsession with it. Published in 1932 (150 copies) by The Black Sun Press, the letters cover his experiences at the front during 1917-18. One finds a boy eager for adventure, patriotic, family-loving, homesick for Boston and reverently hoping to be a hero. His youthful poses and pronouncements are reminiscent of Stephen Crane's Civil War soldier, Henry Fleming who, like Crosby, dreams of Homeric action and heroic moments. "There's one sure thing," he wrote to his mother in 1918, "there's no finer way to die than to be killed in action." Previously he observed to his father: "That God ordained this War is true beyond the slightest doubt and when it's all over the world will be a finer, cleaner, squarer place. This War is all for bettering men and women." But playing against these bright hopes were the days of boredom, bombardment and butchery. As the war grinds on and friends are wounded and killed, the letters darken in tone and mood and the exuberant voice sobers. He saw gruesome sights of young men torn and suffering, one so mutilated "you could see the insides of his face. He had no jaws, teeth or lips left. His nose was plastered in. Blood was streaming all over." Then on November 22, 1917, while driving his ambulance to the front, Crosby was

1

caught in a heavy German barrage that completely demolished his car. Like the wounded Hemingway on the Italian front, he seems to have momentarily died that day. "Talk about being petrified!" he wrote his sister the next day. "We all nearly passed out." In this landscape of geyser-like explosions, dead horses, overturned wagons and smashed cars he saw a friend fall only a yard away with a piece of shrapnel over the heart. During the barrage-ridden trip back, the same wounded friend "got it again" when a piece of shrapnel passed through the nameplate of the ambulance, missing Crosby "by less than a foot." The shrapnel and the screams inflicted psychic wounds that were to ache through the following decade. Crosby remembered the nightmare on all the other November 22's of his life, and also remembered to toast his friends killed in the war. On November 22, 1927, he wrote in his diary:

Ten years ago today the hills of Verdun and the red sun setting back of the hills and the charred skeleton of trees and the river Meuse and the black shells spouting up in columns along the road to Bras and the thunder of the barrage and the wounded and the ride through red explosions and the violent metamorphose from boy into man.

Despite his war experiences, the youthful Crosby was able to maintain a measure of his youthful idealism and optimism until the war ended, and to keep a bright dream of home. During the war he found the French "decidedly lewd" and abhorred "their rotten low morals" though he came to admire the stubborn French *poilu.* However, France made him "feel prouder and gladder that I'm an American citizen and have a home in the best country going." In 1917 he wrote to his father, "you'll have to get a derrick to get me out of Massachusetts. No more travel for yours truly. 'Home Sweet Home' is my motto." He returned to Boston the hero he had hoped to be. He won both the Croix de Guerre and the Field Service Medal he coveted for "l'évacuation des blessés de la division infanterie avec un sang-froid et un dèvouement admirable."

Home, however, did not prove satisfying. He took a Harvard degree and a job in a bank— he was the nephew of J. P. Morgan. Restless with the constricting life of Boston, with his job, with prohibition and with America—"or is it I have the foxes' fear of being trapped?" he wrote in the first entry of his diary for 1922— he found some release in a series of escapades.

One of my wild days when I threw all care to the wind and drank to excess.

. . . At midnight drove old walrus' new automobile down the Arlington Street Subway until we crashed slapbang into an iron fence. A shower of broken glass, a bent axle, but no one hurt. Still another rotten episode to add to my rotten reputation.

Later in 1922, he happily accepted his family's suggestion that he take a position in the Morgan Bank in Paris.

In Paris the tempo of the decade quickened and he began the crescendo toward death. His remarkable diaries, *Shadows of the Sun,* covering the years 1922-1929, and published in 1929 by The Black Sun Press, richly reveal the decade and catch Crosby himself in a series of glamorous and flamboyant incidents. In August of 1921 there was a race in four hacks down the Champs Élysées to the Ritz Bar; at the Bal des Quartz Arts there were "Innumerable glasses of brandy, and home stark naked in a taxicab!" See him in later years climbing a high, greasy crane the better to witness General Foch's funeral, or during a trip through North Africa and the Middle East experimenting with hashish, poking into dives, getting a sun tattooed on his back one night while tied down by a villainous crew in a boat on the Nile. There were parties at which artists, aristocrats and acquaintances gathered at the Crosbys' Paris home and country place, The Mill, at Ermenonville. One hears in Crosby's diaries, in the prose itself, the jazz and syncopated rhythms of the twenties and the effervescence of white cocktails of gin or champagne. And there were games: fast rides in powerful cars, pet racing whippets, pistols, sometimes with books or paintings for targets, a string of burros for polo and racing kept at Ermenonville, a horse racing game with lead horses and a track that rolled out (Crosby often played alone). There was ritualistic betting at the tracks on horses with cabalistic sun names, finally a purchasing and racing of his own horses, and in the years just before his death, heavier and heavier betting with wondrous wins (he always played to win) but more frequent losses. In 1917 Crosby had written home, "You can't feel like playing games after seeing men dying and suffering untold agonies. After the war however no one will be more enthusiastic over games than H. C." The games and gambling all seem part of a prolonged celebration of survival as well as an obsession with the close call. But only a few brief years before, in December of 1917, Crosby wrote to his mother, "I never want to have any excitement for the rest of my days."

Periodic visits to America served to widen the

distance between Crosby and Boston. The Crosby who could not wait to return after the war, and who denigrated the French, now, a few short years after, made Paris his "City of the Sun," venerated French artists, particularly Van Gogh and Rimbaud, and wrote poems glorifying European life and villifying Boston conservatism and "puritanism" and American materialism. In January, 1924 he noted in his diary:

> The horrors of Boston and particularly of Boston virgins who are brought up among sexless surroundings, who wear canvas-drawers and flat-heeled shoes and tortoiseshell glasses and who, once they are married, bear a child punctually every nine months for 5 or 6 years and then retire to end their days at the Chilton Club. Christ what a narrow escape, far narrower than escaping the shells at Verdun.

Eighteen months later, during a visit to America, he recoiled from billboard splattered America, from "an atmosphere of frustration, disillusion" and "smug satisfaction." He found "no contemplation, no melancholy, no imaginativeness" and always the same uninteresting people. He shaped his outrage into a tirade called "Target For Disgust" which appeared in his volume of poems *Mad Queen.*

I curse you Boston
  City of Hypocrisy
  City of Flatulence
    (with your constipated laws)
  Unclean City
    (with your atlantic monthlies
    and your approaching
                  change of life)
I curse you
in the name of Aknaton I curse you
in the name of Rimbaud I curse you
in the name of Van Gogh I curse you

The tirade mounts in fury and invective. Obviously it took less than a "derrick" to move Crosby from Massachusetts to Paris.

Lean, active and handsome, looking something like the Charles Lindbergh he admired, he made a dazzling figure with his deeply tanned skin, his gold necklace and black cigarettes, his red nail polish and black gardenia. To the people on the pavement, Crosby was a brighter Richard Cory who "glittered when he walked."

" 'Yes', and never 'no' was our answer to the fabulous twenties," wrote Caresse Crosby in *The Passionate Years.*

We built a gossamer bridge from war to war, as unreal as it was fragile, a passionate 'passerelle' between a rejected past and an impossible future. Perhaps no such span of years (only two whizzing decades) have ever so amazed and disturbed a generation. Harry Crosby and I briefed the pattern of our times and, unknowingly, we drew the most surrealistic picture of them all.

In the figure and career of Crosby one is often reminded of F. Scott Fitzgerald's Dick Diver in *Tender Is the Night.* Like Diver, Crosby was attractive and attracting. His energy drew around him many diverse people and held them in precarious but graceful configurations; he had kindness, generosity and sympathy and scorned sham and hypocrisy. The twenties exhausted Diver, one may remember; he could not hold the parts of his world together and he could not prevent his own dissolution or renew drained psychic and physical energies. There are parallels in Crosby—the nerves strung tighter than the tightrope he walked, the erratic attempts to find balance, and the fall. Both Crosby and Diver believed in perpetual youthfulness and inexhaustible personal energies. Time defeats these notions. Diver, enervated, fades away into the small towns of New York. Crosby, however, was determined that for him life would not end with a whimper but a bang; he planned to jump from a plane on October 31, 1942. The end came sooner.

In the fall of 1923 Crosby wrote in *Shadows of the Sun:* "My mind has emerged from its midsummer lethargy and I feel creative. . . . But self-expression is cramped in a bank, it needs the forest of freedom if it would flourish. I want to be an individual and move in a sphere of my own. I am in revolt." He gave up his job in the Paris bank and declared himself a poet, much to the amazement of his family and the applause of his wife, herself a poet.

During these Paris years he embarked on a rigorous reading and writing schedule. He made many literary and esoteric discoveries in the 10,000 volume library he inherited from a cousin, Walter Berry, and more and more he interested himself in the literature of his own decade, particularly the experimentalists such as Cummings, Eliot, Crane, Lawrence and Joyce. He discovered the French Imagists, the religious mystics, and was fascinated by all religions and literatures that dealt with the sun. In the last year of his life he wrote, "I am influenced most . . . by Rimbaud, by Blake, by Aknaton, by Van Gogh, by Marlowe."

Along with his dedication to literature he evolved an individual, mystical religion whose

3

God and central symbol was the sun. It is something of a mystery, and something of a mystical experience too, one suspects, how Crosby came to his fierce belief. Nothing in the *War Diaries* gives any evidence of it, though there are a number of conventional references to God. However, by 1922 and the earliest entries in *Shadows of the Sun* his faith is well-developed. All his experiences, with increasing intensity, are focused on the sun; all the spokes of his life run surely to that hub.

Poetry and religion were his fortress against a world that disenchanted and outraged him. The war raped him of youthful illusions; the unrolling decade revealed many hollow men. He had decided in 1923 that "poetry is religion" and that "the sun is the only thing that does not disillusion." Two years later he added, "art is the only clean thing on earth except holiness." Many times in his diary of the decade he elaborated these ideas. In June, 1925 he wrote, "The gorgeous flame of poetry is the moat and beyond, the monstrous (menstrous) world, the world that must be beaten back, the world that is always laying siege to the soul." Inside himself he found glowing flowers, "but outside and all around weeds weeds weeds." By 1927, life was "a ladder of disillusionment," and "the higher one climbs the greater the disillusion. But beyond all ladders thunders the Sun." Visionaries can laugh at the ordinary world, he wrote in "Fire-Eaters" from his volume *Transit of Venus*, "Because we devour the fire / Others have dreamed."

All during the twenties Crosby experimented with a variety of unconventional forms and with a language to express his own vision of reality. He devised a diction and imagery suitable to the mysteries of his religion and expressive of the ecstacies of his experience. Like all mystic poets, he sought a language of purified perception. His poems, generally compact and compressed, employ a vocabulary of fire and explosion and images of light and gold, each poem a gesture towards, a prayer to, the Sun itself. All were preparations for the final act of immolation. Like Van Gogh, wrote Crosby, "he burned with the desire to see the Sun-God face to face to absorb himself forever in his implacable flame."

Crosby's mysticism and ecstatic vision is elaborately expressed in *Torchbearer,* a collection of his prose poems. "I Climb Alone" exemplifies the particular vibrancy of Crosby's work and suggests the ultimate inexpressibility of his experience and quest.

I climb alone above the timber line to
burn with the setting sun. She is my
paramour. Below in the valley the

shadows lurk like a pack of wolves. . . .
And the sun sets. And I leave my flock
of stars and wander all night in quest
of the lost sun. I am impatient desperate
mad. . . . At last there is a filament of
gold. There is the color of the dawn.
There is the rising sun burning with
gold. . . . I feel my eyes filling with
fire. I feel the taste of fire in my mouth.
I can *hear* fire.

When he is most excited, Crosby links fiery metaphors and achieves an ecstatic effect, as in these lines from "103°": "My tongue is a firebrand. My body is the heat of a hundred hells. My eyes are red coins of burning coal. My hair is a forest fire. There is the roar of a conflagration. Is it the echo of the sun?"

The most frequent symbol for the soul in Crosby's work is the arrow. His poem "The Arrow" most directly expresses a crucial religious concept.

A long arrow of gold within is the slender fire which is the spirit—vices virtues
pleasures pains enemies friends fears
hopes—nothing but particles of dust
upon the impenetrable outer surface of
the arrow—these will be blown off as
the arrow shot from the archer of death
carves its track through the wind until
it strikes the target of the Sun. Thus
fire becomes fire. Sun-Infinity.

In his "Notes" at the end of *Torchbearer,* Ezra Pound observed that "the mystic tradition . . . is dependent on direct perception, a 'knowledge' as permanent as the faculty of receiving it." As these poems indicate, Crosby attempts to recreate the intensity of that perception, to give us the "slender fire" of the soul. In other poems Crosby makes the sun a phallic instrument that quickens the enervated spirit. As with many of his American contemporaries, he attempted to shock the bourgeois and outrage American "puritanism" by sexual and erotic imagery. Ultimately, however, this imagery is also a part of his special religious purpose: to symbolize mystical union. Pound read Crosby sympathetically because Crosby's poems answered to Pound's own outrage against the commonplace, against dull and dulled perception and a world of compromise; he also understood the mystical thrust of Crosby's work: "There is more theology in this book of Crosby's than in all the official ecclesiastical utterance of our generation."

It was Crosby's ability to record his exact emotions and his particular way of apprehending life that most attracted T. S. Eliot. In his introduction to Crosby's *Transit of*

Venus, Eliot wrote, "What interests me the most, I find, is his search for a personal symbolism of imagery." This is a "right and difficult method," continued Eliot, and he approves of Crosby's seeking "a set of symbols which should relate each of his poems to the others, to himself, rather than using in each poem symbols which should merely relate it to other poems by other people." In this observation Eliot laid a finger on a cardinal characteristic of Crosby's work and a rubric for American poetry of the twenties. Poetry as personal statement, the shape of vision, is what Crosby essayed.

Crosby did not abandon mysticism in his curious volume, *Mad Queen,* and subtitled "Tirades," but it was mysticism become explosive and destructive. In this volume the poet-worshipper, outraged by a shoddy world, in recoil from the abyss, becomes the assassin who seeks a new, chaste and chastened world cleansed by fire. In "Assassin" he announces:

> I roar with pain
> black-footed ferrets disappear into holes
> the sun tattooed on my back
> begins to spin
>   faster and faster
>   whirring whirling
> throwing out a glory of sparks
> sparks shoot off into space
> sparks into shooting stars
> shooting stars collide with comets
>   Explosions
>   Naked Colors Explode
>   into
>   Red Disaster

One feels in these poems Crosby's attempt to accomplish in poetry what Van Gogh had on canvas. The whole book is driven and obsessed; the poet is the sunstruck agent of an angry God. In *Mad Queen* Crosby recommends a sun-inspired chaos to burn away a dreary and decayed civilization, but he also turns the destructive rays of the sun upon himself. "I burn to gold / fierce and unerring as a conquering sword / I burn to gold / . . . and leave to them the / burning of the dead."

In his introduction to Crosby's *Chariot of the Sun,* D. H. Lawrence saw the poet not as the agent of chaos, the assassin that murders the world, but rather as the rare poet who reveals the "live chaos" of God. "Man fixes some wonderful erection of his own between himself and the wild chaos, and gradually goes bleached and stifled under his parasol. Then comes a poet, enemy of convention, and makes a slit in the umbrella; and lo! the glimpse of chaos is a vision, a window to the sun." Perhaps it is Lawrence's reading of Crosby that

is the most feeling of all his critics. Certainly Crosby felt an affinity to Lawrence. He solicited "The Sun" from Lawrence and brought it out in a Black Sun edition, and then, in his flamboyant way, paid Lawrence in illegal twenty dollar gold pieces, symbolic of the sun. Lawrence had a direct influence on Crosby's poetry too. In *The Passionate Years* Mrs. Crosby recalls, "It was on our return from Egypt that Harry wrote most of "Mad Queen"—he had been reading *The Plumed Serpent* and he was in a spirit of tirade." In both writers' work one finds parallels: the reinvigoration of man by the forces of nature and sex, the restlessness with a complacent world and the thrust of mysticism.

Though Crosby's poetry is luminous with his imagery of light, running through his metaphors of gold is the dark theme of death. Nietzche's "die at the right time" is a refrain in both the diaries and the poetry. He saw suicide as a final refuge for ravaged nerves and as a triumph of imagination over instinct; most of all he was impatient for that ultimate union with the Sun. There are a dozen references in his work to Van Gogh who for Crosby was the "example of triumphant individuality" and "the painter of that Sun which consumed him and was responsible for his final madness and suicide. A Sun-Death into Sun!"

The last year of his diary reveals both frenzy and ecstacy. The intensity of his feeling is reflected in his accelerated activity: editing six books at once for the Black Sun Press, editing for *Transition,* heavier drinking and gambling and bizarre gestures. In September, 1929 he wrote:

> sat in front of the fire drinking champagne . . . until I got quite tight (second bottle of champagne) and I danced and shouted and branded myself with burning coals from the fire (Fanatic) and at last fell asleep under the zebra skin in the corner by the cider barrel.

Then there were flying lessons. In flying he satisfied at once his interest in mechanics, his fascination with speed and his arrowing toward the sun. A few days after burning himself he observed:

> I do know how to fly in the final and real sense of the word that is in the Soul Flights to the Sun but now I want to learn also in the Lindberghian sense of the word and I swear on my gold necklace (O Sorcery O Fire O Sun) to add to my names of lunatic and lover and poet the name of aviator for as Shakespeare would say if he were alive these

four names "are of imagination all compact" and today I read in the White Devil what must be for me prophetic. "Of all death the violent death is best For from ourselves it steals ourselves so fast The pain once apprehended is quite past."

Mad Queen, published the year of his death, also reveals his heightened reactions. In the poem "Sun-Death" all the death-impelling themes are brought together. It is best to die "when your entire life, when your soul and your body, your spirit and your senses are concentrated, and reduced to pin-point, the ultimate gold point, the point of finality, irrevocable as the sun, sunpoint, then is the time. . ." And the piece closes: "we, having set fire to the powderhouse of our souls, explode suns within suns and cataracts of gold into the frenzied fury of the Sun, into the madness of the Sun, into the hot gold arms and hot gold eyes of the Goddess of the Sun."

Caresse Crosby writes that on December 9th, during a Christmas visit to New York, Crosby said to her, " 'Give me your hand, Caresse, our window is wide open. Let's meet the sun death together.' " But Caresse Crosby, who "loved to say 'yes' " was not ready to say it to death. " 'Why, Harry, when we have so much to live for?' " And he answered, " 'That is why, Caresse. There is too much. I cannot endure it all.' He spoke with anguish." Later the next day, leaving no note—what need for a note when the message is loud in his poems and diary—he and a young Boston woman, "The Youngest Princess" of the diaries, were found in a studio apartment, each with a bullet in the head. E. E. Cummings wrote:

> 2 boston
> Dolls; found
> with
> Holes in each other
> 's lullaby.

Both Malcolm Cowley and Frederick Hoffman see Crosby's life and death as a parable of the twenties. "His death," wrote Cowley, "which had seemed an act of isolated and crazy violence, began to symbolize the decay from within and the suicide of a whole order with which he had been identified." Hoffman sees in Crosby's death the logical conclusion of war shock and nightmare. The suicide is "the final act of adjustment" to the horrors of the war. A reading of Crosby's poetry deepens these images of Crosby and further clarifies the motives and meanings of his life. It helps us to understand why Ezra Pound saw in Crosby's suicide a death from excess vitality and his vote of confidence in the cosmos."

In the poet's fascination with speed, with violence and with death, in his search for a personal idiom, in his experimentation with form and the syncopated rhythms of the jazz age, he is part of the American expatriate temper of the twenties. He further identifies himself with the writers of his time by his impatience with and rebellion against the old order, the traditional religious sects, the pre-war America, isolated, innocent and often inhospitable to the artist. His cry against "puritanism" is part of the chorus of youthful war-whoops directed at America from France by the rebellious expatriate writers. Like each of his longer-lived, more talented and illustrious contemporaries, he brought to American literature of the twenties some special qualities.

In his life, work and death Crosby pursued an unusually intense, personal religious vision. His poetry, sometimes clumsy in form and banal of phrase, but when successful, swift, compact and compressed, articulates his mysticism and is unlike the work of his contemporaries. His books attempt to infuse and illuminate our perceptions, to excite us, in the same way that the sun fired his spirit.

Many rich voices were heard in the twenties. Crosby's was not the loudest nor the most subtle, but it was a special and impassioned voice. It chants prayers to the sun; it sings of mysteries and prophecies. Such voices have been rare in American poetry. The voice gains in depth and intensity when one considers Crosby's total work. Pound reached the same conclusion in reviewing Crosby's poetry. "I do not mean this as a slight compliment," he wrote. "It is true of a small minority only."

Crosby's special perceptions reveal to us a level of reality not readily accessible to American poets. In order to gain these perceptions it was necessary for him to disdain and to defy conventional success and sentiment and to escape entrapment by powerful social forces. He is committed to singularity. Powerful tensions in his work result from our sense of the poet poised between the forces of infinity and the abyss, between the fierce, solitary sun and the threat of darkness. From that precarious position he speaks to us of what he feels and knows before his final leap toward the Sun.

How to Read a Canto

by MAX HALPEREN

By 1920, Ezra Pound—the stormiest literary hurricane of the twentieth century—had already led many lives: he had passed through a number of poetic phases; he had criticized art, music, literature, and society; he had been and was a "foreign correspondent" for little magazines like *Poetry* and *The Little Review;* he had helped Yeats redirect his poetry and had beaten the drums for Eliot and Joyce; he had translated Provencal and Chinese poetry and Japanese No plays; he had started or touted literary movements like imagism and free verse, and had passed beyond them. And he had a number of other lives to go, several of which would culminate in a decade in St. Elizabeth's—where he continued writing, criticizing, contributing, translating, touting—and trying to help any young poet who would listen.

As a poet, however, this one-man world had already committed himself to the poem that would take the rest of his life and that would integrate or at least incorporate the entire skein of experience and idea that is Ezra Pound. When he began *The Cantos* in 1917, he described it in a letter as a "new long poem (really L O N G, endless, leviathanic)." He could scarcely have known just where his life, and therefore the poem, would lead him, but he certainly was aware of the ambitiousness of his project. It was and remains his major bid for poetic immortality. No wonder, then, that Pound, far from wrapping himself in a cloak of assumed indifference, has expressed concern more than once that his poem be properly understood, and has lashed out bitterly when he felt he was being misunderstood. Yeats thought he was being helpful when, in *A Packet for Ezra Pound,* he repeated what Pound had told him about the fugal nature of the poem. "If Yeats knew a fugue from a frog," Pound told one of his correspondents, "he might have transmitted what I told him in some way that would have helped rather than obfuscated *his* readers." Two years later, Pound was even more exasperated: "God damn Yeats' bloody paragraph. Done more to prevent people from reading Cantos for what is *on the page* than any other smoke screen."

"Reading . . . for what is *on the page.*" Is it possible to do so? The smoke screen created by both attackers and defenders of the poem seems thick indeed. "Doubtless," wrote one critic,

the reader will already have observed that one of the things I have asked of Mr. Watts is that he should be familiar

with page 38 of the *ABC of Reading;* for unless the critic happens to know that page, he can scarcely be asked to understand Canto LXXV (though with the hint in line 9 a writer with the ability to read music and a knowledge of fifteenth-century musical symbology might possibly puzzle it out alone).

Thick indeed. And is it possible to read for what is on the page despite the inherent difficulties of the poem itself, seeing it neither as "rambling talk" (Allen Tate) nor as a set of obscure statements that can be understood only in relation to their sources?

I think that with a minimum of help—the sort of help provided by very occasional reference to the *Annotated Index to the Cantos of Ezra Pound*—it is quite possible to read the poem as a poem, provided one gives it the same attention one gives any difficult poem, being alive to the tone of each line, awake to its implications, aware of its context. If that is done, one will find, I think, that documents, translations, descriptions, personal comments—all may be read as images, directly reflecting the poet's state of mind or implying his attitude toward what he is presenting.

The following, then, is an experiment in reading, concentrating on the opening cantos. If the poem is at all ascertainable on its own merits, then surely these cantos are acid tests. Rewritten and reshuffled, they can scarcely be read as part of a narrative design. Canto I appeared at the end of Canto III in the first published draft. Canto II, with a different opening, was published originally as Canto VIII. Canto VI has been cut to half its original size. Comment that might have explained some of the material has been cut away. Pound himself admitted privately that some of the early material was presented in a manner "perhaps too enigmatically and abreviatedly. I hope, heaven help me, to bring them into some sort of design and architecture later."

As far back as 1912, Pound wrote: "One wants to find out what sort of things endure, and what sort of things are transient; what sort of things recur. . . ." We may take *The Cantos* as the record of Pound's attempt to "find out." It is, then, a quest. And Pound, wishing to indicate something of his own long poetic journey, begins Canto I with a translation from the *Odyssey* that runs for two pages:

And then went down to the ship,
Set keel to breakers, forth on the godly sea. . .

7

It is a long journey. [Through dark fog and] over "deepest water," the ship moves on its strange voyage, coming at last to the dread shores of Hades. Odysseus and his men need advice on how to get home, and they have been told that only the ghost of the prophet Tiresias can help them. On the shores of Hades they pray, pour libations, sacrifice sheep. At last Tiresias arrives, drinks the sheep's blood, and tells Odysseus what lies in store for him. Then come the rest of the "impotent dead" to drink the blood, be momentarily revived, and tell their tales.

Suggesting an artistic continuity from Homer's time until now, the ancient epic serves as a gateway to Pound's modern epic, for Pound also is about to set out on a journey through mist and over deep water—though his will be an intellectual journey; and Pound also will attempt to inject blood into the ghosts of the past so that they may speak to and comment on the present. "Nothing is new," Pound wrote in the thirties, "and all good is renewal." In fact, Canto I may be taken as an example of such renewal, for Pound has translated, not directly from the Greek, but from a Renaissance Latin pony by the Andreas Divus cited at the end of the Canto, and has employed, not modern English, but the " 'Seafarer' metre, or something like it." The implication is that despite (or because of) these transformations, Homer's book of the dead retains its muscle.

But to read the Canto as though it already incorporated or even implied much about the rest of the long poem is, I think, to miss what is on the page. For the moment, the Homeric vision has renewed itself in Pound's mind, as, presumably, it did in Divus'. But after Tiresias speaks, the vision fades, perhaps because of limitations inherent in the material itself—the translation does, after all, suggest a certain remoteness from our own time; or because of limitations in the experience of the poet him-self—he does, after all, have a long journey to make. In the *Odyssey*, the prophet's advice is quite detailed, but in Pound's version it is cut to a very brief statement that provides no ad-vice at all. In his search for what is recurrent and what is permanent, this new Odysseus will have no Tiresias to guide him. "Lie quiet Divus," says Pound toward the end of the Canto to the Latin translator of the *Odyssey*. "I mean, that is, Andreas Divus." The spell is broken. The excitement of those primitive rituals on the shores of hell has given way to a matter-of-fact comment. And Odysseus ceases to speak in the first person:

And he sailed, by Sirens and thence outward . . .

There are, then, to be no guides to the realm of the permanent. But there are many Scyllas and Charybdises—several of which are singled out in Cantos II and III.

Though sailing into the past over "deepest water," Pound has always denied any senti-mental yearning for the bygone: "It may suit some of my friends to go about with their young noses pointing skyward, decrying the age and comparing us unfavorably to the dead men of Hellas or of Hesperian Italy . . . But I, for one, have no intention of decreasing my enjoyment of this vale of tears by under-esti-mating my own generation." As far as he is concerned, he seeks only what is permanently alive, or what can be made to live. But that is scarcely the only concern; there is also the problem of presenting the past in such a way that it, like Tiresias, speaks directly to the living. For living ideas may easily be stifled by dead forms, by outmoded styles and methods, by words that do not quite suit the material, by minds unable to absorb a new viewpoint. Thus, the need to break old forms and to disrupt old mental grooves, and thus Pound's concern with it. Precisely that need lies at the heart of Canto II.

The point is made rather simply in the opening lines of the Canto:

Hang it all, Robert Browning,
there can be but the one "Sordello."
But Sordello, and my Sordello?
Lo Sordels si fo di Mantovana.

The direct address to Browning suggests a sense of kinship and implies something of an internal struggle—as though Pound had toyed with the possibility of adapting Browning's method and had, regretfully, discarded it. It suggests also, I think, something of the joyous energy flowing into the young poet as he finds it possible—even necessary—to strike out on his own. Much as he might admire *Sordello*—and we have evidence aplenty that he did—Pound cannot simply rewrite the earlier poem either in form or in content. But Sordello as a person —no longer within quotation marks, and thus no longer a literary character—can, of course, be used again; there can be more than one version of the thirteenth-century Italian trouba-dor, and Pound's version, "my Sordello," will necessarily be different from Browning's. Now, as though beginning a fresh appraisal, Pound records the biographical snippet: "the Sordellos came from Mantua."

These lines take us, then, from a fixed form, *Sordello,* to a new form and a fresh look at the source materials. The following lines reverse the order: an ancient image of life and life's energies, the elemental sea itself, is stirred up;

8

however, the result is nothing but a wave running in a beach-groove, reanimating an ancient theme:

> So-shu churned in the sea.
> Seal sports in the spray-whited circles of cliff-wash,
> Sleek head, daughter of Lir,
>   eyes of Picasso
> Under black fur-hood, lithe daughter of Ocean;
> And the wave runs in the beach-groove:
> "Eleanor,

The meaning of these lines is probably clearer in the first version of this Canto, which was prefaced by a rather heavily ironic image of passion and inspiration in bondage to the past:

> Dido chocked up with tears for dead Sichaeus;
> And the weeping Muse, weeping, widowed, and willing,
> The weeping Muse
> Mourns Homer,
> Mourns the days of long song.

Several lines later Pound tells us that

> Tyro to shoreward lies lithe with Neptunus
> And the glass-clear wave arches over them;
> Seal sports in the spray-whited circles of cliff-wash,
> Sleek head, daughter of Lir,
>   eyes of Picasso

and the rest follows.

Three stages seem to be indicated in the earlier version: farthest out to sea, the sea-god; closer, the circles of cliff-wash; finally, the beach-groove. After the images of weeping Dido and the widowed Muse, the appearance of Neptune indicates a new infusion of elemental energy, possibly a new vision. The present tense implies that such energy is always present, always recreative. As we move closer to the shore-line, we see evidence of the creative energies of the sea, first in a physical embodiment: "Seal sports. . . ." But those energies are also mental ("sleek head") and artistic ("eyes of Picasso/Under black fur-hood"); these too are creatures, "daughters," of the elemental natural forces represented by the sea god, whether he is named Lir (Irish) or Ocean (Greek).

And yet, when the fresh spurt of energy comes ashore, when the creative impulse spends itself, it may well result in nothing more than the repetition of an old idea, it may move in an old groove—the theme of destructive beauty. There is renewal here, but of a sort that deadens instead of enlivening. The Greek epithets describe Helen as ship-and city-destroying (derived from Aeschylus' *Agamemnon*—a fact which may content some but which is quite beside the point). Eleanor, however, is not simply another Helen; she is, as Canto VI describes her, also "domna jauzionda," the joyous lady capable of attracting and encouraging the troubador elite. Thus Pound restates the need to break old forms and to look at materials afresh. The beach groove ignores differences; it would lose whatever is unique in Eleanor.

In the present version of the Canto, So-shu (whose identity has never been settled) clearly replaces Neptune as the instigator of fresh power. The shift from Mantua to China in itself suggests an infusion of new materials and forms. Churning in the sea, So-shu is in touch with the infinite and the elemental; by stirring, he creates new combinations. But even his Oriental waves slip into the old Occidental groove. It is difficult to break an old habit of mind.

The problem is scarcely a new one; it was discerned and described by Homer. He might have been blind, but his ear was precise, his technique certain:

> And poor old Homer blind, blind as a bat,
> Ear, ear for the sea-surge, murmer of old men's voices.

He could fix both the surge of new energies already noted in the Canto and the fears of old men. We are given the speech of the elders of Troy as they watch Helen on the wall:

> Moves, yes she moves like a goddess
> And has the face of a god
>
> . . . .
>
> And doom goes with her in walking,
> Let her go back to the ships.

This, of course, is another version of the beach-groove. Beyond, the sea's energies forever enter man:

> And by the beach-run, Tyro
>   Twisted arms of the sea-god,
> Lithe sinews of water . . .

But on the beach no new groove is carved; there is only a "Quiet sun-tawny sand-stretch."

Even the assurance and energy provided by the vision of a god may be lost. It is possible to be certain of an immortal truth, yet be unable to convince others. In fact, a group faced with the same experience may see it quite differently from the one perceptive visionary. In Canto II, the god Bacchus appears to a sea-captain. Far more than Ovid, the source of the tale, Pound stresses the certainty of the vision. Twice the captain repeats:

I have seen what I have seen.

He insists:

Aye, I, Acoetes, stood there,
    and the god stood by me,

and again:

When they brought the boy I said:
"He has a god in him,
    though I do not know which god."
And they kicked me into the fore-stays.

The last line quoted indicates the connection between this episode and the rest of the Canto. Acoetes sees the god, but none of his men do. King Pentheus of Thebes, to whom Acoetes tells his story, refuses to believe it. And the Canto fades out into a world, not of certainty, but of instability:

The tower like a one-eyed great goose
    cranes up out of the olive-grove.

The instability of the world in which the poet seeks the recurrent and the permanent— this seems to be the central theme of Canto III. On the slither of time the poet must seek the eternal—the gods. In an early draft of the first Canto, Pound wrote:

And shall I claim;
Confuse my own phantastikon,
Or say the filmy shell that circumscribes me
Contains the actual sun;
    Confuse the thing I see
With actual gods behind me?

At the opening of Canto III, Pound describes himself as a young and impecunious aesthete, alone and idle in Venice:

I sat on the Dogana's steps
For the gondolas cost too much, that year,
And there were not "those girls," there was one face,
And the Buccentoro twenty yards off, howling "Stretti,"
And the lit cross-beams, that year, in the Morosini.

The repetition of "that year" calls attention, here as elsewhere, to the temporal and impermanent nature of these experiences, while the third line suggests their personal, accidental quality (if one is diligent and devoted to such matters, one may trace "those girls" to Browning; but Pound expunged Browning from the passage and I see little reason to insist on writing him back in; the line stands as a statement about two different experiences and that is what matters). But against these fragmentary experiences, Pound places an image of the gods, who—representing immortal truth and immortal vigor—are ever-present:

Gods float in the azure air,
Bright gods and Tuscan, back before dew was shed.
Light: and the first light, before ever dew was fallen.

They are presented as an idle young aesthete might see them or intuit them: beautiful but unrelated to the world of men. Upon entering that active world—as Pound does through the tale of the Cid—

My Cid rode up to Burgos,
Up to the studded gate between two towers,

one finds it difficult to engage the gods; one finds not eternity but death and destruction:

Ignez da Castro murdered, and a wall
Here stripped, here made to stand.
Drear waste. . .

In Canto IV Pound asserts the method, already implied in a number of places, by which he hopes to overcome time and change. Joining and juxtaposing images, he outlines, in a tentative way, several recurrent attitudes. He also asserts—and this too has been implied—that it is not enough for the poet to discover what recurs and what endures. Odysseus may return with the wisdom of the prophet, but loses all companions. Acoetes is firm—"I have seen what I have seen"—but he is the only one to see it and is destroyed. The artist's knowledge must somehow be related to the active world of men. Otherwise, as Pound has never tired of insisting, such knowledge is useless.

Recalling the end of Canto III, Canto IV opens with the destructive vision that animated Homer's pen:

Palace in smoky light,
Troy but a heap of smouldering boundary stones.

But as the artist who would preserve rather than destroy, and who is concerned with the vision and the spirit that can animate an entire community, Pound appeals:

ANAXIFORMINGES! Aurunculeia!
Hear me. Cadmus of Golden Prows!
The silver mirrors catch the bright stones and flare,

Dawn, to our waking, drifts in the green
cool light;
Dew-haze blurs, in the grass, pale ankles
moving.
Beat, beat, whirr, thud, in the soft turf
under the apple trees,
Choros nympharum, goat-foot, with the
pale foot alternate.

"Anaxiforminges"—"ruling the lyre"—opens Pindar's second Olympian Ode, and suggests a community event in celebration of the gods; Aurunculeia is the bride in whose honor Catullus wrote his wedding song, another ceremonial at whose center is the god of marriage; Cadmus is, of course, the legendary founder of Thebes. All suggest communal enterprise centered in communal belief. They are presented too cryptically, perhaps, but the very brevity of these allusions indicates, I should think, that Pound has not discovered in these earlier suggestions very useful guides for his purpose. His mind slips from these fragments to the reality of an ever-present dawn alight with creative vigour; and in the dance of nymphs and fauns there is a suggestion of joy and freedom expressed, though not confined by, the pattern of the dance. The pattern implied by Pindar can be but a pallid reflection of this dance.

In sharp contrast to the imagery of "green cool light" and "pale ankles moving," we are shown an old man "by the curved, carved foot of the couch." Like the old man of Troy, he will speak of doom, and we may expect the "beach-groove" of Canto II to be explored, as indeed it is, with allusions to the dark stories of Tereus' passion and the destruction of Acteon, and with suggestions of their Provencal counterparts: the wave of renewal and recurrence runs in the beach-groove. The first half of the canto focuses on a vision of Diana at her bath, a vision that includes both a sense of ecstasy and a sense of mystery:

Not a ray, not a sliver, not a spare disc
of sunlight
Flaking the black, soft water;
Bathing the body of nymphs, of nymphs,
and Diana,
Nymphs, white-gathered about her, and
the air, air,
Shaking, air alight with the goddess,
fanning their hair in the dark.

Out of such a vision emerges poetic energy and productivity, but, for the community at large, the will to secrecy may be destructive of whatever is fine and innocent:

And she went toward the window,
the slim white stone bar

Making a double arch;
Firm even fingers held to the firm pale
stone;
Swung for a moment. . .

But there is another way in which the gods may manifest themselves: publicly and communally, by the light of the sun:

The liquid and rushing crystal
beneath the knees of the gods.
Ply over ply, thin glitter of water;
Brook film bearing white petals.
The pines at Takasago
grow with the pines of Ise!

"Ply over ply" indicates Pound's attempt to see through cultural levels for what recurs. In reaching around the globe for his imagery of order Pound is, of course, preparing the way for the Confucian and Chinese Cantos, and he is suggesting as well that the East provides a necessary counterpart or corrective for the basic patterns of the West. He returns briefly to Catullus' wedding song and makes it a reflection of the "Choros nympharum": "Blue agate casing the sky" recalling "the green cool light"; "saffron sandal so petals the narrow foot" recalling the "pale ankles moving." Here is recurrence, though scarcely a very exact one.

But between what the artist perceives—such perceptions as Pound is currently piecing together—and the spirit that drives the community, there ought, Pound insists, to be some correlation. That is the note on which the Canto closes.

Canto VI restates the problem in a new guise. A group, "we," is opposed to the one, "you." The many may know what the one has done, for action is readily perceivable. "We" may also know what Guillaume, one of the founders of the troubador tradition, has done. These are fairly public matters:

What you have done, Odysseus,
We know what you have done . . .
And that Guillaume sold out his ground
rents
(Seventh of Poitiers, Ninth of Aquitain).
"Tant las fotei com auzirets
"Cen e quatre vingt et veit vetz. . . ."
The stone is alive in my hand, the crops
will be thick in my death-year. . .

But as the following lines indicate, there are mysteries to which the many, though having access to common knowledge, do not possess the key—that of language, for example, and that of sensitivity. The Provencal couplet stands for precisely what it is—something most of us will not understand and a sense of pagan joy our society has dispensed with ("I copulated with them as you shall hear/One hundred and eighty-eight times"). The next two lines suggest the perception of the one, the artist perhaps, capable of sensing the spirit in what otherwise would be dead matter. Like the Greek gods, the spirit is universal and immortal, and the artist to whom the stone is alive may, like an ancient demigod, bring the wasteland to life. The line also suggests that there is a connection between the artist's perception and the health of the land—a point Pound will make time and again in the course of *The Cantos*—and it suggests further the possibility of combining perception and power in one man—another idea that Pound will harp on in the course of his long poem.

The transmission of such perception depends, as the poem has already suggested, on receptive mentalities. They are not easy to find. Eleanor is of the line of Guillaume, and we meet her later in the Canto as the "joyous lady" of the troubadors. But then "Louis is wed with Eleanor," and a new, unperceiving mentality is introduced. To Louis, the line of Guillaume has nothing to do with the poetic and the spiritual; it is purely political:

And had (He, Guillaume) a son that
    had to wife
The Duchess of Normandia whose
    daughter
Was wife to King Henry e maire del
    rei jove. . .

The spirit of the Odyssean voyage, as Pound defined it in Canto I, has nothing to do with Louis' crusade:

Went over sea till day's end (he, Louis,
    with Eleanor).

The first half of the line is derived from the translation in Canto I, while the second half recalls the foolishly pedantic "He, Guillaume." We are in different mental worlds, though in the same physical ambience.

The spirit in the stone is a mystery. But even public documents may hide the truth to the artist who is not willing to play the part of historian. After taking us through the divorce between Louis and Eleanor and the marriage of Eleanor and Henry II, Pound presents a wedding agreement:

Nauphal, Vexis, Harry joven
In pledge for all his life and life of all
    his heirs

Shall have Gisors, and Vexis, Neufchastel
But if no issue Gisors shall revert . . .

Here as elsewhere the ellipsis is intended to suggest a good deal that remains unstated—

for, as an earlier version of Canto VI reports at great length, Harry joven, Henry II's heir, died before the wedding, but Henry steadfastly refused to return Gisors. Another agreement follows, one between Richard III and Philip of France:

"Need not wed Alix . . . in the name
Trinity holy indivisible . . . Richard our
    brother.

Again, the dots hide a good deal; the simple fact that something has been left out is all that Pound wishes to indicate here; it is not terribly important to note that the agreement was signed in an atmosphere of ungodly hate that scarcely warrants the references to the Trinity and to "our brother."

But when one has all the facts, both documents and poems may, if properly aligned, prove useful in shaping the form of a recurrent mood or idea. At long last the fact that Sordello came from around Mantua is to be given a place in the story—as part of an emerging idea or spirit, linked to another fact and thus suggesting that Pound may have something solid to work with. Bernart de Ventadorn sings of his lady as one who, like Diana, "sheds such light in the air." But, concerned with the spirit, not with private possession of the beloved, Bernart asks:

"Send word I ask you to Eblis
    you have seen that maker
"And finder of songs so far afield as this
"That he may free her,
    who sheds such light in the air."

It is now that Pound returns us to Sordello:

E lo Sordels si fo di Mantovana,
Son of a poor knight, Sier Escort,
And he delighted himself in chancons
And mixed with the men of the court
And went to the court of Richard Saint
    Boniface
And was there taken with love for his
    wife Cunizza, da Romano,
That freed her slaves on a Wednesday
Masnatas et servos, witness.

This Sordello is one who recognizes in others such as Cunizza the same freedom of spirit he possesses himself; Sordello's biography and Cunizza's testament reveal the same order of mind as Bernart's. A new groove begins to be shaped.

* * *

The discussion above is scarcely designed to prove that everything in Pound's long poem is self-evident. That cryptic passage at the opening of Canto IV is enough to bury any such nonsense, and it takes only a glance at the rest of the poem to discern many such passages. But whatever source-hunting is needed to clarify an allusion, the reader's first task is to ascertain its force and meaning in *The Cantos,* not its position in the source. In fact, anyone who has read carefully both *The Cantos* and Pound's major sources—Pére de Mailla's multi-volume history of China, for example, or the collected works of John Adams—must conclude, I think, that the sources are often beside the point, and often misleading. Only "on the page" can we discover Pound's intentions. Only "on the page" do we find, if we look closely, a carefully designed set of themes and variations for each Canto—themes and variations usually announced at the opening of the Canto.

Perhaps—and one must confess to a certain wistfulness at this point—if the poem acquires enough readers who are willing to read the poem, not poetry-substitutes, it may become possible to assess it sanely and meaningfully, saving it from both the Pound cult and the anti-Pound cult.

Robinson Jeffers and the Torches of Violence

by FREDERIC I. CARPENTER

In *The Novel of Violence in America*, W. M. Frohock comments that "Violence is epidemic in such novels. They are, like Jeffers' poems, 'Crusted with blood and barbaric omens/Painful to excess, inhuman as a hawk's cry.' " To the critic the extreme exemplar of the violence which characterizes modern American literature is not Hemingway, or any recent novelist, but rather the California poet of the late 1920's, whom conservative critics have ever since been trying to forget. And just as the problem of literary violence has increasingly obsessed the writers of our most modern generation, so the poetry of Jeffers has come to seem increasingly significant. After the assassination of President Kennedy, some moralists blamed the act on the violent emotions stimulated by modern literature, and traced this evil to D. H. Lawrence and to Jeffers. From the perspective of the 1960's, this earlier grappling with the "modern" problem of violence seems crucial.

Like many writers of the 1920's, Jeffers came to artistic maturity during World War I. He had already published two volumes of minor poems, in which he had echoed the optimistic idealism of the generation whose political spokesman was Woodrow Wilson. But America's entry into the war brought Jeffers face to face with the problem of violence in its most fundamental form. And he, more than any of his contemporaries, was disturbed by it: after two years of anguished self-searching, he finally reached a total disillusionment with his own earlier idealism, and rejected both the traditional forms and the idealistic contents of his own earlier poetry. In the early 1920's he began writing the poetic narratives of physical and emotional violence which made him famous. And in one of the best of his new poems he addressed "Woodrow Wilson," mourning the tragic heroism of the idealistic president, and rejecting "the huge delusion" of his dream of "establishing the earth on peace."

But Jeffers is best remembered for those narrative poems which make no reference to the external violence of Mr. Wilson's war or to the resulting destruction of American idealism. *Tamar* and *Roan Stallion* deal, rather, with man's inner violence and emotional disturbance. Not the legalized slaughter of war, nor the rational crusade of American patriotism became Jeffers' obsession, but rather the irrationality of familial violence, and the unspeakable emotions which lead toward human self-destruction. And because he dealt primarily with this introverted form of violence which all the taboos of Western civilization have conspired to repress, his poetry first achieved spectacular fame, but then suffered the repeated attacks of a generation of conservatives. And these moralistic attacks—sometimes justified—have tended to make modern readers overlook both the significance and the unique historical importance of his poetry.

After publishing the early poetic narratives of emotional violence which culminated with *The Women at Point Sur*, Jeffers was forced by the attacks of his enemies and by the doubts of his friends to reconsider his poetic motives. And he formulated some logical answers to these criticisms in prose letters, explaining (for instance) that his theme of incest was really intended as a symbol of racial introversion. But more significantly, these criticisms inspired him to formulate his artistic credo in a series of meditative poems and fables: "Apology for Bad Dreams," "An Artist," and "A Redeemer," And his "Apology for Bad Dreams" has increasingly been recognized as one of the best single poems he ever wrote. Since it deals both subjectively and objectively with the problem of violence in literature, its very success emphasizes the crucial nature of that problem.

The vivid language and poetic imagination of "Apology for Bad Dreams" contribute most to its power and its excellence, but the rationale which it suggests for the theme of violence is equally challenging. The author explains:

> . . . .I said in my heart,
> "Better invent than to suffer: imagine
> victims
> Lest your own flesh be chosen the
> agonist, or you
> Martyr some creature to the beauty of
> the place."
> And I said,
> "Burn sacrifices once a year to magic
> Horror away from the house."

"Bad dreams" (Jeffers suggests) may, if formulated by means of poetic art, prevent "suffering," both for the author and perhaps the reader. These poetic "sacrifices" may "magic" (and the use of "magic" as a verb makes it more emphatic) "horror away from the house." And later he repeats: "remembered deaths be our redeemers;/ Imagined victims our salvation."

But if these poems which Jeffers imagined to describe the rationale of his poetic violence are vivid and challenging, they are also ambiguous. The overt expression of violent emotion by means of poetry may achieve a kind of therapeutic value for the poet: "Better invent than suffer." But how effective may this poetic therapy be for the reader? Will the overt expression of repressed violent emotions prevent his "suffering" also? And if these poetic "sacrifices" possess a certain "magic" power to dispel the psychological "horror" of "bad dreams," can they ever achieve any practical power to protect any actual "house"? Does our modern poet really believe in this "magic"? In a later poem Jeffers imagines "A Redeemer" who deludes himself into the belief that he is making "anti-toxin" for his fellow men by keeping open stigmatic wounds in his own hands; but Jeffers seems to discern a touch of madness in this "Redeemer." Is his belief in the therapeutic effectiveness of his own narrative poetry any less deluded?

If Jeffers' poetry suggested these questions, it never succeeded in answering them. Yet the true function of poetry has never been to answer questions—even those which it has suggested. And Jeffers' later poetry continued to explore the basic problems of literary violence, and sometimes to suggest partial answers. Sometimes by means of logical assertions of his own poetic belief (as in "Crumbs Or the Loaf"); more often by means of narrative explorations of violent actions (as in Dear Judas); but most successfully by means of imaginative metaphors and images (which are the essence of all poetry) Jeffers continued to illuminate this basic problem. If his own poetic creed sometimes seemed ambiguous, and if his violent narratives sometimes led the reader down blind alleys of the mind, his brilliant metaphors often suggested imaginative answers to the problems which neither the logic of his poetics nor the architecture of his narrative poetry could fully solve.

The most extreme (and the least successful) of all Jeffers' narrative poems focused most sharply on the problem of violence. In The Women at Point Sur an apostate minister consciously performed acts of extreme violence in order to "burn the world down to significance." He described this purpose at the beginning:

". . .I shall not die blind, Jesus did:
'Why hast thou forsaken me, my God?'
I not his son take him by violence. This
     is that hybris in the tragedy, that
     brings destruction.
Content. I will buy."

And throughout the rest of the long narrative poem, this "hero" repeated acts of conscious violence in the hope of finding significance in life. But repeatedly he failed, and his violent acts increasingly produced a kind of emotional numbness, whose effect was to negate all significance whatever. Extreme literary violence resulted in complete literary failure.

Halfway through The Women at Point Sur, Jeffers seems to have become conscious of this failure. In section XII of the poem, he apostrophized himself:

I made glass puppets to speak of him,
     they splintered in my hand and have
     cut me, they are heavy with my
     blood.
But . . . . I sometime
Shall fashion images great enough to
     face him
A moment and speak while they die.
     These here have gone mad: but
     stammer the tragedy you crackled
     vessels.

The "crackled vessels" of his imagined tragedy "stammered" to a dead end. But their very failure (and their author's) underlines an important fact: absolute violence in literature often results in absolute insignificance.

When Jeffers' historic revolt against the pre-war idealism of his youth became most extreme, it became least successful. And this fact explains, I think, both his success and his failure. His historic significance lies in his extreme and exemplary expression of that rebellious disillusion which followed World War I. But the very extremity of his rebellion warped the literary expression of it, so that his strength sometimes became his weakness. He often confused blind violence with significant tragedy.

He then attempted to formulate the rationale of this literary violence in short poems, and in prose. "Crumbs Or the Loaf" suggested by its title something of his literary practice of extremes. Tragic tales are fables whose effect is merely practical:

It is better no doubt to give crumbs than
     the loaf,
     make fables again,
Tell people not to fear death, toughen
Their bones if possible with bitter fables
     not to fear life.

Readers may be conditioned to expect the worst of life, by means of narratives which describe violent experience. But this practical purpose of tragic poetry is minor: ideally, Jeffers says, the author of literary violence should describe the inevitability of destruction so that the reader will be induced to love even that which may destroy him. "But it's quite true/

15

The invulnerable love is not bought for nothing." But since most readers will be incapable of this mystical love of an absolute God, the tragic poet should offer "crumbs" of practical comfort, rather than the whole "loaf." Between the extremely practical purpose of tragedy, and its extremely mystical purposes, Jeffers offered no middle ground.

His prose interpretations of the function of tragedy continued to emphasize its merely practical purpose. In a letter (to the present writer, dated March 31, 1932) he suggested the ideas which had lain behind his "Apology for Bad Dreams":

"Imagined victims our salvation" I think represented two strains of thought 1) There was a time when human sacrifice was needed to save the people; then a sheep could be substituted, or some kind of Guy Fawkes image. Or an imagined victim in a story, suffering things we all feel liable to and hope to escape. Wasn't this one of the perhaps unconscious functions of Greek tragedy? 2) More practically, we endow a person in a story with certain excesses of thought or passion and see what their logic leads to, and are thus perhaps warned ourselves, so he suffers instead of us.

I think one of the most common intentions in tragic stories, from the Oedipus down, is to build up a strain for the sake of the explosion of its release, —like winding up a ballista.

Tragedy—Jeffers seems to say—serves some very useful purposes. It may substitute for the practice of human sacrifice in primitive societies. Or it may explore imaginatively the probable practical results of violent actions. Or it may merely provide a release from tension—"like winding up a ballista." But all three of these explanations have one quality in common—their extraordinarily practical and prosaic nature. The high religious quality of Greek tragedy did not enter into his theory, and the traditional "purgation of pity and terror" seemed to him a release from nervous tension. Indeed, in his narrative poems, the tragic emotion of pity was to be exorcised, rather than cultivated.

One significant fact, which Jeffers himself seems never to have realized emerges from all this. Although Jeffers repeatedly described acts of tragic violence, neither his poetic theory nor his poetic practice was truly "tragic." In spite of his expressed conviction, his fictional characters achieved neither the necessary heroism, nor the necessary self-awareness to "face Him

and speak," while they died. They remained, rather, the blind creatures of their instincts, like the heroine of *Roan Stallion*, "moved by some obscure human fidelity." Because they could not believe in any idealistic morality, they could never die heroically for any purpose beyond themselves. And because their rebellion against existing society was instinctive rather than conscious, they never achieved the ability to "speak" while they died. They remained "puppets," both of their own instincts and of their author's imagination, who "stammered" rather than spoke. And because readers could identify with them only on the instinctual level, they never aroused the conscious tragic emotions of pity and terror.

Jeffers' partial failure, which both caused and gave justification to the attacks on his poetry during his lifetime, lay in his own inability to realize this crucial fact. If he had recognized that the purpose and essential nature of his poetry was not tragic, in the traditional sense, confusion might have been avoided. For his poetry was actually of a different nature, inspired by a different purpose. His narratives were often (as he suggested) exemplary fables, or allegories, rather than tragedies. And his purpose was not so much tragic, as prophetic. Although some of his poems (especially the California narratives of his middle period) attempted to approximate the traditional patterns of tragedy, his most distinctive poems were prophetic.

"The Tower Beyond Tragedy," for instance, dramatized the traditional tragic events of the Greek Oresteia, and much of it was even cast in the dramatic form of conventional tragedy. But the center of the poem consisted of the imaginative poetic prophecy by Cassandra of the fate of the world's empires of the future— ending with America. And the climax of the poem consisted of the attainment by Orestes of a mystical love of nature, which exalted him beyond the power of the tragic furies. At the beginning of his career, Jeffers' narrative poem exemplified his later assertion that "the invulnerable love is not bought for nothing," and emphasized the tower *beyond* tragedy, rather than tragedy. And the poetic prophecy of Cassandra repeated the briefer poetic prophecy of the author: "Shine, Perishing Republic."

In like manner, *Dear Judas* later recalled the story of the crucifixion, not for the sake of the tragic drama itself, but for the perspective it offered on the larger tragic drama which is history. The poem begins with a conscious invocation of the spirits of the past: "passions too violent to vanish/ Still haunt the garden" But then Mary and Judas began "to remember the future."

Life grows transparent: what's left us
   but to light the torches of violence,
   to line it with visible fire?

And as the imagined drama unfolds, it illuminates the future, so that the tragic suffering of Jesus becomes the prototype of all the agonies of future leaders and heroes, and history is seen as a recurrent series of tragedies. The purpose of the poem is not to suggest identification with the historic hero. It is, rather, to suggest a perspective beyond history, from which all these violent dramas can be viewed with equanimity and understanding. And the violence symbolized by the cross of Jesus becomes the archetype of all violence.

Meanwhile, that element of imaginative reality which is the first essential of all literature—especially of all narrative and dramatic literature is achieved not by the tragic identification of reader with fictional protagonist, but by poetic metaphors and images. The purpose of "the torches of violence," which have been lighted by the author, is not heat, but light. The violent actions of history and of fiction, translated into poetic imagination, illuminate the meaning of life. Thus Jesus is described as "the greatest of all torch-like men." And he imagines that: "I am making a new thing in the world,—a power weaponed with love not violence; a white/ Dominion; a smokeless lamp; a pure light." But Jesus also recognizes that "Only a crucified/ God can fill the wolf-bowels of Rome," and chooses a violent death to become a God. And by this suffering he lights the brightest of all "the torches of violence."

These poetic metaphors suggest a rationale of literary violence different from that of conventional tragedy, and also from melodrama. Violence is not so much to be condemned as the result of some tragic flaw, or some hybris in the hero, as it is to be illuminated, and recognized as a necessary part of the nature of history. And violence itself—when seen in the perspectives of myth and of history—is recognized as contributing to that illumination. Only when its meaning is denied—"smothered by its own smoke in the human brain-vault,"—does the illumination fail.

The prophetic and symbolic violence which

lies at the heart of Jeffers' poetry, and which increasingly has dominated the fiction and drama of the modern world, has value on different levels. It may have psychological value. The dominant idealism and moralism before World War I caused many readers to repress their violent emotions as evil, and to deny them literary expression. But the literary revolt of which Jeffers was the extreme exemplar, effected a liberation of this repressed violence. Although conservatives and moralists viewed this revolt with alarm, and still continue to denounce it, many other serious and religious men have born witness to its value. The powerful Catholic poetry of Brother Antoninus, for instance, is desended directly from the seemingly irreligious poetry of Jeffers—to whose memory the younger poet has published an eloquent "Tribute." Readers, critics, and fellow poets have testified to the "redemption" effected by the "remembered deaths" of Jeffers' poetry.

But on a deeper level, the prophetic and historic importance of Jeffers' literary revolt is becoming increasingly apparent. The vision of violence which he first described in the 1920's has become the obsession of the 1960's. His realization of the absolute absurdity of the historic idealism which would make the world safe for democracy by inventing the bomb which could destroy the world, was prophetic in every sense. His repeated warnings that violence is intrinsic in history, and that this unpleasant fact must be faced, rather than repressed, was prophetic. He first dared to "think the unthinkable," and to imagine total violence in literary terms. And he first emphasized that violence had value—that it was, metaphorically, "The Bloody Sire" of all the world's values. He proclaimed that the true love of God must include also the mystical love of a destructive God. And his knowledge that this "invulnerable love is not bought for nothing" has recently been translated roughly into the terms of popular cinema by "Dr. Strangelove."

If Jeffers' imagination and literary rationalization of the problem of violence was sometimes confused, it is not surprising. After his death we are only beginning to recognize the illumination which "the torches of violence" may produce.

Of Prayer and Praise: The Poetry of Hart Crane*

by HILTON LANDRY

Every sentence has meaning . . . by convention. Yet every sentence is not a proposition; only such are propositions as have in them either truth or falsity. Thus a prayer is a sentence but is neither true nor false. Let us therefore dismiss all other types of sentences but the proposition, for this last concerns our present inquiry, whereas the investigation of the others belongs rather to the study of rhetoric or of poetry.

Aristotle, *De Interpretatione.*

We know truth not only by the reason, but also by the heart, and it is in this last way that we know first principles; and reason, which has no part in it, tries in vain to impugn them. . . . Principles are intuited, propositions are inferred, all with certainty, though in different ways.And it is as useless and absurd for reason to demand from the heart proofs of her first principles, before admitting them, as it would be for the heart to demand from reason an intuition of all demonstrated propositions before accepting them.

Pascal, *Pensées.*

Whether we be young or old,
Our destiny, our being's heart and home
Is with infinitude, and only there.

Wordsworth, *The Prelude*

The very Absolute, in all its fulness of life, is even now the object that you really mean by your fragmentary passing ideas. . . .

Royce, *The World and the Individual,*
First Series.

The models, theories, and methods of Hart Crane are unanimously identified with romanticism, a literary party which has long been out of favor. This is a great convenience for his detractors, especially those who also pose as defenders or at least objective assessors of his work. It enables them to point to him as a spectacular horrible example of the dangers of a one-hundred-fifty-year-old condition which has become overripe, not to say decadent, and to imply delicately their own immunity and superiority. Comments on Crane's undisciplined life, often delivered in the form of gnomic

*With the support of a grant from the American Philosophical Society.

utterances, inevitably intrude in the criticism of the poetry, with the result that what seems to be a discussion of poetry is at least in part the condemnation of a private life. Thus a writer like Yvor Winters is a "classical" moralist disguised as literary critic in his essay on Crane, and the subject of discourse gives him a welcome opportunity to display the symptoms of the disease he calls romanticism (*In Defense of Reason,* 1947).

However much authorities like Pound, Hulme, and Winters deplore romanticism or some of its manifestations, it still remains one of the principal movements, if not *the* principal movement, of modern literature. Although its future may be limited, its vitality has been maintained to the present by a series of renewals and reinterpretations accomplished by some of the best writers of the last hundred years. To effect a renewal has been the task of the poets and novelists; to offer the metaphysical and critical basis for renewal, the vital reinterpretation, has been the task of the critics and philosophers. In one sense the first European romantics were also the last, but variations on the basic "themes" have produced a long continuation of the tradition. For example, the German idealists Kant, Schiller, Schelling, Hegel, and Schopenhauer, however vaguely known or freely distorted, were the intellectual heroes and allies of the French Symbolists in their struggle with the dead romanticism of Hugo and the "scientific" positivism of Taine. In England, Arnold inherited and reinvested the poetic legacy of Wordsworth, Yeats that of Blake and Shelley, and I. A. Richards inherited the intellectual estates of both Coleridge and the empiricists Bentham and Mill. (Remy de Gourmont, one of Pound's favorite critics, offers a rough parallel to Richards in his combining idealism with some principles borrowed from the psychologist Ribot.) In America, Emerson's version of romanticism was further transmuted by Whitman, the careless "trancendentalist" from New York, and Emily Dickinson provided a unique example of the effects of planting the romantic seed in puritan soil. But Emily Dickinson was not the "last romantic" in America; that role was reserved for Hart Crane. In his valuable and influential essay on the poet Allen Tate remarked, "Crane not only ends the romantic era in his own person; he ends it logically and morally" (*On the Limits of Poetry,* 1948). Tate followed this assertion with the wise concession that "this does not mean that the romantic impulse may not rise and flourish again," for even as he was pronouncing its doom that impulse was flourishing in the poetry of E. E. Cummings and Wallace Stevens. Some writer is always being called, in accents of delight or despair, "the last romantic," but another always comes to take his place. When Yeats, in "Coole Park and Bally-lee, 1931," said of Lady Gregory and himself, "We were the last romantics," he was quite wrong; not long after Yeats wrote his elegy for Lady Gregory, Dylan Thomas published his *18 Poems* (1934).

What I am trying to establish by listing names and sketching relationships is that the reinterpretation and renewal of romanticism is a major characteristic of modern poetry and one that deserves respect in view of the excellence of many specimens of its theory and practice. Crane's practice has always been accorded a certain measure of respect, but his theory has been frequently attacked for its "errors" and "confusion" and used as a stick with which to beat his poetry, although its central principle is clearly in the main stream of modern criticism. There can be no doubt, especially since Crane referred to them, that Coleridge and I. A. Richards, Baudelaire and Rimbaud, lie behind the distinction he makes between the logic of metaphor and "pure" logic, between the use of language in poetry and its use in science. In "General Aims and Theories" Crane states that

the motivation of the poem must be derived from the implicit emotional dynamics of the materials used, and the terms of expression employed are often selected less for their logical (literal) significance than for their associational meanings. Via this and their metaphorical inter-relationships, the entire construction of the poem is raised on the organic principle of a 'logic of metaphor,' which antedates our so-called pure logic, and which is the genetic basis of all speech, hence consciousness and thought-extension.

The final sentence of the essay makes explicit what this passage implies and what his critics are apt to forget: "Language has built towers and bridges, but itself is inevitably as fluid as always." A fuller statement of his critical position appears in his letter to Harriet Monroe in defence of "At Melville's Tomb." Here, in a declaration of creative and critical independence, he asserts his right to have assumptions about poetry different from Miss Monroe's (or Winters' or Tate's) and to compose poems embodying his responsible "inflection" of language. After stressing his interest in the inter-

action of words through their connotations rather than their "logically rigid significations" and discussing some of the implications of this principle, he equates the logic of metaphor with I. A. Richards "pseudo-statement" and reminds us that the house of poetry has many windows: "Much fine poetry may be completely rationalistic in its use of symbols, but there is much great poetry of another order. . . . " He then summarizes his main views:

It all comes to the recognition that emotional dynamics are not to be confused with any absolute order of rationalized definitions; ergo, in poetry the *rationale* of metaphor belongs to another order of experience than science, and is not to be limited by a scientific and arbitrary code of relationships either in verbal inflections or concepts.

The basic distinction which Crane makes approximates Coleridge's distinction between the intuitive reason, the power which operates by an "intuitive or immediate beholding, accompanied by a conviction of the necessity and universality of the truth so beholden not derived from the senses," and the discursive understanding, "the faculty judging according to sense" and "contained within the sphere of the senses." Reason (Kant's *Vernunft),* the "organ of theology and philosophy," is the source of universal principles; understanding *(Verstand),* the great classifier, "in generalizing the notices of the senses constitutes sensible experience." The relationship between reason and understanding corresponds to that between imagination and fancy; for the members in each pair differ in kind and not merely in degree and they share the same intellectual instruments. The peculiar instrument of reason and imagination is the symbol, that of the understanding and fancy is the allegory or the image.

Now such distinctions by Coleridge and Crane may seem to provide arms and ammunition for those who maintain that one of the persistent features of romanticism is the division between sensibility and intellect. But any careful reader of *Aids to Reflection, The Friend,* or the *Biographia Literaria* knows that this is not the case; for the sentence in which Croce attempted to sum up the esthetic theory of the German idealists applies equally well to Coleridge, the disciple of Plotinus and Plato:

The road they tried to follow was to conceive a faculty which should be neither imagination nor intellect but should partake of both; an intellectual intuition or intuitive intellect, a mental imagination after the fashion of Plotinus (*Aesthetic,* 1953, p. 301).

In short, the main endeavor of the leading theorists of romanticism, however much some of their emphases may appear to deny it, has been the restoration, the rehabilitation of the whole man. This is true of Croce in the *Breviary of Aesthetic*, despite his insistence that it is feeling which gives coherence and unity to the "lyrical" intuition of art, and it is obviously true of Bergson in *Creative Evolution*, for his intellectual sympathy or intuition is "instinct that has become disinterested, self-conscious, capable of reflecting upon its object and of enlarging it indefinitely."

Although I. A. Richards is hardly sympathetic toward either Croce or Bergson, his division between science and poetry, between the symbolic (or descriptive) use of words and the emotive use, between statement and pseudo-statement, not only corresponds to their general distinction between concept and intuition (*The Meaning of Meaning*, 1936, p. 153), but his concern with pseudo-statement or the emotive use of language in poetry is as much a recognition of the needs and interests of the whole man as their emphasis on intuition. The chief difference is that he is a rigorous student of language, a man with a wide but discriminating knowledge of modern psychology and philosophy, an empiricist as well as something of an "idealist." He has always been an empiricist as well as a follower of Coleridge (and Plato), despite the common tendency to condemn his early works as "positivist" (see *Speculative Instruments*, p. 48, n. 1) and to praise his later ones as Coleridgean, and his emphasis on the difference between the emotive and descriptive uses of language has been apparent from *The Meaning of Meaning* (1923) to *Speculative Instruments* (1955). This crucial difference is best presented in terms of the chief speculative instrument of the last work, the diagram (p. 26) summarizing Richards' classification of the functions of language.

According to this classification, in the referential or descriptive hierarchy of language functions, Valuing and Influencing are subordinated to Indicating and Characterizing, and Realizing is more or less ignored. In the emotive organization of these functions Realizing, Characterizing, and Indicating are under the control of Valuing and Influencing (*Speculative Instruments*, pp. 26-38). The control of the referential functions by the influential is the case in most poetry and religion and much philosophy; the domination of the referential functions pertains in natural science, radical empiricism and positivism, and in some branches of "social" science. Although this division is made in the interest of poetry, it also recognizes the opposing claims of science and in fact is an honest attempt to settle the conflict between science and religion and poetry which reached a peak in the later nineteenth century. Rightly understood, it does not, as critics contend, leave everything of importance and value to science and nothing but trivia and froth to poetry; on the contrary, it simply recognizes that each belongs to a different order or ordering of experience, to paraphrase Crane; that each has its own kind of truth and its own kind of knowledge. In the realm of emotive meaning, of poetry, truth and falsity have to do with "the worth and justice of appraisal, the authority and scope of the aim, and the judiciousness of the selection of what is to be thought about, and how, in the interests of the maximum development of realization." (Here and in preceding remarks on the relations of language functions in science and poetry I am indebted to Richards' lectures on "The Conduct of Language" at Harvard in 1948.) For this realm "truth" is equivalent to "troth" or "fidelity, loyalty, constancy"; it is acceptability or adequacy (*Principles of Literary Criticism*, 1926, pp. 269-71; see also Maritain's *Creative Intuition*, ch. 4). For the realm of science, truth pertains to what is verifiable by the correspondence, coherence, or pragmatic tests (cf. *Phaedo*, 92, 93-94. 101); it is conformity to fact, system, or experience.

All this is to carry the subject beyond the limits of Crane's reading and formulations, but not beyond the scope of his intentions and his elective affinities. One cannot, in all fairness, deny intellectual respectability to a view which has been continually represented by a succession of philosophers, theologians, and critics from Aristotle to T. S. Eliot. Sometimes the line between science and poetry or between philosophy and religion has been drawn in the interests of one side, sometimes in the interests of the other; but the distinction continues to be made, whether in terms of nature and grace, prayer and proposition, or evaluation and description, simply because it divides the subject at the *natural* joints. However much one may resent the arrogance and partiality or even blindness with which the division is often made, the very act itself is implicit recognition that, as Eliot said, "There is a logic of the imagination as well as a logic of concepts" (introd., St.-John Perse's *Anabase*, 1949) and that neither is necessarily inferior to the other.

2

Hart Crane's most important and most characteristic work is *The Bridge*, a series of lyric poems loosely held together by certain unifying features. The most obvious of these features is the journey or quest, by sea and by land, a quest that begins with Brooklyn Bridge in "Proem," takes the speaker backward and forward in history and time, and formally ends with the bridge in "Atlantis" as the speaker utters prophetic visions of the future. What the object of this quest is may be variously stated—"the greatness of America"; "spiritual harmony and order"; Cathay as "consciousness, knowledge, and spiritual unity"—but is clearly the Absolute in some form, in some, if not all, of its manifestations. The Absolute is the Whole or All of which we are condemned to know only a part, to know only in certain aspects and in limited ways, of which the leading ones (for purposes of this poem) are symbol and myth. There is no coherent myth in *The Bridge*, only proliferating symbols groping towards myth, but these symbols exert a second unifying influence in the poem. The proem suggests the class of symbols and metaphors that will recur throughout the work as the speaker proceeds on his quest for the Absolute: the circle or wheel representing closure, completeness, perfection and the curve or arc representing the incompleteness and striving which seek perfection. In the first stanza the seagull's wings shed "white *rings* of tumult" and then "with inviolate curve, forsake our eyes"; a few lines later, to note a more ambiguous example, cinemas are called "panoramic sleights," and in the fifth stanza a "bedlamite" leaps to his death with "shrill shirt ballooning." At the end of the proem the bridge itself, exemplifying stasis in motion, is "vaulting the sea," and the speaker entreats it to descend to his level and "of the curveship lend a myth to God." In fact, the poem as a whole describes a large circle, for like Columbus, the persona of "Ave Maria," the speaker is sustained by faith and hope as he pursues his partially successful quest and ends where he began.

Brooklyn Bridge is a work of art as well as the product of science and labor, and because it is it becomes a central symbol in another work of art which is named after it. To say that the bridge is the "symbol of our constructive future, our unique identity, in which is also included our scientific hopes and achievements of the future" is not enough, as Crane knew, for in the proem he apostrophized it thus:

O harp and altar, of the fury fused,
(How could mere toil align thy choiring
  strings!)
Terrific threshold of the prophet's pledge,
Prayer of pariah, and the lover's cry.

It is an object that is at once scientific, religious and artistic, an object that has been made all things to all men, perhaps because as Denis de Rougemont said,

> Art is an exercise of the whole being of man, not to compete with God, but to coincide better with the order of Creation, to love it better, and to reestablish ourselves in it. Thus art would appear to be like an invocation (more often than not unconscious) to the lost harmony, like a prayer (more often than not confused), corresponding to the second petition of the Lord's prayer—"Thy kingdom come" (*Spiritual Problems in Contemporary Literature*, ed. Hopper, 1957, p. 186).

This statement is more Christian than Crane would care to be, yet it fits his work extremely well. Over and over again we encounter the invocation, the apostrophe, and the prayer addressed either to the Absolute or some aspect or symbol of it and coming at strategic points in the poem as a whole. The last four stanzas of "Proem: To Brooklyn Bridge" comprise an apostrophe and entreaty to the bridge; "Ave Maria" finds Columbus invoking two "partisans of his quest" in the first stanza and praying to God in the last five; Maquokeeta is entreated and apostrophized in the last fifteen stanzas of "The Dance"; in "Cape Hatteras," a kind of ode to Whitman, Walt is often invoked and especially in the last four stanzas; various apostrophes appear in the last half of "The Tunnel"; and "Atlantis" ends with a kind of dythyrambic prayer to the bridge in five stanzas. Crane, in short, is the superlative poet of the imperative subjunctive mood, the reviver and invigorator of a mode of speech which has languished since the Romantic poets.

The richness and fecundity of his vocative metaphors are remarkable as a few elementary comparisons will make clear. In stanza ten of Shelley's "Ode to Liberty" there appears this series of vocatives: "Thou huntress swifter than the Moon! thou terror/of the world's wolves! thou bearer of the quiver,/Whose sunlike shafts pierce tempest-wingèd Error." The second and third members are in apposition to the first and are really elaborations upon it, specifying metaphorically the character of Liberty and the nature of her prey. Shelley is giving us here variations of a formula and variations on a theme. In a roughly similar series of vocatives, the lines just quoted from the proem, Crane gives us more novel metaphors and more subtle variations of his theme. The bridge is at once harp and altar, both united or "fused" by the *furor poeticus;* its

21

parts have been put together by the "fury" of machinery and toil. "Choiring strings" points to its duality in unity again, for "choiring" reminds us of the religious significance of "altar." (The bridge is an altar because, like the eyes in "At Melville's Tomb," it is raised toward heaven and because it is the product of a certain faith.) As entrance to the promised land, the hope of refugees, it is the "threshold" of the prophet's pledge, "terrific" because of the burden of hopes and fears placed upon it. In the same way it represents the outcast's "prayer," the object of his petition, and it resembles his prayer in its striving for heaven. The "lover's cry," last in the series for heaven metaphors, provides a further dimension, although the basis of relationship is still ascent and faith (cf. "Legend," 11. 20-21; *Letters,* ed. Weber, p. 181).

Hopkins, one of the most "metaphorical" of all modern poets, is the only one besides Crane who makes much use of the vocative metaphor; yet if one compares a typical passage of "Atlantis" with the opening lines of "The Starlight Night" or those of "The Wreck of the Deutschland," he seems tame and highly traditional.

> Thou mastering me
> God! giver of breath and bread;
> World's stand, sway of the sea;
> Lord of living and dead,

That is partly because he is realizing highly traditional ideas of God and His relation to the world—He is both power and peace, the giver and taker of life—but it is mainly because, in comparison with Crane's, his metaphors lack grammatical elaboration and complex grounds of identification or predication. Consider, for example, the following stanza from the prayer which concludes "Atlantis":

> O Thou steeled Cognizance whose leap commits
> The agile precincts of the lark's return;
> Within whose lariat sweep encinctured sing
> In single chrysalis the many twain,—
> Of stars Thou art the stitch and stallion glow
> And like an organ, Thou, with sound of doom—
> Sight, sound and flesh Thou leadest from time's realm
> As love strikes clear direction for the helm.

Here Crane apostrophizes the bridge as symbol of Atlantis or Cathay, "Eternity or the Absolute," and thus as bridge between the "world of Eternity" and the "world of Time." Like the Absolute itself it unites the many in the One and may be conceived in various ways, none of which is adequate to convey its "meaning." However, through the logic of metaphor, through metaphorical language that is essentially "irreducible," i.e., "not susceptible of explanation by analysis and substitution," the speaker can approximate the accommodation of the symbol to the discursive understanding.

This eighth stanza of "Atlantis" consists of a long complex sentence which contains two parallel subordinate clauses, a parenthetical compound sentence, and a final temporal clause. Syntax and grammar are relatively clear and simple, though not without some ambiguity, in contrast to the density of imagery in each element of the sentence. The skeleton of main elements has the speaker saying that the "steeled Cognizance" which is the bridge leads "Sight, sound and flesh . . . from time's realm" while "love strikes clear direction for the helm." However, the "leap" of the bridge "commits/The agile precincts of the lark's return," and within its "lariat sweep encinctured sing/In single chrysalis the many twain." Furthermore, the bridge is "stitch and stallion glow" of stars as well as "like an organ . . . with sound of doom."

We are back in the world of stanzas eight and nine of the proem, but we are moving in a different direction. There the bridge was threshold of a promised land firmly placed in the world of time; here, like Moses, it leads us away from "time's realm" into another better realm, Atlantis or the Absolute. "Cognizance" suggests, among other things, the bridge's knowledge or recognition of its significance—the sense "emblem or badge" fits here—and its destination (the "incognizable Word" of "Ave Maria"). Its outline reaches confidently from earth to heaven and returns again, hence its leap encloses rather than imprisons, or perhaps commits itself to, the agile environs of the lark's ascent and return. Also, within its sweep, composed of cables flexible as a lariat and like a lariat encircling its structural elements, the parts of the great musical instrument and "Choir," though separate ("twain"), sing as a unit within the hard shell. Perhaps the regular pattern of lights on the bridge, echoing the stars, suggested the use of "stitch," while the glowing shape and motion of the whole led to the stallion metaphor. (Compare lines in "Cape Hatteras" for vehicles of metaphors from horses—the "wind's withers" and "wind's flank," and "flaked like tethered foam/Around bared teeth of stallions"; note also "saddled sky" in "Faustus and Helen, III." An earlier draft of "Atlantis" printed in Brom Weber's *Hart Crane,* p. 431, gives a version of this stanza suggesting further possibilities for "stitch" and "stallion glow.") The organ simile brings us back to the musical instrument, now filled with the sound of doomsday, when we will all pass from time's realm. And as the steeled Cognizance leads sight and sound, partly by means of the imagery it has evoked, and flesh from the world, love, like a captain on the bridge of his ship, determines the direction.

The most arresting metaphor of the next stanza (nine) appears in the first line, "Swift peal of secular light, intrinsic Myth," where the relevance of "peal," ordinarily applied to some kind of sound, to light is fairly clear even though its relevance to the bridge is not. (Instead of an outburst of sound, "peal" here signifies a flash of light.) The shape of a segment and the sway of the bridge may suggest a connection with "peal" by way of a bell, but we are being invited to regard it as "secular light." Crane may be referring to a flash of spiritual illumination provided by the "intrinsic Myth," may be saying elliptically, to paraphrase the Psalmist, "in thy light we see light." In that case "secular" would indicate the origin of the bridge rather than the meaning or nature of its light; after all, as the "fell unshadow" that is "death's utter wound" its light is immortal. "Intrinsic" also supports this view: the bridge is a myth through its essential character (to those like the inspired speaker who have eyes to see it) and not by reason of the builders' intention.

There is little in stanza ten ("Forever Deity's glittering Pledge . . ." ff.) that is new, hence its apparent simplicity. (A new stanza begins with this line, as it should, in the Anchor edition of Crane's collected poems; in the Liveright edition [1933] these lines are part of a double stanza, nine.) Not only is there some repetition within the stanza, but the vehicles of certain metaphors recall some of those in the proem and others in earlier stanzas of "Atlantis." Rhetorically religious in tone and diction, it is an attempt to render the rapture of ascent toward Deity. Retrospection dominates the last two stanzas as Crane reflects on history, then rises to new heights as he shifts his apostrophe from the bridge to Atlantis, and comes to a quiet close with a reprise of some of the main motifs of "The Bridge" as a whole.

Stanza eleven offers some characteristic problems, for there is no immediate reference for either "migrations" or "inventions," and the syntax of the third line is awkward if not confusing:

Migrations that must needs void memory,
Inventions that cobblestone the heart,—

Unspeakable Thou Bridge to Thee, O Love.
Thy pardon for this history, whitest Flower,
O Answerer of all,—Anemone,—
Now while thy petals spend the suns about us, hold—
(O Thou whose radiance doth inherit me)
Atlantis,—hold thy floating singer late!

"Migrations" might point to earlier stanzas in "Atlantis," to the "labyrinthine mouths of history" in the second or the mythic Greece of the fifth, but it would be more appropriate as a regretful reference to parts of "Quaker Hill" (written a few years after "Atlantis"), "The Dance," or "The River." Perhaps the motion defined in the preceding stanza induced Crane to use the idea here, though with a marked difference in attitude. There the movements were warmly espoused, while here, like the inventions that harden or wear down the heart, they are "unspeakable" to the bridge as love. Because they destroy the basis of tradition and faith, the way of preserving the mythic past, they are unspeakably bad. (The account of Atlantis itself depended upon the goddess of memory as Plato remarked in the *Critias*, 108D.) Furthermore, such migrations are inexpressible and thus incomprehensible to a bridge between past and future, time and eternity, to a symbol of love "whose stems inherit gods and drink the sea." In the remainder of the stanza the bridge becomes a white Anemone identified with Atlantis, not a "wind flower" or sea animal but a flower rising in radiance from the sea. Since it represents the Absolute rather than an earthly paradise, it is "Answerer of all" — answerer of all questions and of all men, although only the inspired poet-priest is aware of this. He especially is inherited or possessed by the radiance of the flower which sheds its light on all; indeed, it is a mutual possession—for the singer a kind of knowledge or illumination by identification analogous to the highest level of mystical experience. When he implores Atlantis to hold its "floating singer late," he is asking that his ecstatic state be prolonged so that he may more fully celebrate the Absolute, may enable others to see what he has seen.

Thus, toward the divine, transcendental, and eternal presence of the Absolute, the mystical and musical "strings" of the bridge "leap and converge." Its cables are like spears colored by one summoning star which sheds "infinity," and they are starry masses armed in steel. Yet from the many comes the One, the "Psalm of Cathay," the Bridge of Fire.

So to thine Everpresence, beyond time,
Like spears ensanguined of one tolling star
That bleeds infinity—the orphic strings,

Sidereal phalanxes, leap and converge:
—One Song, one Bridge of Fire! Is it
   Cathay,
Now pity steeps the grass and rainbows
   ring
The serpent with the eagle in the leaves
   . . . ?
Whispers antiphonal in azure swing.

In this final stanza Crane is merely speaking of the bridge as symbol, but he might well be speaking of the entire poem. "Atlantis," he wrote Otto Kahn, is the "mystic consummation toward which all the other sections of the poem converge," and "their contents are implicit in its summary" (*Letters*, p. 240). "The Bridge" itself is one Psalm of Cathay and one bridge of fire. The flame and fire of "Ave Maria" and "The Dance," and perhaps the embers, blood, and fire of "Southern Cross," are recalled here; the tolling or "telling" star that bleeds infinity may be the same as the "one star" that "immortally . . . bled into the dawn" in "The Dance"; and the serpent with the eagle in the leaves are the serpent of time and eagle of space in "The Dance," "The River," and "Cape Hatteras."

When the speaker asks, "Is it Cathay?" he is repeating the question of "Ave Maria" which Columbus thought he had answered. Despite this question, one has no reason to assert, as so many critics have, that Crane ends the poem with a query or an expression of doubt; for not only is there an answer in the last line, but within the lines in which he is asking what the bridge signifies in relation to the land that produced it he is answering by means of the symbolic rainbow. The celestial analogue of the bridge, the rainbow is a sign of affirmation, hope, and approval, like the shimmering arch vindicating the vision of Whitman at the end of "Cape Hatteras" or the bow set in the cloud in Genesis (9:13-16). In effect, the last line of the poem is elliptical: the azure swing of the bridge whispers "yes" in a devout musical response to the crucial question. This "yes" is whispered in the sense that only those who have the sensitivity of the seer can hear it.

To some critics, whether hostile or neutral, what Crane is conveying in "Atlantis" and certain other poems is "some vague transcendental experience that had no basis in clear thinking or controlling feeling." It is claimed that he used words "merely as an excitant, blurring all coherent vision in confused declamatory resonance," and the last stanza of "Atlantis" is cited as an example (Drew and Sweeney, *Directons in Modern Poetry*, p. 70). What I have been trying to suggest, in the face of such opposition, is that much poetic *mania* makes divinest sense, that in typical stanzas of "Atlantis" a reasonably sympathetic reader who is willing to work seldom encounters confusion or lack of control. There are local difficulties which arise from the radically metaphorical nature of Crane's style and the complexity of his syntax, but the more carefully one studies the poem, the more one becomes convinced that he knew what he was doing. By eighteenth-century standards Crane, like Shakespeare and other exploiters of the full resources of language, is occasionally guilty of "mixing" metaphors, yet this is not the major source of his alleged obscurity. A principal cause of his legendary difficulty is his heavy reliance on emotive rather than sense metaphors, on metaphors that are essentially untranslatable even though they have some basis in "sense," combined with a habit of viewing the subject of discourse from multiple metaphorical perspectives. Almost any of the stanzas I have briefly discussed will support and illustrate this assertion.

Finally, one must point to the fundamentally religious character of his outlook as another source of his comparative obscurity. By nature and nurture a transcendental idealist, he embraced no formal philosophy and no organized religion, despite his reading of Plato and Nietzsche and his exposure to Christian Science. His religion became the pursuit of the Absolute, conceived not as God but as the equivalent of God and experienced as a living ideal whose reality transcends space and time. His pursuit of this ideal is manifested in religious diction which may often appear Biblical or Neoplatonic yet has no specific traditional content, no reference to a text which would guide us to his meaning. It is not so much the confusion of his "vision" as the relative lack of a traditional vocabulary that leads to the charge of unintelligibility. In short, Crane is one of the many who, through no fault of their own, have been largely deprived of the common sources of the western tradition—the Bible and classical mythology and philosophy. The proper attitude to take toward this deprivation is not the pitying superiority implicit in some criticism of his work, but a charitable sympathy based on an awareness of the abysmal ignorance of even the wisest men.

Cummings the Chivalrous

by ROBERT G. TUCKER

There is something chivalric about e.e. cummings' poems. Beyond the lower-case protestations of his own nonheroism, he gallantly jousts with all modern monsters—constrictive conventionalism, eyeless impersonality, merciless mobbism, rampant regimentation—as though to clear the air of lovelessness, that he may do the other, the chief thing: celebrate to the Nth the love that he and his Lady share.

Like Shakespeare, cummings is convinced that "Love's not Time's fool," and like Shakespeare, he presents us with the range, all the way from spontaneous, juvenile eroticism through joyous, mature marriage and costly, courageous compassion to the love of God. But though Shakespeare shows us the loveless for a time enough sustained, after their being confronted with their own wretchedness, that we may realize the confrontation as healing, cummings, having thrust the fierce lance, does not stay at the scene to watch any dragon turn into a prince, but immediately after the encounter departs to sing lovesongs to his Lady. When next the loveless or the partial enter the field of vision, cummings' celebration is interrupted, it ceases, and he sallies forth again, clad in the armor of indignation, brandishing satire as though it were still in its pristine power when the satirist's tongue alone could kill, could ridicule literally to death, obliterate along with the offender the offense forever.

Why, then, do not cummings' monsters stay dead? I submit that the quality of the long love which he celebrates and the quality of the ridicule with which he swiftly strikes and departs represent notably distinct, finally incompatible feelings. His expression of this cleavage, felt apparently as in his characters or his audience, despite frequent liveliness, always reveals some attendant anguish in its valorous host. And, to some degree, though somewhat subdued, this anguish remains in the last book, 73 Poems (1963), not only in lines like this (from poem 45):

. . .

—not though mankind would rather know
    than feel;
mistrusting utterly that timelessness
whose absence would make your whole life
and my(and infinite our)merely to undie

but the anguish also remains even as late in the sequence as poem 70, as witness the concluding lines:

and partially imagine whose despair
when every silence will not make a dream
speak; or if to no millionth metaphor

opens the simple agony of time

—small wonder such a monster's fellowmen
miscalled are happy should his now go then

For it is, we may recognize, a cultural as well as a personal cleavage in which cummings finds himself; he is responding in kind, though more skillfully, to those who most bluntly display the ill temper of our time. Compare a much earlier poem from is 5 (1926), approved for collection in Poems 1923-1954 and again for 100 Selected Poems (1959); I refer to "my sweet old etcetera," and (in this war-poem) particularly to the lines

. . . my

mother hoped that

i would die etcetera
bravely of course my father used
to become hoarse talking about how it was
a privilege and if only he
could meanwhile my

self etcetera lay quietly
in the deep mud . . .

The awareness that parents anywhere could conceive their child as, for whatever cause, expendable is presented as thoroughly loathsome, and we are invited to share a sort of universal abhorrence of such confused parental attitudes. To be sure, in W [ViVa] (1931) we find "if there are any heavens my mother will (all by herself)have/ one;" in 50 Poems (1940) we find "my father moved through dooms of love;" and pages 8-13 of i:six nonlectures (1953) also show cummings' admiration for the heroic personalities of his mother and father.

Nevertheless, there is, if only culturally speaking, enough pressure behind the sentence, "my/ mother hoped that/ i would die," to express and emotionally account for cummings' unflagging distrust of and contempt for anything like the frequent callousness of authority, whether parental, social, religious, scholarly, scientific, military, or national. The Enormous Room (1922), his first book, is concerned with that grotesque Kafkaesque World War I experience: his being imprisoned (although he was a volunteer in the Norton Harjes Ambulance Corps) for three months in a concentration camp as the result of a mistake by a French official. Why, then, wouldn't he, at the least sound of "must" on the wind, even like Hotspur, rush from his Lady's bower to do bold justice (and balance the scales by his might), then at the faintest hope of "may," swiftly himself again, happily return to songs of love?

As is feuding and war on tribes and nations, though, satire is fundamentally hard on the satirist. It may briefly relieve his irritation, but it cannot cure it, since he, too, must consciously adopt the "villain's" role and express it exactly, while in his depths abhorring such a role. It is an anguished projection of, in reaction to, a felt hostility, no matter how gallantly or gleefully conducted on the surface. No man is an island at heart. Cummings, in correspondence with me, once implied an associated difficulty. I had said that I believed men capable of mercy, but not of true justice (which, in our ignorance of all the ramifications, therefore seemed to me more appropriately left to God); cummings replied (July 18, 1954),

· · ·

as for "justice" versus "mercy": our non-hero would doubtless exclaim (with his dark taxidriving friend) Heartily Agreed, if showing "mercy" didn't strike me as significantly easier than doing "justice" . . .

I didn't then, I don't now believe that ease or difficulty are crucial to the question of exercising capabilities which are given, and I have never contended elsewhere (see *The Massachusetts Review* 1, Spring, 1963, pp. 497-498) and I am not contending here that cummings' satirical poems are not valuable and exemplary in their intent to present to our awareness, as they do, dreadful inhumanities. My sole concern here is to note that the presentations express a personal anguish (hard on cummings) and a cultural anguish (hard, in the fashions of lovelessness, on us all), an anguish which has never been and cannot be permanently resolved by satire, however acute, because of the simultaneously contradictory stances which writer and reader alike must adopt in order to achieve satire's judgmental effect, though that be only one of its effects.

Bearing this effect of cummings' chivalry in mind, then, we turn to consider some of its other effects. As implied above, cummings' indignation is related to the way in which he values individual freedom as against all creeping tendencies toward callous inhumanity, the monsters cited above: *pro-patria*-tism, corporatism, groupism—I needn't extend the list. His Lady is much more closely associated with

La Liberté in his love than any abstract nationalism ever could be. And the expression of the range of his feelings has had the valuable effect of awakening us to possibilities beyond the conventional, setting us to think and feel about our valuation of freedom for ourselves and freedom for others. Similarly, the notorious liberties which cummings takes with the conventions of our most permanent public/private intermediary, written language—the rejection of capital letters, save for irony or special effects; the setting-forth of words on the page in such arrangements that he could dispense with almost all conventional punctuation (or, when using it, could omit conventional spacing between a comma, say, and the following letter), yet still (or even more precisely) express his meaning; even dividing words into their syllables or separate letters, putting these in unique and expressive spacial relations with one another—these liberties enable one to catch quite accurately the snap and the nuance of his human speaking-voice, all its tones alive. Cummings takes liberties as Walt Whitman takes liberties, and we, poetry, and the language are the richer for it.

Moreover, cummings' free style is exemplary in the sense that he seems never to imply, "Exactly imitate me!" but rather, "Here is what one of us can do with the conventions and still communicate effectively (at least on a par with most attempts); so why not go and see what you can do in *your* way? Each of us is valuable to others chiefly as he is honestly himself." Together, the love-poems and the satires, the many pages of vital, maturing poetry from *Tulips and Chimneys* (1923) to *73 Poems* (1963), present a broad spectrum, from brutal irony against what he felt unworthy of human beings to pure lyricism, celebrating the love which he found inseparable from truth and beauty, and the best, even the noblest, human experience. If he shocks, it is not to lower standards but to raise them—invariably in the direction of valuing and respecting individual worth and freedom, toward realizing and cherishing the dignity in each created soul.

I want therefore to be as honest and clear as possible in what follows. Though I can truly sympathize with cummings, I cannot be unqualifiedly grateful for whatever persisting in him made him suffer so long the satirical sense of alienation, division, cleavage, as though this were some half-life which all (except he and his Lady and individuals already matured by love) were doomed to lead on earth—especially when, often in the same poem, he expresses the maturing-agent, the remedy, fully, apparently without fully realizing it. Consider, in its order of culmination, the very last poem we have from cummings' hand, poem 73 of *73 Poems*, in its entirety:

all worlds have half-sight, seeing either with

life's eye(which is if things seem spirits)or
(if spirits in the guise of things appear)
death's; any world must always half
   perceive.

Only whose vision can create the whole

(being forever born a foolishwise
proudhumble citizen of ecstasies
more steep than climb can time with all
   his years)

he's free into the beauty of the truth;

and strolls the axis of the universe
—love. Each believing world denies,
   whereas
your lover(looking through both life and
   death)
timelessly celebrates the merciful

wonder no world deny may or believe

I want to say "Yes" to everything here concerning your lover and love. But I ask, why "must" (? line 4) love—the whole vision, not the half—be at all exclusive of time and the world? If the beauty of truth, the axis of the universe, really be love, then that's forever thankfully that, and cummings often elsewhere and here can happily transcend the Platonic, Pauline cleavage between things and spirit. Even the ancients cannot keep the breach from healing: Plato is never so felicitous as when creating a parable which does *not* completely divide the world from the ideal (see his Ladder of Love, his Cave, for instance), nor was Paul ever more effective than when, as the Christ of the gospels often does, he celebrates love as both a present and eternal possibility for all men.

Surely the mature artist is largely responsible for his art, a place marvelously designed for patience, for taking time to find a way to resolve hostilities, to show reconciliation, a secular scripture, if you like, whose values can be transferred to life, as in teaching, on occasions, or perhaps as often in family, social, business, political, international, and religious affairs on earth. In his art, the artist has the greatest privilege of performing for the full house, the total audience, not as divided into sheep (for praise) and goats (for judgment, ridicule, wrath, damnation). Come hell or high water, rejection or acceptance, in art and joy one may speak as to all, performing his praiseful act of, by, and for humanity whole.

David R. Clark, a staunch friend and colleague, and I accomplished, over nearly ten years, the half-hour act of getting broadcast an unexpurgated tape of cummings (reading a sequence of his poems chosen to express his idea of freedom). The Educational Radio Network thankfully carried the half-hour in an hour-program from WFCR, Amherst, January 14, 1963. Clark and I played our parts on- and off-stage thus, simply to let cummings' voice be heard reading. I do not now propose to cramp cummings' style (even were that possible); I have intended only to suggest what culturally seems behind and involved in that style. To understand his work as well as possible, in no way precludes my love for so human a poet, AS IS.

If repeated reading of the enduring masters from Homer and Job onward, and continuing thought about it, is valid, I would prophesy that those poems in which cummings accepts and celebrates (without sensing in his audience a single mind divided) are those which will be cherished longest. And he accepts, celebrating as only he can, in poem after poem, his Lady, spring, the sea, sky, mountains, birds, roses, handorgans, mud, balloons, clowns, streets, wind, a leaf—each singular, unique, and God-given creature whom he could wonderfully, humanly love. The jousts and the forays, the savagery, are the work of a time that passes so swiftly as to make even anguish seem poignant. For in the everlasting NOW, as his Lady knows, and as cummings sings, in his most chivalrous voice (at the conclusion of "my father moved through dooms of love"),

Love is the whole and more than all

"No Ideas but in Things":

William Carlos Williams in the Twenties

by RICHARD J. CALHOUN

The most surprising thing about an attempt to evaluate William Carlos Williams' poetry in the 1920's is that after four decades the job still needs to be done. (Linda Welschimer Wagner's *The Poems of William Carlos Williams,* which appeared while this essay was in proof, makes a partial contribution but places primary emphasis on Williams in the 1930's and the 1940's.) Perhaps Williams, himself, serves as the best guide to the reason for this sorry state of affairs. In his *Autobiography* he recounts how he felt in 1922 when the thunderbolt of T. S. Eliot's *The Waste Land* struck.

It wiped out our world as if an atom bomb had been dropped upon it and our brave sallies into the unknown were turned to dust.

To me especially it struck like a sardonic bullet. I felt at once that it had set me back twenty years, and I'm sure it did. Critically Eliot returned us to the classroom just at the moment when I felt that we were on the point of an escape to matters much closer to the essence of a new art form itself—rooted in the locality which should give it fruit. I knew at once that in certain ways I was most defeated.

This quotation has been frequently cited as an example of Williams' antipathy to the Eliot tradition in American poetry. On first thought, I am tempted to comment that Williams was wrong in only one respect: his directions in American poetry received a setback of not twenty years—but almost forty.

On second thought, however, this assessment of Williams' fate seems a bit facile. The truth of the matter is that Eliot's rise to such a great position of influence was not the only reason Williams did not receive his critical due for what he was attempting in the 1920's. His poetry obviously offers difficulties for critical evaluation, since on the surface it does not seem to be concerned with ideas. In addition, Williams was not entirely defeated: he always had a pleasant relationship with poets whom he desired to influence. He was correct, however, in asserting that there was little evidence of any direct influence. In his early years, he knew but apparently did not influence Pound, Hilda Doolittle, and Marianne Moore. Theodore Roethke, whose work Williams admired, never

spoke of any direct influence in the thirties or forties so far as I know; and Robert Lowell has recently written of his early period that he admired Williams but could not enter into him. The title of one of his poems written in the 1920's seems prophetic—"To a Solitary Disciple."

Recently, the situation has changed. Professor Glauco Cambon has pointed to Williams' influence on the recent movement in American poetry toward open forms by poets like Donald Hall, James Wright, and the recent Robert Lowell, as well as on the "beats" and near-"beats." Karl Shapiro, certainly the strongest opponent of the Eliot tradition in the present decade and currently the most vocal advocate of a Whitman tradition in American literature, now pays Williams the compliment of including him with the master, Whitman, as the only truly American poets we have so far produced. This current movement in poetry away from tradition, away from the academic, away from the objective correlative, is another reason for a reexamination of what Williams was attempting in the 1920's. He fought some of the same battles then.

Certainly Williams was productive enough in the twenties to deserve detailed critical notice from someone other than his friend, Kenneth Burke. This was the period when the many fine poems in the *Collected Poems 1921-1931* (New York, 1934) were published. Most of these appeared in periodicals or in three principal poetic works, *Kora in Hell: Improvisations* (1920), if not poetry, a prose poem; *Sour Grapes* (1921); and *Spring and All* (1923), with its prose manifestoes about his poetry. *Al Que Quiere!,* which Kenneth Burke called the real beginning of his major style, had been published just three years prior, in 1917. In addition, there were such prose works as *The Great American Novel* (1923), *In the American Grain* (1925), and *A Voyage to Pagany* (1928).

Although there has not been much perceptive criticism on Williams, he is usually given credit for at least two contributions to American poetry during the twenties. First, he often did what the good artist should do in that in his concentration on familiar materials he managed to transcend them and reveal things as we have not quite seen them before. Second, he helped to open up the restricted, late nineteenth-century and early twentieth-century catalogue of usable poetic materials. Of course, most modern poets, even those not called "anti-poetic," have done this; but I believe Williams' contribution has been rather special.

It is not so much this diction that is different from that of his contemporaries as it is the poetic objects—the "things"—that he describes. But then again, such a statement is very likely only partially accurate. A fuller statement should indicate that the striking difference between Williams and his contemporaries is that he used these objects as the subjects for *entire* poems. Other poets have used them *in* poems, but not *as* poems as consistently as Williams did. Two poems which express very well the poet's awareness of his absorption in unorthodox objects are the first two poems called "Pastoral" in the *Collected Earlier Poems*. The first makes clear his preoccupation.

> When I was younger
> it was plain to me
> I must make something of myself.
> Older now
> I walk back streets
> admiring the houses
> of the very poor:
> roof out of line with sides
> the yards cluttered
> with old chicken wire, ashes,
> furniture gone wrong;
> the fences and outhouses
> built of barrel-staves
> and parts of boxes, all,
> if I am fortunate,
> smeared a bluish green
> that properly weathered
> pleases me best
> of all colors.

And it concludes with stress on his awareness of how others will regard his intense interest in such things.

> No one
> will believe this
> of vast import to the nation.

The second poem is based on two contrasts between an apparently lower and a higher form of life. The first contrast is between the quarreling "little sparrows" and the "wiser" human kind capable of guarding their emotions. The second contrast features the gait of an old man "gathering dog-lime," whose

> tread
> is more majestic than
> that of the Episcopal minister
> approaching the pulpit
> of a Sunday.

His conclusion is a statement of amazement at his own observations.

> These things
> Astonish me beyond words.

Finally, in a poem significantly entitled "Apology," he confesses the reasons for his choice of subjects.

> Why do I write today?
>
> The beauty of
> the terrible faces
> of our nonentities
> stirs me to it:
>
> colored women
> day workers—
> old and experienced—
> returning home at dusk
> in cast off clothing
> faces like
> old Florentine oak.
>
> Also
>
> the set pieces
> of your faces stir me—
> leading citizens—
> but not
> in the same way.

It is Williams' absorption in such objects as these which earned him the designation of being "anti-poetic," a charge first made by Wallace Stevens in his "Preface" to the *Collected Poems 1921-1931*. Since Williams always felt that this description misrepresented his intentions, perhaps a better authority is his own statement in the "Prologue" to *Kora in Hell*. Here he makes it clear that his poems represent a struggle, sometimes a successful one, sometimes unsuccessful, to lift to "the imagination those things which lie under the direct scrutiny of the senses, close to the nose."

This concern with immediate experience explains why Williams has been sometimes slighted as merely a regionalist, because the task he set forth led him to champion the use of the local and the familiar. T. S. Eliot, perhaps deliberately, took Williams' stress on the local and on place as meaning that Williams could be only of "local interest." Again, Williams was the victim of a critical injustice. What he really advocated, of course, was not local color in any sense of the term but the use of familiar materials as the means to general truths. He has always contended that the local is the universal. Perhaps Eliot was aware that Williams' stress on the importance of the local was in part a rejection of Eliot's own brand of literary symbolism. Williams had always objected to Eliot's symbols as being incapable of dealing with life directly or of communicating except to "the instructed few." In addition, as he made clear in an essay in the late thirties, Eliot's supernaturalism was an affront to Williams' humanism. Because of it Eliot failed to show that man "is mysterious in his own right and does not submit to more than his common sensual relationship to explain him." (*Selected Essays*, p. 212) Williams' own focus was on man and the relationship of his consciousness to his physical surroundings.

In order to understand the importance of the local to Williams one must come to grips with his concept of "place." It is hard to define, because "place" is a rather general term which nevertheless performs the specific purpose of making effective in his poetry his view that "the local is the only thing that is universal." In fact, one might say that in a sense "place" to Williams is his twentieth-century substitution for what in the nineteenth century poets called "nature." It refers to man's immediate experience, to what confronts him directly in his world. One of Williams' clearest definitions of "place" occurs in a discussion of the local; it is the "local (in the sense of being attached with integrity to actual experience)." (*Selected Essays*, p. 118) Not surprisingly, a fellow writer in the twenties who found it easy to grasp Williams' stress on the importance of both the local and place was D. H. Lawrence. At work himself on *The Plumed Serpent*, Lawrence took time out to review *In the American Grain (The Nation,* 1928). He found himself in perfect agreement with Williams' stated preference for the local in literature. With characteristic eloquence he made it clear that the local "is the very opposite of the parochial, the parish pump stuff. The local in America is America itself. Not Salem, or Boston, or Philadelphia, or New York, but that of the American subsoil which sprouts up in any of these places into the lives of men." Lawrence also saw that "place" is what makes such creative art possible, for it must "rise out of a specific soil and flicker with a spirit of place." Finally, as the author of a study of American literature himself, Lawrence endorsed one of the major arguments of *In the American Grain*— that America has only been infrequently realized as a place, as a "thing" to be experienced and consequently more than a means to some end, such as the Puritan end with its abstract or theological view.

In a 1933 essay on the photographer, Alfred Stieglitz, Williams made another statement as to the importance of "place" in his poetry in the twenties. He had been attempting to respond to a "burning need" of American culture. In his view what was needed and what the poet could attempt to supply was

> realization of the qualities of a place in relation to the life which occupies it; embracing everything involved, climate, geographic position, relative size, history, other cultures—as well as the character of its sands, flowers, minerals and the condition of knowledge within its borders.
> (*Selected Essays*, p. 157)

He was also confident that art like Stieglitz's and poetry like his own would find a response in a love of the actual which underlies "all American enjoyment." And if I might append a final note, there is a rather obvious relationship between Williams' theory of language, of an American diction for American poetry, and his concept of "place." Like his contemporary, H. L. Mencken, he was undoubtedly a believer in an American language, which because of its different place must be different from English.

Most discussions of Williams start with another quotation, not with "the local is the only universal" but with the better known "Say it, no ideas but in things," which first appeared in the early "Paterson" sketches. No statement in Williams is more important if properly understood. Unfortunately, too many critics have placed their stress on the two words "no ideas" and have simply classified Williams as some kind of Imagist, or as he called himself, an Objectivist,—at any rate, one who lacked the serious concern with ideas of a poet like T. S. Eliot. I should like to place the stress where it properly belongs, on the entire phrase, and consequently correct some misapprehensions about Williams' relationship to Imagism and Objectivism. No greater service can be performed for Williams' status as a poet, unless it would be to crack the mystery of the remarkable effectiveness of his unadorned diction, a service requiring the concentrated critical efforts of a Randall Jarrell or a Robert Lowell.

Obviously Williams owed much to Imagism. Professor Stanley Coffman in his history of the movement regards Williams' poetry as a beautiful illustration of the objectivity of Imagism, of its desire to use language to reproduce the appearance of things as concisely and as scientifically as possible. Another authority on Imagism, Ezra Pound, was willing to take Williams' own statement of his difference with the Imagists at face value and judge him in the 1920's as an Objectivist. To Pound "Objectivism" simply meant that poetry was in the object itself. What he failed to consider, however, was Williams' own insistence on form. In his *Autobiography* Williams defines Objectivism as the view that the poem is an object that states its meaning by the very form it assumes. The form is something created by the poet, an artifact that makes the difference.

In the poem "The Wind Increases" Williams asks the question: "Good Christ what is / a poet—if any / exists?" His answer stresses not only the accuracy of the portrayal of what he sees but the novelty of his observations, the force of his words, and the rhythm of his lines. The answer is that a poet is

```
a man
whose words will
          bite
              their way
home—being actual
having the form
                  of motion
At each twigtip

new

upon the tortured
body of thought
        gripping
the ground
a way
        to the last leaftip
```

What these lines imply is something that always made Williams a bit more than an Imagist. He felt that truth lies in the province of the poet and that it is by staying close to the actual, the "thingness" of things, that the poet reveals his truth. He often commented sardonically that John Dewey might have explained him to the public. This comment makes sense to the extent that there is something very practical about his emphasis on the local and about his belief that there are "No ideas but in things." His view might be regarded as just a good American pragmatic stress on knowing the nature of things because we need to have practical knowledge of their utility and function in order to avoid living too abstractly on the mere surfaces of actuality. But this explanation does not take into consideration Williams' apparent belief that he is making an important truth claim for art. Dewey's *Art as Experience* might serve as a gloss on Williams' intentions.

Or, granting that Williams had no knowledge of Dewey's works, one might nevertheless give a measure of philosophical validity to Williams' ideas by going far from American empiricism and pointing out a similarity to Martin Heidegger's view of the relationship of art to things. According to Heidegger an artist like Van Gogh in his painting of a peasant's shoes reveals to us what these shoes really and truly are, what the true nature of things for daily use is—in short, what the true *being* of things is. Art brings to the fore the true nature of existing reality, as the phenomenologists say, by the act of getting us to transcend the "natural attitude," which with all its presuppositions keeps us from really seeing the object. Probably Williams would have been flattered by this comparison since he wanted to be explained by more than just Dewey.

As further proof of Williams' concern with ideas one might turn to his strong personal belief that poetry is never escape from a serious concern with life. To Williams it is escape only from the false illusions, the failure of the imagination of the masses. As he wrote to John Crowe Ransom in the thirties, "It is not, in other words, evasion. But it *is* escape—from the herd." (*Selected Letters,* p. 273)

Williams believed that the only approach to reality is through the details of actuality because that is where we are. Consequently his objects are chosen from the commonplace of the American scene — a red wheelbarrow, sparrows, the young housewife, a laundryman, a crowd at the ballgame, and so on. The tangible, everyday world and workaday people are the materials of his poetry; but, in order to convey the truth in the things, he tries to avoid either a sentimental or a commonplace view. In his best poems he succeeds; in his worst, he fails. In the best, he escapes from the mass view, from the world where so little "depends" to that where "so much depends." Both his poems and his prose essays insist on the importance of this endeavor.

> To be an artist, as to be a good artisan, a man must know his materials. But in addition he must possess that really glandular perception of their uniqueness which realizes in them an end in itself, each piece irreplaceable by a substitute, not to be broken down to other meaning. Not to pull out, transubstantiate, boil, unglue, hammer, melt, digest and psychoanalyze, not even to distill but to see and keep what the understanding touches intact—as grapes are round and come in bunches.

The function of the artist is to "discover and separate these things from the amorphous, the conglomerate normality with which they are surrounded. . . ." (*Selected Essays,* p. 233)

One might draw up a much longer list of quotations, but perhaps the most significant commentary lies imbedded in a poem previously mentioned, "To a Solitary Disciple." The advice to this "disciple" might be summed up in the verbs, all verbs of seeing—"notice," "observe," "grasp," "perceive," "See." But what the disciple is directed to *see* is not the usual color of the morning scene but the *relationships* of the objects.

> Rather notice, mon cher,
> that the moon is
> tilted above
> the point of the steeple
> than that its color
> is shell-pink.

A truth emerges from the fact that there is an observable opposition at work. The little "ornament" (ironically, the cross) at the pinnacle of the steeple tries to stop the converging lines from reaching the moon but fails as they enclose the moon in a momentary image of beauty, or so it appears to the poet's imagination. Only through the contribution of the imagination made possible by seeing the relationship of the two (the moon and the steeple) from the particular point of view of the poet at that particular moment, does the truth come that there are moments of observed beauty in opposites, "weight" and "lightness," earth and air. But with Williams' characteristic realism, the poem concludes with attention called to those opposites in their ordinary states, apart from this momentary relationship.

> But observe
> the oppressive weight
> of the squat edifice!
> Observe
> the jasmine lightness
> of the moon.

Another key statement of Williams is "Divorce is the sign of knowledge in our time." (*Paterson*, Book I) "Divorce" is a theme in many of his poems long before *Paterson* because one of his major aims as a poet was the search for relationships between "things." A sizeable body of his poems start with apparently diffuse objects and arrive at some sort of "apperception" by showing how they are related within the field of perception; in a second large group of poems Williams is merely content to concentrate on a perception regarding a single object. In some of these, the most Imagistic, the "perception" fails to come off. Roy Harvey Pearce has commented that some of his poems reflect the poet's failure to understand what he sees.

The theme of "divorce" is so important to Williams that it has been called by at least one critic his equivalent for sin. (The best discussion of "divorce" and fragmentation in Williams is the unpublished Columbia University Dissertation (1959), "The Poetic World of William Carlos Williams," by Alan B. Ostrom.) Unlike Eliot, Williams is concerned with evil not in a theological sense but in what might be called an existential sense. Evil is the separation of anything from its true nature or its real place in the world. Since to Williams the artist should be the whole man, he is even more opposed than the early Eliot to any type of dissociation of sensibility; the poet's rational powers must not be separated from his emotional resources. In his poetry Williams is seeking to unify experience by showing us either his own relatedness to an object or the internal relationships of objects taken from his own location in time and place. Or, as suggested above, he simply "presents" his failure to "reconcile." Consequently his concern with "divorce" is additional evidence for my contention that ideas have a place in his poetry in that it provides him with "theme" and "symbols."

Let me elaborate further. First of all, he does not make any distinction beween body and mind as sources of knowledge. Man's emotional life is part of his existence, his life of actuality; it is part of his total adjustment and response and consequently not inferior to reason. Every part of the body is engaged in a response. This insistence on the integrity of the body is even given comical treatment as when the nose is given its due in the poem "Smell!"

> Oh strong-ridged and deeply hollowed
> nose of mine! what will you not be
> smelling?
> . . . .
> Must you taste everything? Must you know
> everything?
> Must you have a part in everything?

Or with a bit of metonomy added, in the poem "The Eyeglasses" it is the eyeglasses (not eyes) that are drawn by the "universality of things . . . toward the candy / with melon flowers that open" rather than to "A letter from the man who / wants to start a new magazine / made of linen."

Second, as a consequence of his obsession with "divorce," Williams is almost the polar opposite of Hart Crane in at least one important respect. Crane desired to absorb the machine; Williams is almost Blakean in his rejection of the mechanical because he regards it solely as a product of man's abstracting mind. He views technology as having promoted dissociation by encouraging us to transform even the most concrete aspects of human experience into ideas. As a result, we are concerned not with things but with abstractions. Once more we have an explanation for his insistence, "No ideas but in things."

To Williams, the preoccupation of our technological society with the mechanical deprives man not only of a needed contact with "things" but also of time for other human beings. It makes something as natural as love almost impossible. Many poems make it clear that man needs love, but Williams usually avoids the sentimental in stating his view. On occasion he spices his point with a bit of irony, for instance, in "Riposte."

Love is like water or the air
my townspeople;
it cleanses, and dissipates evil gases.
It is like poetry too
and for the same reasons.
Love is so precious
my townspeople
that if I were you I would
have it under lock and key—
like the air or the Atlantic or
like poetry!

At times for the physician, love takes the form of compassion for the patient, as in the poem "Complaint," when he enters the dark room where there is "a great woman / on her side in the bed." He notes that "Night is a room / darkened for lovers," and concludes:

I pick the hair from her eyes
and watch her misery
with compassion.

At times he regards it as something just for the young.

An old willow with hollow branches
slowly swayed his few high bright tendrils
and sang:
Love is a young green willow
shimmering at the bare weed's edge.

Sometimes metonomy is used and an object associated with the loved one becomes an object of love, as in "Thinker," as the speaker views his wife's "new pink slippers" and concludes about them:

And I talk to them
in my secret mind
out of pure happiness.

In the poem "Blueflags," as he lets the children play at the marsh edge he employs a symbol from Whitman of his love: "there comes the smell / of calamus / from wet, gummy stalks." In poems in the later twenties and the thirties this theme is replaced by a pessimistic awareness that social conditions demean it.

The justice of poverty
its shame its dirt
are one with the meanness
of love

Third, perhaps partly as a reaction to the Eliot tradition, Williams also laments our modern tendency to "divorce" the conventional or the traditional from the natural. This theme is particularly important in the poems concerned with art and the artist. There are more of these than one might think at first glance. It has been suggested that even his poem "Tract" might be interpreted not so much as about a funeral as a statement of the artist's preference for the natural over the conventional. In order to stress the necessity of the artist's rootedness in the natural a good many of his poems are landscape poems which tend to reverse the order of the eighteenth-century prospect poem by beginning with a general scene and then narrowing it down to one particular object on the natural or human scene. Poems with this type of structure include "Approach of Winter," "Spring Storm," "The Farmer," and "Tulip Bed."

If it is partly as a result of his hatred of "divorce" and his consequent desire for relatedness that Williams, like Frost, tends to accept the naturalness of mind and nature, then his mode of acceptance is not a "what is —is right" view. Like Frost he does not necessarily approve of what he accepts but is simply realistic to the point of excluding any false illusions. In *Kora in Hell* he wrote: "Out of bitterness itself the clear wine of the imagination will be pressed and the dance prosper thereby." Twenty years later, he wrote in *Paterson*, Book II: "Be reconciled, poet, with your world, it is the only truth." This sanity, this acceptance, marks a difference between Williams and many of the writers of the 1950's and the 1960's who posit an absurd world.

His view of the artist's role of defiance is also different. In an essay for his architect brother, Williams made it clear that a poet may write out of defiance, "but it is a defiance because he sees something worth having. He must shake himself free, he himself as one man, from the destroying horror of an oppressive existence." (*Selected Essays*, p. 180) In 1928 Kenneth Burke, reviewing Williams' work for *The Dial*, aptly summed up what I would regard as the difference between Williams' "lostness" and the present-day theme of absurdity by remarking that he "has learned to be lost without pretence or despair. He does not attempt to palm off horrors as facts. It is from curiosity that his ideas derive rather than from unrest."

To turn to another form of Williams' acceptance, I feel that his poems on another modern theme, death, deserve more critical attention than they have received. Williams' view is utterly realistic without any hope of immortality. It is one of the major themes of his poetry in the twenties. He views death as an equalizer in the early poem, "Spring Song," where he pretends there is

> some subtle difference,
> one last amour
>
> to be divided for
> our death-necklaces, . . .

But this hope is only an illusion, and the poem becomes a love poem with the conclusion.

> I would merely lie
> hand in hand in the dirt with you.

This emphasis on death as "dust unto dust" is the usual view in Williams. One of the most vivid poems insisting on this theme but still understating its horror is "K. McB."

> You exquisite chunk of mud
> Kathleen—just like
> any other chunk of mud!
> —especially April!
> Curl up round their shoes
> when they try to step on you,
> spoil the polish!
> I shall laugh till I am sick
> at their amazement.
> Do they expect the ground to be
> always solid?
> Give them the slip then;
> let them sit in you;
> soil their pants;
> teach them a dignity
> that is dignity, the dignity
> of mud!
>   Lie basking in
> the sun then—fast asleep!
> Even become dust on occasion.

Death is "complete destruction"—a view concisely stated in the poem by that title.

> It was an icy day,
> We buried the cat,
> then took her box
> and set match to it
>
> in the back yard.
> Those fleas that escaped
> earth and fire
> died by the cold.

Occasionally he invokes authority on death, his own as a doctor, one who has lived and fought with it, as in the poem "Death the Barber," when he tells the barber of

> the newest
> ways to grow
> hair on
> bald death.

It is as a doctor that Williams admires the struggle of life against death, evident in even the simplest forms of life, as in one of his best known poems, "By the Road to the Contagious Hospital," where he views the first signs of rebirth in the grass and thinks of the courage involved in birth in any form.

> They enter the new world naked,
> cold, uncertain of all
> save that they enter.

Then, the doctor has occasion to view the struggle of the patient with death as when he sees the "Old Jaundiced Woman" rolling her "saffron eyeballs" and moaning, "I can't die / I can't die."

It might be wondered whether an account of Williams as a poet in the twenties can conclude without consideration of his dissatisfaction with free verse, the consequent importance that the line unit assumed for him, and his search for a measure in terms of the triadic line. Since this is a subject that has been well covered by Vivienne Koch, Randall Jarrell, John Malcolm Brinnin, Roy Harvey Pearce, and others and since Williams himself regarded his search as not completed until the "variable foot" of *Paterson*, I shall exclude it from my account of Williams.

My concern with William Carlos Williams in the twenties has been rather with a poet who cannot be classified as just an Imagist, a continuator of Whitman, a better Sandburg, or as of local interest because his poetry seems to lack the depth that tradition, ideas, and symbolism impart. Even to regard him, apart from *Paterson*, simply as an impressionistic painter in verse, as Kenneth Burke and John Malcolm Brinnin tend to do, is sufficient to explain only certain poems—often his least successful ones, like "The Great Figure." Instead, I have tried to show that prior to *Paterson* Williams was interested in his own kind of ideas. We can understand this interest only if we understand his qualification, "No ideas but in things." The ideas come about only through language formed from an observer's response to objects in concrete situations. Hence his opposition to preconceived ideas and literary symbolism. His view has its analogies in such divergent theories about the relationship between thought and language as John Dewey's *Art as Experience* or the phenomenological aesthetics of Martin Heidegger and Maurice Merleau-Ponty.

The reason he seems to slight ideas in the traditional sense is that, first of all, his view of poetry was based on a belief in total response of the human body: the artist avoids "divorce." As he expressed this point in "How to Write," poetry involves "the middle brain, the nerves, the glands, the very muscles and the bones of the body itself speaking." (*Selected Essays,* p. 213) Second, his view stresses a discovery of form in the materials themselves by the imagination when freed from concepts and literary associations: "No ideas but in things."

In summation, there is a sort of up-to-date Emersonian self-reliance in Williams. Man must be self-reliant and free himself from the modern-day distractions of the technological world and rediscover a unity between the self and the natural world by avoiding "divorce" and discovering "place." I have also tried to show that a good many of Williams' prose statements serve as guides to his intentions; they should not be disregarded as polemical. If Williams' view of the "local," "place," "divorce," and "things" led him to be defiantly anti-literary in his techniques, I shall let him have the final say about this aspect of his endeavors as a poet. It was all

a reply to Greek and Latin
with
the bare hands.

Our Number is Her Nature

by FRANK DOGGETT

A naturalistic conception of things is a great work of imagination,—greater, I think, than any dramatic or moral mythology; it is a conception fit to inspire great poetry, and in the end, perhaps, it will prove the only conception able to inspire it.

Santayana

1

At the time of his first book, Stevens had already conceived for his poetry a minimum basis of thought, or, if not thought, at least a consistent view of things. In *Harmonium* he expresses a rudimentary naturalism that is usually little more than a sense of the reality of things about him—things moving and changing in the flux of time and experience. Its basis is an inherent skepticism that rejects the transcendent and can never rest in any explanation or circumscription of the world. Limiting the scope of his confidence to the immediate, he conjectures an indefinite and unknowable expanse beyond the impression of the moment.

To hold that the world is an indeterminable presence is to reject the idea of the microcosm. Stevens is too much of a skeptic to feel that he can gain the whole through a part, that like Blake he can see the world in a grain of sand. The "Indigo Glass in the Grass" explicitly states that in no object nor conjunction of objects can the world be contained. And in "The Comedian as the Letter C" the poet doubts that the world can be comprehended in one man's vision of it or even in any conjunction of human points of view:

What is one man among so many men?
What are so many men in such a world?

In an illimitable and incomprehensible world of continual flux, the human element is only one among many elements. The unity of the world as composed by one mind is only the unity of one life lived, and even that, like Crispin's, involves a continual readjustment of the sense of the world; for as the poet asks in extenuation of these readjustments, these vicissitudes of anyone's idea of the world:

Can one man think one thing and think it long?
Can one man be one thing and be it long?

The unspoken reply is the obvious negative. Crispin's, or anyone's, next moment will differ from the last and most probably resemble it as well.

Resemblances and differences are significant elements in experience for Stevens. They structure the natural world for him and are constituents of his naturalistic emphasis on the appearance of things in poems like "Sea Surface Full of Clouds" or "The Load of Sugar Cane." Some years later than *Harmonium* he wrote "Three Academic Pieces," whose opening essay is a brief account of the unity that resemblance gives to one's sense of the world. Simple resemblance itself is considered here to be "one of the significant components of the structure of reality." Resemblance of one thing to another is part of the continuity of experience. "It binds together. It is the base of appearance," the essay explains. Several poems in *Harmonium* anticipate the idea discussed in his essay, the idea of the unity that resemblance gives to the content of experience. In "Domination of Black" for instance, resemblance binds together everything named, and is the significant component of the sense of reality of the poem. The colors of the bushes and of the leaves recur in the color of fire, movement of the leaves in the wind is repeated in the turning of shadows and flames, and the color and movement of the leaves suggest that of the peacocks' tails:

The colors of their tails
Were like the leaves themselves
Turning in the wind.

The pivot of all these resemblances is the image of the movement of things in wind, and wind brings the idea of the flux of time to mind. By the same process of connotation, "peacock" symbolizes mind or self (at least for the speaker of the poem) with all its color turning in the flux and its cry against mortality. Connotation itself is created by the activity of a mind tracing resemblances. "Perhaps the whole field of connotation is based on resemblance," the essay conjectures. In the poem, connotations for the idea of mortality shared by hemlock, shadow and night are emphasized by resemblance; for all these things share a symbolic darkness. Stevens' essay says of this enhancement of a shared element or quality: "If resemblance is described as a partial similarity between two dissimilar things, it complements and reinforces that which the two dissimilar things have in common."

Resemblance is a thread of continuity from one impression to another followed by the mind seeking relations among things. Stevens probably was familiar with the chapter on "The One and the Many" in William James' *Pragmatism* and the discussion there of the various kinds of lines of continuity that bind the world together. James indicates the necessity of a sense of the continuity of things on the field of consciousness, notes that the mind can pass in many ways from one thing to another, speaks of the lines of influence or relationship that can be traced: "Following any such line you pass from one thing to another till you may have covered a good part of the universe's extent." He says that to follow simple continuity it is even enough to move from one thing to another and say that there is this and this and this.

Tracing the structure of reality through the discernment of resemblance or of any other lines of continuity that bind the world together, the mind is engaged in its natural activity and becomes the "secretive hunter" of "Stars at Tallapoosa":

> Let these be your delight, secretive hunter,
> Wading the sea-lines, moist and ever
>   mingling,
> Mounting the earth-lines, long and lax,
>   lethargic,
> These lines are swift and fall without
>   diverging.

The swift lines falling without divergence and the lines between the stars of the first stanza are all lines of relationship and cognitive interconnection, as even the imaginary lines of starlight must be. All these lines are part of the continuity of experience and compose what William James describes as "innumerable kinds of connection that special things have with other special things." The poet finds this tracing of relations and interconnections is like the interior life of feeling and association:

> But in yourself is like:
> A sheaf of brilliant arrows flying straight,
> Flying and falling straightway for their
>   pleasure.

Then the poet reconsiders and discards the old figure of the arrows of thought to describe the successive impulses of immediate experience. The quick activity of memory is a closer parallel, its "nimblest motions" as the poet beautifully describes the instant and straightway recoveries of the fervour of past experience hidden in the darkness of possible remembrance:

> And the lost vehemence the midnights
> Or, if not arrows, then the nimblest motions
> Making recoveries of young nakedness
>   hold.

The mind, the secretive hunter that seeks within itself the various forms of relationship, imposes the unity of its own being upon all of its experiences. As Stevens goes on to explain in "Three Academic Pieces," a spontaneous mythology results when the mind projects the human image outward and interprets the world anthropomorphically. Like Narcissus discovering himself in the mirror of the pool, the human self sees his humanity reflected in the world around him: "he sought out his image everywhere because it was the principle of his nature to do so." The image seen may be no more than a formulation of a feeling of simple pleasure in normal experience; it may seem to be a discovery of the appealing nature of the scene, although only an echo of inner health and wakefulness.

Personification is the verbal form of this spontaneous mythology. Stevens' own use of myth usually goes no further than a basic central image that embodies a complex of feeling and desire related by metaphor to the natural world. In "The Paltry Nude Starts on a Spring Voyage," there is the first bare showing of the season, a few weeds seen in thin sunlight, and above them, the symbolic figure of the early year, the paltry nude starting on the spring voyage that would assuredly transform her into summer's goldener image of spontaneous desire. Spring is the time of year associated with the archetypal image of bareness and immaturity, the Kore or maiden, and the poet remembers her even in the midst of summer as a time "When radiance came running down, slim through the bareness." Long awaited before it comes, its weather and its essence are desired like the desired image of woman. "Depression Before Spring" expresses this desire in the figure of one expected in "slipper green"—in the verdure of the season. It is one of Stevens' many adaptations of the archetypal image of woman projected as a personification upon the world of one's impressions.

The crow of the cock in "Depression Before Spring" carries an echo of the idea of the procreative urge: for the cock elsewhere in *Harmonium* represents the primal creative element in a pun that recurs as "damned universal cock," in "Bantams in Pine Woods," and as "the perfect cock" of "The Bird with the Coppery Keen Claws." Finding in the desire of male for female an analogy to the desire of life for springtime, the poet sets up in "Depression Before Spring" a series based on the analogy: cock for hen, man for woman, poet for springtime personified as woman. Male calls, cock crows, but no hen answers:

But ki-ki-ri-ki
Brings no rou-cou
No rou-cou-cou

The male "Ho! Ho!" or even the poem itself
that seems to be a poet's invocation of the
longed-for season, brings no apparition of the
first green answer to desire:

But no queen comes
In slipper green.

"The divine ingenue" of "Last Looks at the
Lilacs" is also a personification of reality manifested in the essence of a season. Her indifference to what it is that embraces her innocence
is consistent with the usual indifference of
nature to man in Stevens' work, and her innocence is that of the undirected accidental
course of reality: personified as one having the
innocence that is an ignorance and an absence
of any ill intention. She does not care who
"marries her innocence thus,/So that her
nakedness is near."

Her companion, the analytical but unintui-
tive caliper, is man in his practical, unimagina-
tive relationship with earth; he is a boorish
instrument of measurement, who has lost the
mythic vision of things and is no longer able
to sense the primal heat of the season of
procreation, the Floreál or month of flowering.
Practical, reasonable man is adjured to take
his last look at the lilacs, whose lavendar
bloom displays the proliferation of things in
nature; for seeing this flowering as no more
than meaningless detail, as trash, he cannot see
it as the outward manifestation of the vital
principle of natural growth, and no longer
feels

Her body quivering in the Floreál

Toward the cool night and its fantastic star,
Prime paramour and belted paragon,
Well-booted, rugged, arrogantly male.

Union with the male principle, "Patron and
imager of the gold Don John," is a metaphoric
account of the fruition of the year—the springtime earth suffused in the warmth and light
that transforms it into the earth of summer.
"O Florida, Veneral Soil" uses a kindred
body of personification. Addressed to the archetypal woman as earth image—here identified
with the actual place, the soil of Florida—the
poem beseeches her to reduce the meaningless
variety of disparate objects that distract the
consciousness, and asks her to conceal herself
in darkness and quietude. After the dreadful
sundry of miscellaneous reality and the con-
fusions of daylight, the mind is tormented
even at night by the ferment of undirected

feeling. What the poet seeks instead is the
calm of the night sea and sky and its simple
composition of cloud and stars:

Donna, donna, dark
Stooping in indigo gown

And cloudy constellations.

Invoking the vision of myth, the poet asks of
the symbolic figure of earth that she reveal to
the lover of reality, to the consciousness, no
more than the few specific things that the mind
can attend when it gives something significance
or regards something for its own sake. "Conceal
yourself," the poem entreats, or if you manifest
yourself in the darkness, disclose through the
mythical vision:

Fewest things to the lover—
A hand that bears a thick-leaved fruit,
A pungent bloom against your shade.

These are significatory images for the consciousness that is the lover of reality—an image of
creativeness (from the hand symbol) holding
an emblem of fruition, or a perfection, some
ideal form, emerging out of creative darkness.

3

Male and female principles in the poetry of
Stevens are often representations of consciousness as male lover and of reality as anonymous
woman—unknown because reality can never be
realized objectively. "Le Monocle de Mon
Oncle," however, presents the male-female relationship as simply what it is; for this poem
is a discourse by man to woman on love looked
at through the monocle (the point of view) of
middle age. In the opening poem the poet,
from the vantage of his years, addresses the
beloved, mocking her as the mythical goddess
of love. He deprecates her powers, for he has
come to the time of life when love is not all.
And, now, there is nothing that can overwhelm
him like the magnificence of poetry and its
sharp verbal paradoxes:

There is nothing, no, no, never nothing,
Like the clashed edges of two words that
kill.

The poem clashes its negatives against each
other with a display of the combat of words
and their cancellings. And then the poet remembers his beloved in the time of youthful
love—and, from deep within him, sorrow for
what love once was rises into expression as
from a well of tears:

And then
A deep up-pouring from saltier well

Within me, bursts its watery syllable.

The naturalistic significance of the poem, and its major theme, is revealed in the poet's recognition that the course of love is only the course of nature. There is first the common ground of human experience. "Shall I uncrumple this much-crumpled thing," this common theme of love, the poet asks, and in the eighth stanza he finds love to be a cycle whose stages are repeated for each individual:

An ancient aspect touching a new mind.
It comes, it blooms, it bears its fruit and
dies.

And they, the poet and his beloved, have come to that time in the course of love (and its course is only an aspect of the course of nature) when they are the overripe fruit of that tree. The tree he has in mind has a certain tip, he says, indicating by the phallic image the fact that the sexual nature of love remains while the individual passions that visit it come and go:

It stands gigantic, with a certain tip
To which all birds come sometime in their
time,
But when they go that tip still tips the tree.

The law of sexual motivation is not the sole factor, the poet maintains in the eleventh stanza; for choice of one by another is selective and passionate. The stanza concludes with an image that illustrates the ambivalent nature of love—its primal organic basis and its shared imaginative quality. Lover and beloved sit beside the pool of pink, "Clippered with lilies scudding the bright chromes," depicting the conceptual nature of their affections, while a frog "Boomed from his very belly odious chords." The image of the frog is one of many that sets forth as the major theme of the poem the idea that love, with all its imaginative and affective involvement, is a natural event emanating from an organic source.

4

Just as the course of love is no more than the course of nature, so in "The Comedian as the Letter C," is the course of thought in Crispin only the natural course of a man's life. Crispin, like any man, must live by synechdoche, and conceive, in terms of the small part known, the indefinite unknown. Reconstituting his philosophy, his idea of the nature of the world, over and over, Crispin composes each time out of his miniscule point of view and out of his vagrant subjectivity what he trusts at the moment is a true, a permanent conception of reality, as valid for the next altered moment as for the present.

To illustrate the fact that the human idea of the world is a continual revision, Crispin's life is traced in terms of shifting perspectives of reality. From sea to tropics and then to North America, from introspective sea voyager to settler in Carolina and father of four—these changes of place are also changes of mind. Crispin's continual effort to adjust his philosophy to reality is only a form of adaptation to place and condition. During his voyage he loses the beliefs of his homeland and sees himself as diminished in the midst of ocean. Confronted by the blankness of matter during his ocean voyage, Crispin assumes that now he is able to see the veritable thing in itself. He looks at vast sea and endless sky and asks what it is that all this mystery of appearance could be, since apparently it has no source in anything as human as a deity; for all the pretences and strategems of the human ego are lost in the blankness of the non-human.

Crispin seeks to intuit the reality of things, wishes to realize them as he trusts they may be in their own objective existence. Just as the later poet of "An Ordinary Evening in New Haven" sought "nothing beyond reality," the younger poet of *Harmonium* refused to look beyond reality, because he believed there was nothing beyond it. In a naturalistic conception, the sole ground of an existence is its reality. To be real is almost a quality in itself; for reality is the truth of existence, a feeling of the verity of things. Since a trust in the reality of things and selves fills out the void that would otherwise exist without a belief in a transcendent ground of being, the word "reality" holds an unconscious store of feeling in Stevens' use of it.

Even the self becomes a configuration and essence of surrounding reality in a naturalistic poem. And it is fitting that Crispin consider man to be only a product of the complex of what is specific for a certain place and time. This is a conclusion offered by "Anecdote of Men by the Thousand," with its statement that the self is formed by its perceptions:

The soul, he said, is composed
Of the external world.

The poet of "Theory" in like manner accepts David Hume's notion that the self is composed of the floating empirical moment and flatly asserts that "I am what is around me." In like manner Crispin concludes that "his soil is man's intelligence," and this remark holds many of the implications of the assertion many years later in "Things of August" that "the world images for the beholder" and that the self is "the possessed of sense not the possessor." All of these assumptions about the nature of the

39

self make it a natural part of a natural world.

At the end of "The Comedian as the Letter C," Crispin is the realist for whom "what is is what should be." He discovers that the good of experience emerges from the fecundity of the natural world and that its events include him and its forces impel him. And if the ordinary round, composed of daily joys and evenings that disclose the infinity of night—if the succession of days "saps" any man as it does Crispin, it is not that it diminishes or draws away his hopes and ambitions, but that the quotidian "saps" as the sun does, draining away each day and giving another.

Crispin's last deduction is that the world, simple and familiar as a turnip, is the same unknowable but ponderable reality, for, as a totality, the world is only an imagined thing, and at the same time it is the true substance of experience. Hence, it is "its ancient purple" according to Stevens' blue-red color symbolism (blue for imagined, and red for real), with the imagined-real colors merging into purple; for the world, that in itself is the essence of the real, is only a conception carried wherever man goes and reproduced in each generation. It is always the same incomprehensible whole, "the same insoluble lump;" and the fatalist who believes that what is is what must be:

> Stepped in and dropped the chuckling
> down his craw,
> Without grace or grumble.

To swallow the realization that the world is unknowable is a simple and spontaneous act for the naturalist who assumes that man and his works are a part of the natural order and do not transcend it.

The poet concludes that all of Crispin's philosophising, all his attempts at

> Illuminating, from a fancy gorged
> By apparition, plain and common things,
> Sequestering the fluster from the year,
> Making gulped potions from obstreperous
> drops,

are a natural effort to comprehend the nature of reality in the midst of the confusion of the flux of feeling and thought and changing appearance—an attempt to understand a whole from a part and to see the world in an impression. For Crispin's philosophizing is a natural response of the conceiving creature. Like Santayana, the poet realizes that "thought is a form of life, and should be conceived on the analogy of nutrition, generation and art." If Crispin has proved nothing by all his speculation, his shifting philosophy is the natural course of one man's mind, and his life only another incident in the course of human life:

> What can all this matter since
> The relation comes, benignly, to its end?

> So may the relation of each man be clipped.

The end is benign because the course of Crispin's life is the course of nature. Crispin's vain attempt to understand a world from the small vantage of an impression, confused and muddled by the subjectivity and irrational reflection of selfhood, is only the tale or relation of each man. It is an expression of the human nature that is only a part of the larger nature of things and events. And so, the poet concludes ambiguously, may the account of each man be ended; or (as the alternate meaning) the account of each man may be ended thus.

5

According to the narration of Crispin's peripatetic speculation in "The Comedian as the Letter C" and the explanation of the organic nature of love in "Le Monocle De Mon Oncle," thought and affection are conceived to be parts of the natural world. In "Sunday Morning," Stevens places the whole man in the natural order. And in the skeptical tradition of naturalism he draws a parallel between the indigenous life of man and that of the wild creatures: man is a natural creature like the deer and the quail and has his cycle of maturity like the wild berries. His descent to death is represented symbolically by the descent of pigeons to darkness at evening, sinking downward with "ambiguous undulations." The world that man inhabits is the chaos of chance and accidental being of naturalism; he is isolated from all other moments other than his own by the inescapable separations of expanses of time:

> We live in an old chaos of the sun,
> Or old dependency of day and night,
> Or island solitude, unsponsored, free,
> Of that wide water inescapable

Since for Stevens nothing is truly credible except present being, happiness occurs only in immediate experience. The earth itself offers man his only possible paradise, because it is the only possible location for his existence. Therefore the proper subject of the poet who is also a naturalist is his individual sense of the world. This is a continuing conviction of Stevens and, many years later than *Harmonium*, he observes in "A Collect of Philosophy" that the poet's world is his constant subject: "the poet's world is intended to be a world yet remains to be celebrated and which, at bottom, the poets hope will probably always remain to be celebrated." And in the same essay he says that the poet's world is his native sphere, the sphere that he has made his own by the individual version of it he conceives: "The poet's native sphere is the sphere of which duBellay wrote: 'my village . . . my own small house.' " And when Stevens adds that "the poet's world is this present world plus imagination," he means that the poet's world is the world that he knows and continually realizes in the many variations of his own individual conception of it. Thus the poet's world is the same world that any man finds in his vivid actual apprehension of it—that he finds

> In comforts of the sun,
> In pungent fruit and bright, green wings,
>   or else
> In any balm or beauty of the earth.

In the infinite complexity of multiple experience, the world continually opens out for the endless celebration of poetry or the endless enrichment of the self by its occasions. The symbolic image of the ring of men of the seventh stanza of "Sunday Morning" chanting their celebration of the paradise of present being and "their boisterous devotion to the sun" represents the celebration of poetry and the enjoyment of sensibility. By their devotion to the sun, they address themselves to both a symbol and instance of the objective reality about them—objective only as a source because existing in the inner conceptual life of organic being. Their chant arising "Out of their blood returning to the sky" is addressed to the non-human or savage source of experience and they address it

> Not as a god, but as a god might be,
> Naked among them, like a savage source.

In this early presentation of the sun symbolism that recurs in all the successive volumes of Stevens' poetry, the basic elements are present. The reality for which the sun stands is, as a savage source, a primal base from which the elaborations of an individual understanding of it may arise. It is naked in the special sense that Stevens has for the word: naked in that it is unconscious and is a presence in itself before it is clothed by conception. Santayana uses the word in this sense in the long philosophical metaphor from *Skepticism and Animal Faith*

in which ideas are clothes and things are bodies. Reality is base of conscious thought, or as Santayana says,

> All nature runs about naked, and quite happy, and I am not so remote from nature as not to revert on occasion to that nakedness—which is unconsciousness—with profound relief.

The chant of the ring of men is a poem to the reality of existence and a hymn of faith that men themselves are only a manifestation of the natural world and part of the infinite variety of the natural order. The dew upon their feet, from the grasses of that earth from which they come and to which they will return, symbolizes the likeness of man to the natural growth of the fields:

> And whence they came and whither they
>   shall .go
> The dew upon their feet shall manifest.

As to this origin and destination, "Anatomy of Monotony," a poem that substantiates the naturalism of "Sunday Morning," is even more explicit. Earth, the mother, and all its creatures share, the poem implies, the same nature and the same fate. Man emerged from the creative energy of earth—lewder or more procreant in its creative phase. Whatever he may be, his nature can never transcend hers.

> If from earth we came, it was an earth
> That bore us as a part of all the things
> It breeds and that was lewder than it is.
> Our nature is her nature.

Stevens' naturalism is immediately apparent in the basic mythic vision of nature as woman whether mother or beloved. The apparent duality of mind and world that permeates his poetry may seem, in a superficial view, to be at variance with a naturalistic conception of things; but mind in Stevens, as in Schopenhauer or Santayana, is only nature looking at itself. If the world exists as it is only in a particular experience of it, if the world that we know is a conceived world, the one who conceives is only a part of that world. His nature is her nature; or, to state the figure in an abstraction, the subject is part of the object.

41

T. S. Eliot: Christian Poetry Through Liturgical Allusion

by MALCOLM S. GLASS

To speak of T. S. Eliot as a Christian poet should not surprise many readers today; to suggest such an epithet thirty-five years ago would have evoked reactions of shock and dismay. Indeed, Eliot's commitment to Anglo-Catholicism in 1926-27 and his famous declaration of this commitment in the Preface to his collection of essays, *For Lancelot Andrewes* (1929), provoked the critics to scorn and to despair at the loss of a spokesman for the twentieth century. Paul Elmer More, in his essay, "The Cleft Eliot," (*The Saturday Review of Literature* for November 12, 1932), regarded Eliot's declaration a *"volte face,"* an irreconcilable contradiction. Thomas McGreevy in *Thomas Stearns Eliot: A Study* (1931) sneered at Eliot's conviction as

. . . the bastard, schismatic and provincial if genteel kind of Catholicism that, for the time being, at any rate, he has, somewhat New Englishly stopped at . . .

We should leave such skeletons in their graves and say that in the intervening years—and the perspective they have afforded—attitudes have changed.

Despite the growing recognition of Eliot as a poet speaking of and from a strong Christian conviction, his poetry is, nonetheless, often misunderstood. Wherever there is misunderstanding, the source of trouble is usually found to be a lack of understanding of the poem's intellectual background or context. Students of Eliot quickly realize that allusion is a common technical device in his poetry. Allusions are often many and rich, and they may serve varied purposes. Yet these allusions supply the reader with keys that unlock the poem's deeper meanings. A poem does not release its full meaning unless the reader understands the source of an allusion and the significance of its original context. A knowledge of source and context reveals the function and significance of the allusion in the poem, thereby illuminating the meaning of the poem.

This technique is commonly recognized, and critics have assiduously hunted out literary, architectural, and musical allusions. However, there is a kind of allusion which many critics have apparently slighted, ignored, or failed to notice—liturgical allusion. It is a kind of allusion peculiarly Eliot's, and it is of special importance to a consideration of Eliot as a Christian poet. The label, *liturgical allusion,* is meant to include references to liturgy and prayers used by the Church of England (Anglo-Catholicism is a movement within the framework of this church) either for corporate worship or private devotion, to traditional Christian symbolism, or to Holy Scripture. (Symbolism is frequently an adjunct if not an integral part of liturgy; liturgy is based on Holy Scripture.)

It is largely through his allusions to Christian liturgy and liturgical elements that Eliot informs his poetry with Christian meaning; such allusions are the background, at times the very framework, of a poem. Of course, liturgical allusion is more prevalent in poems written after Eliot's formal acceptance of Christianity. A close re-examination of Eliot's poetry preceding his conversion reveals a tendency to employ liturgical allusions even in the early poems; and the progression of these early poems, when viewed in light of the later, more explicitly Christian poems, suggest a movement through skepticism toward an orthodox Christian viewpoint. Eliot's conversion seems a culmination and fulfillment of that progression.

A careful study of liturgical allusion in a single representative poem will best demonstrate the means by which Eliot informs a poem with Christian meaning. "A Song for Simeon" (October, 1928) is the second of a group of lyrics known as the "Ariel Poems." These poems have more in common than the general title: all of them deal with the ambiguity of different kinds of births and deaths, and all deal with the theme of spiritual rebirth. Like the first Ariel poem, "Journey of the Magi," "A Song for Simeon" is concerned with the revelation of the Incarnation, and it dramatizes a personal experience of this revelation through a monologue.

The event of the manifestation of the Word in "A Song for Simeon" follows the story of the Magi chronologically, and neither of the protagonists of these poems was permitted to see the full revelation of Christ. "A Song for Simeon" takes its title from the Song of Simeon which is the canticle appointed to be said or sung after the reading of the New Testament lesson in the service of Evening Prayer. The source of Simeon's song is the second chapter in St. Luke in which it is told that Simeon was a just and devout man of Jerusalem who was blessed, for

. . . the Holy Ghost was upon him. And it was revealed unto him by the Holy Ghost, that he should not see death, before he had seen the Lord's Christ. (Luke 2:25).

At the time that the Virgin Mary was to offer a sacrifice to accomplish the Jewish custom of Purification after child-birth, the child Jesus was presented also in the Temple, according to the custom of the law. (Luke 2:22-28). (Both of these events are recognized on one festival which falls invariably on February 2.) Simeon was guided to the Temple at this time that the promise that he should see the Messiah before he died might be fulfilled. He took Jesus in his arms and blessed God and spoke what is now known as the Song of Simeon, the canticle, *Nunc Dimittis* (based on Luke 2:29-33):

> Lord, now lettest thou thy servant
> depart in peace, according to thy word:
> For mine eyes have seen thy salvation,
> Which thou hast prepared before the face of all people;
> To be a light to lighten the Gentiles,
> and to be the glory of thy people Israel.
> *(The Book of Common Prayer*, p. 28).

This is the setting against which Eliot's poem is intoned. Most of the liturgical allusions of the poem are to the *Nunc Dimittis*. In fact, references to this canticle act as a governing principle in the poem: the allusions (here, fragmented quotations) to the same or a similar source are dispersed throughout the poem so that they act as a framing device giving the poem structural cohesion.

We have given a full account of the liturgical matters upon which the poem is based because a failure to understand Simeon's situation seems to be the cause of misinterpretations. The poet has assumed, wrongfully I fear, that his reader will know the incident in the Gospel narrative from which the canticle is taken.

Simeon was an old man at the time that he received Christ, and it has occurred to some critics that Simeon should be identified with other of Eliot's "old man" figures, Tiresias of *The Waste Land* and Gerontion. But it must be pointed out that both Simeon and Gerontion are not despairing, hopeless old men, but they are, to an extent, old men in the Pauline sense of the phrase "old man." Paul uses the phrase figuratively to symbolize unregenerate man—sinful man who is not yet spiritually reborn but who may be, nonetheless, actively seeking rebirth of the spirit through self-examination, repentance, and penance:

> Knowing this, that our old man is crucified with him that the body of sin might

be destroyed, that henceforth we should not serve sin. (Romans 6:6).

That ye put off concerning the former conversation the old man, which is corrupt according to the deceitful lusts; And be renewed in the spirit of your mind; And that ye put on the new man, which after God is created in righteousness and true holiness. (Ephesians 4:22-24).

Lie not to one another, seeing that ye have put off the old man with his deeds; And have put on the new man, which is renewed in knowledge after the image of him that created him. (Colossians 3:9-10).

The opening verse paragraph of "A Song for Simeon" is indeed reminiscent of "Gerontion" and the early poems in imagery and phrasing. Simeon, like Gerontion, is awaiting death in a land that is dominated by a foreign power symbolized by the "Roman hyacinths." Winter has made its stand against the coming of spring; Simeon awaits death which will not come for him until he has seen the Messiah. He waits for the "death wind," "The wind that chills towards the dead land." All that remains for him are memories, the past, and one hope: to see the salvation of the Lord. The petition "Grant us thy peace" is not from the *Nunc Dimittis,* but from the *Agnus Dei,* an anthem of devotion which derives from St. John 1:29: "Behold the Lamb of God which taketh away the sins of the world." In the *Agnus Dei* the phrase, "O Lamb of God, that takest away the sins of the world," is repeated three times by the Priest, the congregation responding, "Have mercy upon us," two times and "Grant us thy peace," the third. The anthem is commonly said or sung before the Communion in the Holy Eucharist; it also appears in The Litany or General Supplication, the greater doxology, *i.e.,* the hymn, *Gloria in Excelsis,* and, also, in the Litany of the Dying. The meaning of this petition for the poem becomes clear when we understand it as a humble petition for mercy and peace, in some cases the peace of death. Simeon was by no means a faithless or despairing man, as Gerontion seems to have been; rather, he was "just and devout . . . and the Holy Ghost was upon him."

The old man, Simeon, considers all of his past life and sees it as a just and devout one; for he has been faithful, has fasted and done good works. He is also able to foresee future events which the Magi could not even guess. Perhaps by the guidance of that same Holy Ghost, Simeon foresees the sorrow which must come to Christ in His death and passion. Here is an ironic concurrence of a foreboding of the

43

crucifixion even at the hour when the infant Jesus is presented in the Temple. The Magi encountered the same irony, but they did not know it; Simeon is aware of what is to come, but is, nonetheless, perplexed by it. Again through the petition of the *Agnus Dei* Simeon asks that he be granted a peaceful death "before the time of cords and scourges and lamentation." He prays that he may receive the blessing of Christ, though Jesus is but an "Infant, the still unspeaking and unspoken word." Simeon feels that he must be blessed before it is, seemingly, too late; "Before the stations of the mountain of desolation," *i.e.*, the stations of the Way of the Cross, the climb up Calvary; and "Before the certain hour of maternal sorrow," *i.e.*, the hour of the five sorrows of the Blessed Virgin. Simeon does not wish this blessing and a peaceful death so he can avoid these sorrows; it is not as Mr. G. C. Smith believes, that Simeon is "unwilling to be caught up in a life inflicting violence and calamity," or that he is "unprepared" to face the sorrow. [See Mr. Smith's *T. S. Eliot's Poetry and Plays* (1956).] If Simeon could have full knowledge of the Gospel revelation, he might choose to remain alive; but he is already an old man, approaching death; Simeon sees only the impending sorrow; he cannot see beyond to the joy of the resurrection. The possibility of Christ's coming to die to save man, that His resurrection might be a sign to men of his redeeming action, is just as incomprehensible to Simeon as it was to the Magi and, later, to the disciples. Simeon knows only half of the meaning of the Gospel; he knows no more. Simeon is not afraid of what is to come; he is simply bewildered, as bewildered as the disciples were even unto the last hour; and the disciples were told what was to happen more plainly than was Simeon. Simeon knows that it would be impossible to live to see these things, for he is an old man, his death has been delayed only so that the promise "that he should not see death, before he had seen the Lord's Christ," might be fulfilled. He is a man of "eighty years and no tomorrow." Now that the revelation has been accomplished, death is at hand, and Simeon is ready for it. He can do nothing about the future; it is not his, but Christ's. He can only thank God and pray that he may depart into death peacefully according to God's promise; for he has seen the Lord's salvation. As Eliot expresses it:

Grant Israel's consolation
To one who has eighty years and
no to-morrow
According to thy word.

Luke 2:25 describes Simeon as "waiting for the consolation of Israel," and "according to thy word" is the *Nunc Dimittis* reference to God's promise.

Simeon foresees more than sorrow in the life of the Infant, for he tells Mary that "this child is set for the fall and rising again of many in Israel" (Luke 2:34), and in Eliot's words, men ". . . shall praise Thee and suffer in every generation / With glory and derision." Nevertheless, Simeon's death is nigh and he will not be numbered among the martyrs and saints who will ascend the stairs of contemplation. Ironically, Simeon himself refers to his half-knowledge of the meaning of the Word in the words Eliot has him speak: "Not for me the ultimate vision." Simeon sees, also, the inevitable sorrows of the Virgin as he says, "(and a sword shall pierce thy heart, / Thine also)," lines which Eliot quotes from Simeon's words to Mary, Luke 2:35. Yet Simeon does not wish to be preserved from such future vicissitudes, as Mr. Smith suggests; rather he has received the fulfillment of God's promise and wishes peace in death. He may be tired with his own life and the lives of those after him, but he is not afraid to live; he feels only that there is nothing further for him to live for, since he has seen the Messiah. And in a sense, even in his own death he dies the temporal and spiritual deaths of those who come after him: "I am dying in my own death and the deaths of those after me." He does not fully comprehend the truth he has seen, but it does not really matter. He lived only so long as it was promised. For him it is finished, and he would commend his spirit into the hands of the Lord: "Let thy servant depart, / Having seen thy salvation."

As for the relation of "A Song for Simeon" to the liturgy, it is notable that the more ancient services of Evening Prayer of the Church of England carried overtones of death, and the repose of the dead; hence the *Nunc Dimittis* was a fitting canticle for this service, as the Reverend John Henry Blunt notes in *The Annotated Book of Common Prayer* (1908). Mr. Blunt goes on to point out that there is

. . . a close connection between the Song of Simeon and the idea of our Blessed Lord's Passion [which] arises out of the occasion on which it was first uttered, the Presentation, which was in effect a Sacrifice.

This connection is poetically realized in Eliot's poem.

The tenor of Evening Prayer today is similar to the words of David: "I will lay me down in peace and take my rest, for it is Thou, Lord, only, that makest me dwell in safety" (Psalm

4:9, the response to the fifth suffrage or versicle of that service).

The peaceful rest of the night symbolizes peaceful rest in death. This mood Eliot recreates poetically, also. In order to be able to go to death in perfect repose a man must needs have strong faith.

It is Simeon's faith and composure even in the face of death that Eliot expresses in his poem, not Simeon's anxiety or fear of future things. Simeon, like the Magi, cannot fully know the significance of that which has been revealed to him; he does not need to know, for his faith sustains him; he has as much, if not more, faith after having seen but one sign of salvation than the disciples had after many signs, wonders and explicit explanation from Christ himself. The poem expresses the strength of faith of a man who knew but half of the truth in which he had faith. Eliot may portray Simeon as bewildered in his ignorance, but not as a man for whom the new birth is a complete loss as far as he is concerned, nor as a man who is "haunted by the pain and disquiet of the revelation," as Elizabeth Drew says in *T. S. Eliot, The Design of his Poetry* (1949). And if it is Simeon's faith that matters most, then his faith stands in comparison to men's faith today, as in "Journey of the Magi." The judgment of modern man is not favorable in either poem.

In both "Journey of the Magi," and "A Song for Simeon," there are implications of the necessity for forsaking the old laws, the "old dispensation," in order that the new covenant be accepted. Although the Magi and Simeon may feel a sense of inadequacy in making the change for themselves, it is an inadequacy growing out of ignorance, and is no fault of their own. There is more of affirmation in these poems, implicit though it may be, than the "failure of affirmation" which Mr. G. C. Smith sees. Both of the poems are based on events associated with the Nativity. They deal, ostensibly, at least, with the Christian revelation which is, for Eliot, the most important, the Incarnation. In these poems rebirth is seen as a kind of death, or death as a kind of rebirth; even Simeon's death is a rebirth, a rebirth in the Lord.

The importance of liturgical allusion should be clear. This essay has examined one poem against its background, the contexts of its allusions; if the examination was thorough, that is because there is no other way to study T. S. Eliot's poetry. His poems are highly complex and difficult; a study of them is likewise complex and difficult. The reader should understand the true meaning of the context of an allusion and then understand how the meaning of the allusion is related to the meaning of the poem. Superficial study will yield only superficial, and often erroneous, understanding. Of all the kinds of allusion in Eliot's poetry, liturgical allusion is most rewarding, especially to the reader interested in the Christian dimension of Eliot's poetry; and this kind of allusion is still the least thoroughly examined and the least perfectly understood. Further exploration of this aspect of Eliot's poetry will bring significant and exciting discoveries to the reader who pursues the kind of study conducted here.

John Crowe Ransom: The Evolution of His Style

by GUY OWEN

John Crowe Ransom, now that Robert Frost and Wallace Stevens are dead, may very well be the greatest living American poet—in spite of the fact that he himself has said that he was "deliberately minor." In fact, Allen Tate pronounced recently, with perhaps pardonable pride, that Mr. Ransom is "the dean of American poetry." Although he has never been a fashionable poet, Ransom has been an important seminal influence: without any question he has, through both example and teaching, changed the shape of Southern poetry and criticism and made a profound impact on modern American letters.

And yet, curiously, there has been rather little written about him. No doubt part of the reason for this comparative neglect is that Ransom chose to write in an unfashionable mode; in addition, the body of his poetry is quite small, most of it written in a five year span in the 1920's. Except for the issues of *The Sewanee Review* and *Shenandoah* which commemorate his 60th and 75th birthdays, written and edited by his friends and former students, there are only scattered essays here and there that examine his poetry, such as Robert Penn Warren's brilliant study of his irony and John L. Stewart's introductory essay, *John Crowe Ransom*. However, he does come in for extended comment in the two recent books on the Fugitives, John M. Bradbury's *The Fugitives: A Critical Account* and Louise Cowin's *The Fugitive Group*, where his role as the leader of the Vanderbilt poets is made clear.

Whether Ransom is a major poet or a very fine minor poet is debatable (I incline to the latter view), but no one can deny that he is one of the most important poets to emerge during the 20's. Certainly no study of American literature of this vital decade would be complete without a chapter devoted to him. And since Ransom's style is the most interesting, as well as influential, facet of his poetic achievement, I propose in this introductory essay to examine the dynamic development of his technique. For the sake of convenience, and since it does not impose a distortion, I suggest that his style can be divided into three stages: (1) the early and open style of *Poems About God* (1919), (2) the mature middle period of *Chills and Fever* (1924) and *Two Gentlemen in Bonds* (1927), and (3) the late, rather turgid style of such poems as "Address to the Scholars of New England." (Perhaps there are not enough poems in this last group to speak with confidence about Ransom's final development.)

Of course, I do not wish to imply that there is a clear-cut division between these three stages; there is, inevitably, considerable overlapping in technique and themes. Nevertheless, I feel that the point is worth making that Ransom is a master of a number of styles—though he is prone to leave the work in his plain style out of his collected editions.

John Crowe Ransom made a late start as a poet; he developed rapidly in a few years during the middle 1920's, then gave up poetry for criticism. He was thirty years old when his first volume was published in 1918. Most of these poems were written during a two-year period at Vanderbilt, before the exciting days of the Fugitives. Ransom sent the poems to Christopher Morley, a friend he had made while a Rhodes scholar at Oxford, and on the recommendation of Robert Frost the volume was brought out, to a mixed reception, by Henry Holt.

Poems About God is not a distinguished volume, though the astringent tone must have seemed fresh in 1918. Ransom, a severe critic of his own work, has never reprinted a single poem from his first book, although it includes a few accomplished short pieces, such as "The Four Roses" and "Moonlight," and is clearly a cut above the run-of-the-mill collection of verse being published at the time. The collection, for the most part, is unified around the theme of man's relationship to God—though this motif is stretched at points, and abandoned in a number of poems. As Richmond Beatty noted in an early essay on the poet, Ransom has been concerned, early and late, with fundamental issues. No one can doubt the seriousness or the intellectual motive of the poems, nor fail to note the awkwardness of the lines and an occasional stridency.

Poems About God reveals, perhaps inevitably, an inexperienced poet groping for his voice—and not quite finding it. Perhaps the opening of "April" is closest to the mature Ransom manner:

> Savor of love is thick on the April air,
> The blunted boughs dispose their lacy
> bloom,
> And many sorry steeds dismissed to pasture
> Toss their old forelocks. . . .

Only a few of the poems seem derivative, a rare thing for a first volume. "The School" is in part a reworking of a Robinson theme ("I kicked his clods for being common dirt, / Worthy a world which never could be Greek . . ."); "Under the Locusts" and the end of "November" owe something to Housman; and "The Lover" seems a mixture of Donne and Housman. If there is one main influence, the honor must go to Hardy, a poet whom Ransom avowedly admires and has written about and edited. Unquestionably, Hardy has had an impact, especially in those poems where Ransom is most critical of God:

> For all his mercies God be thanked
> But for his tyrannies be blamed!
> He shall not have my love alone,
> With loathing too his name is named.

In addition, John Stewart has called attention to the influence of Browning. (Later Ransom would turn to Yeats and Hopkins, even occasionally to Eliot, as in "Good Ships.")

If Ransom cannot be said to base his style on one master, neither can one discover here more than hints which point to his later mature style, which has made him world famous as a craftsman, even as a poet's poet. To put it negatively, there is little in his early work of the elegance and sophistication of *Chills and Fever* and *Two Gentlemen in Bonds*, to say nothing of the perfect balance and skillful texture of the poems written in the mid 1920's. The diction of the majority of the early poems is anything but bookish; it is, on the contrary, realistic, rather simple and for the most part "unpoetic." One can readily see why the volume appealed to Robert Frost. Except for rare exceptions (*escheat, damozel*), he avoids archaic words, though he does not mind using archaic sentence structure for the sake of a rhyme—a practice which mars, at times, an early poem, as well as later ones. Similarly, he does not often use such colloquial words as *gallivanting* and *over yonder*.

On the other hand, there is a good deal of irony, much of it obvious and heavy-handed, even bitter, as in "Prayer" and "Dumb-Bells." Ransom seemed to deliberately shock his contemporaries by flaunting his criticism of God in their faces:

> What can one hope of a crazy God
> But lashings from an aimless rod?

Instead of relying on explosive or fresh imagery, he resorted more often than not to an easy irony. Finally, there is a good deal of sly humor, some of it turned against the poet himself.

In contrast to many of his contemporaries—notably Cummings, Pound and Eliot—Ransom chose not to experiment with form and meter. Instead he opted to work his innovations in tone and diction, like Robinson and Frost, within established forms, normally employing an iambic measure. As one might expect, *Poems About God* shows the poet trying his hand at sonnets—later a favorite form—quatrains, couplets and a kind of loose blank verse. His first poem, "Sunset," was an attempt at free verse; it is so clumsy and diffuse that the apprentice poet must have felt safer thereafter working within the harness of established patterns. His rhymes are also quite traditional; he seldom employed an oblique rhyme or the delightful fresh rhymes of his later witty poems. The pairing of *Jesus* and *tease us* in the satiric "A Christmas Colloquy" is a noticeable exception, pointing the way to one of Ransom's signatures in his next two volumes.

Although Ransom was a harsh critic of southern poetry, the world of his poems is unmistakably southern. However, he avoids local color for its own sake, sentimental and picturesque "nature" poems, together with the legends of the South that were the stock-in-trade of such Dixie bards as the Charleston group. Obviously from the outset, Ransom was antiromantic, a poet who trusted the head rather than the emotions. After all, it was he who wrote later, these mischievous couplets:

> Sing a song for Percy Shelley
> Drowned in pale lemon jelly,
> And for precious John Keats,
> Dripping blood of pickled beets.

Yet, since as a poet Ransom began with "a fury against the abstract," he is driven to selecting particulars in order to give his ideas substance. The particulars and the characters, then, in these poems are Tennessee folk whom he knew well. For example, his own father in "Noonday Grace," and a hired plowman in the bitter "Grace"—though few of his people come to life in the manner of Frost's or Robinson's, doubtless because Ransom was from the beginning more interested in ideas than in personalities. Always in these early poems there are other references to provide what Ransom called "the texture of the world's body": home-cured country ham, canned fruit, blackberry pie, and the sullen heat of dog days. The poet, however, seldom allows local references to weight his poems down with provincialities, a characteristic which distinguishes his verse from that of the majority of his southern contemporaries.

If Ransom's mature style is not clearly adumbrated in his first volume, his chief themes are —though naturally they are not developed with his later subtlety and impeccable craftsmanship. Nearly all of the motifs that obsess him are here; for example, the dual nature of man or the conflict between the material and the spiritual can be seen in "Morning." Since Ransom is a poet of narrow range, his later volumes do little more than elaborate on the themes he treats in his early work. From the very first, the world he creates is a thwarted one, where "in the finest flesh/ There isn't any soul" and men "who might be angels" are "fastened down with bodies. . . .", and "the whole world crumples in disease. . . ."

One gathers from the preface to *Poems About God* that the author was already a little ashamed of the first fruits of his muse. At any rate, he subjected himself to a further period of apprenticeship, and when he published *Chills and Fever* in 1924, it was obvious that his poetry had taken a great leap forward. In a few years his style underwent a change that has been called miraculous. No doubt the close study and teaching of English poetry at Vanderbilt aided Ransom in developing his mastery of technique. Perhaps too the perfection of many of the new poems owes something to the dialogue the poet carried on with the other Fugitives during the heady years between 1922 and 1925 when they were publishing their famous and influential little magazine. It was Ransom's custom to read one of his poems at their weekly meetings, absorbing the criticism of his fellow poets Donald Davidson, Merrill Moore, Robert Penn Warren and Allen Tate, as well as the lesser lights of the Nashville group. Later he would revise his poem for an issue of *The Fugitive*, often re-working it again before including it in one of his collections. (Always a fastidious craftsman, Ransom has continued to revise poems that have been often anthologized and considered modern classics.)

Whatever the reason for the transformation, *Chills and Fever* and *Two Gentlemen in Bonds* represent Ransom's "new style," a style less open and more concerned with the subtleties of meaning and the fine nuances of sound. Here we note at once the elegant manner that has made him famous, perhaps as best exemplified in such poems as the early "Dead Boy," "Bells for John Whiteside's Daughter," "Conrad in Twilight," "Blue Girls," "Captain Carpenter" and "Janet Waking." But there are a dozen other poems I could cite whose art is near perfect, including the richly textured and more ambiguous "Antique Harvesters."

As Cleanth Brooks has said, these poems are obviously *made;* the poet takes pride in calling attention to the carefully controlled texture of his art. Clearly, nothing accidental is allowed to intrude in Ransom's work; if there is an awkwardness or harshness, then it has its contribution to make to the total design of the poem.

These poems are brilliant examples of Ransom's cool detachment, his ironic tone, the often imitated "mixed mode," the wit and metaphysical conceits. Most of the poems are fairly short, for Ransom has difficulty in sustaining longer pieces. Here are the small dramatic crises, compressed to the barest essentials, told in a conversational voice that is often charming and brutal—poems that seem impersonal, yet release emotional power.

Perhaps the prologue to *Chills and Fever,* "Agitato ma non troppo," will suggest the poet's mature manner:

I will be brief,
Assuredly I know my grief,
And I am shaken; but not as a leaf.

Ransom has asserted that he is not the "I" of this poem; he has recently revised it to point this up. Yet he makes clear in this lyric the kind of poetry he is rebelling against in his own work; the contemporary poetry that leaned heavily on emotion and romantic trappings, symbolized by Shelley's reed that too often "sang tremolo."

As "Agitato" suggests, however, its creator has a "grief in his mind," and the themes of these two volumes betray Ransom's obsessions, many of them explored tentatively in *Poems About God*. As one discovers in *Chills and Fever,* Ransom's world is anything but a pretty one—his is a "dwindled" world. In it one confronts the decay of old age, death coming to the young, the beautiful losing their beauty, the inability of man to realize his potentials, the divided nature of the modern psyche, materialistic values triumphing, the values of the old world perishing, evil lurking everywhere. And always there are lovers—parting, quarreling, caught between passion and honor, marrying for wealth instead of love, most often dying without fulfilling themselves.

Randall Jarrell has described, in part, the world Ransom created as follows:

In the center of everything . . . is the practical world of business and science and morality [which Ransom deplored], a vortex that is laboring to suck everything into its transforming revolutions. In the foreground there is a girl weeping for a dead pet; or simply a girl, dead; and her parents are mourning—in their dry, wistful, pedantic way . . . Nearby the girl, grown up now, stands under the great hollow oak that whispers gently to its daughter—stands torn with pure love, pure pain, as she watches the "serpent's track" of the bicyclist pumping his winding way up hill. . . . Children are playing in the vacant lots, animals are playing in the forest. Everything that the machine at the center could not attract or transform it has forced out into the suburbs, the country, the wilderness, the past: out there are the fairy tales and nursery rhymes, chances and choices, dreams and sentiments and intrinsic aesthetic goods—everything that doesn't pay and doesn't care.

If Ransom's themes are relatively few—and some of them rather shopworn—the kind of poem he writes is limited, too—especially when he is compared to such contemporaries as Eliot or Pound. With only a little difficulty, Howard Nemerov has reduced all of the poems included in the first *Selected Poems* to five categories: (1) elegies—a favorite with Ransom during the 20's—("Dead Boy," "Here Lies a Lady"), (2) bestiaries, or fables about animals and birds ("Lady Lost," "Dog"), (3) fables about people ("Our Two Worthies," "Judith of Bethulia"), (4) poems about lovers—which cannot be called love poems—("The Equilibrists," "Two in August"), and (5) meditative poems about art and knowledge—a type that Ransom is drawn to in his later development—("Philomela," "Painted Head").

So much for the limited world of Ransom's themes; now to return to the style of the poetry he was writing during the middle 20's. Ransom's typical poem presents a small drama, often a dramatic crisis, usually narrated by an observer not involved in the action. As Randall Jarrell has noted, here is a modern poet who tells *stories*. But it is not the story or the characters—much less the setting—that interest the poet: it is the conflict of the ideas presented—for example, honor versus passion in "The Equilibrists" and the active versus the contemplative life in "Two Gentlemen in Bonds." The urbane, witty, even aristocratic narrator reveals what Robert Penn Warren calls "the kernal" of his little fables in a dry, cultivated voice in a conversational flow. The language is in the so-called mixed mode, and it is often a curious mixture of ornamentation and bluntness, of courtesy and rudeness, of the pedantic and the colloquial. As Robert Lowell, one of Ransom's students, has said, Ransom's "is the language of one of the best talkers that has ever lived in the United States":

Autumn days in our section
Are the most used-up thing on earth
(Or in the waters under the earth)
Having no more color nor predilection
Than cornstalks too wet for the fire. . . .

It has been often noted that Ransom keeps himself out of his poems after his apprenticeship period. Perhaps he felt ashamed of having presented himself and his kinsmen so nakedly in *Poems About God;* perhaps he merely revolted against the example of sentimentality that pervaded contemporary southern verse in the 20's. No doubt his training in the classics helped to serve as a guide (he read "Greats" at Oxford). In any case, Ransom speaks for himself in only two of the poems in his new *Selected Poems.*

It follows, then, that Ransom is almost always careful to keep an aesthetic distance from his subjects. As critics have observed, his dramas are set in the past, his lovers are already dead, often his world is drawn from books, as in "Armageddon," and thus twice removed from life. If there is an "I" involved in the poem, Ransom characteristically keeps this hidden until the action is over, or almost over. Cleanth Brooks has compared this strategy to the technique employed by Milton; he suggests that "it is in this control of perspective that constitutes Ransom's special claim to a kind of classical decorum."

This is another way of approaching tone. As John Bradbury writes in *The Fugitives,* "various critics have described the peculiar attitude or tone which constitutes the essential Ransom as 'wrinkled laughter' (Morley), 'acid gayety' (Van Doren), 'detached, mock-pedantic, wittily complicated' (Jarrell), 'ambiguous and unhappy' (Winters), 'suave,' 'mixed,' or simply 'ironic'." Whatever it is labeled, it can be seen that Ransom's style depends on his being detached from the subject which he is presenting.

One of the most striking qualities of Ransom's new style was his reliance on a diction that seems "old-fashioned," language that harks back to Caxton and Malory. There was a mere suggestion of this in *Poems About God,* but with *Chills and Fever* the poet's style became heavily flavored—perhaps even weighted down at times—with medieval words and the latinate language of the Renaissance. As Stewart has observed, Ransom taught Milton at Vanderbilt and was fascinated by his Latinism, as well as by the diction of Sir Thomas Browne and Jeremy Taylor. And since his father was a Methodist minister, the influence of the King James Bible was inevitable.

Whatever the reason for the change from a simple, realistic vocabulary to a more learned and bookish one, the change is obvious and dramatic. Perhaps a short list of such words will suggest this aspect of the poet's style: *bruit, lissome, thole, chevelure, diuturnity, estranger, transmogrifying, saeculum, stuprate, perdure* and *pernoctated*. What other American poet would risk such language in the 1920's? In one poem alone, "Necrological," Ransom employs *albeit, ogive, leman* and *wight*. Furthermore, at this stage in his development he seemed drawn to such "poetic" words as *fabulous, casement, dolorous, vaunting,* and *hyacinthine,* to cite a few examples at random.

This use of medieval and renaissance diction is a trademark of Ransom's style, and, in my opinion, it became at times a mannerism. The poet has often been twitted for his use of *escheat,* etc. Yet, to be fair, the justification for such language in Ransom's poetry is easily found. Perhaps his penchant for an almost Spenserian vocabulary can be explained in part by the fact that Southerners take an unusual interest in the trappings of chivalry and often seem fascinated by rhetoric—witness southern political oratory or southern sermons of the old school. More important, Ransom is often dealing with medieval subjects, wherein archaic language is not only fitting but inevitable. "Armageddon" and "Necrological" are two examples. Elsewhere the poet is employing such medieval forms as the ballad, as in "Captain Carpenter." But there is a more significant reason for his use of an outrageously poetic and archaic diction. Ransom's language is often deliberately over-inflated for ironic effect; that is, to call attention to the contrast between the language and the subject of a poem, or to help puncture a threatening sentimentality. The *transmogrifying* bee of "Janet Waking" is a famous example of this strategy.

There is a danger here, of course, in singling out Ransom's polysyllabic and antiquarian language. It must be remembered that he continued to write in the 1920's poems that were as much in the "plain style" as most of the work included in *Poems About God.* In fact, some of his best poems—"Blue Girls," "Piazza Piece" and "Vision by Sweetwater"—are written in a language that is classical in its purity and lucidity. And there are other poems written as simply as a Wordsworthian ballad—"Jack's Letter" and "Little Boy Blue"—though Ransom, as a rule, has not revised such poems for the editions of his selected poems.

In addition to the archaic diction emphasized in the poems of the 20's one might also note in passing Ransom's use of archaic word order, which becomes more obvious, and deliberate, in his second and third volumes. Ransom's is a conversational voice, not a singing one. Yet, unlike Frost, he does not always employ the natural word order of ordinary speech; the structure of his lines is more formal. For example, he seems deliberately to make use of inversions for the sake of a rhyme, as well as

for emphasis: "But strange apparatus was it for a Carmelite" and "But with much riddling his head became unruly" are two lines from "Necrological." "Alone in the press of people travelled he" appears in "The Equilibrists." There are numerous examples of such inversions, some of them too obviously calling attention to themselves, scattered throughout *Selected Poems.* Perhaps Ransom would cite the example of his old master Thomas Hardy to justify the use of such a poetic device. However, in his latest poems he seems to take care to achieve a more natural word order.

I have said enough to indicate that Ransom is given to writing witty poems. His wit is not only seen in the content of such poems as the saucy and irreverent "Survey of Literature" and the satiric "Amphibious Crocodile," it also manifests itself in his oblique rhymes, for which he has a special fondness. Ransom seems to have been one of the first southern poets to experiment with this device; in fact, he is the only one to do so in Addison Hibbard's anthology, *The Lyric South* (1928). No doubt he saw this as one way to avoid poems that jingle, as well as a way to work innovations within fixed stanzaic patterns. At any rate, he became a master of slanted rhymes in his middle period —though his latest poems avoid rhyme altogether. For example, in "Bells for John Whiteside's Daughter" we note his use of such rhyming pairs as *body-study, window-shadow, little-scuttle* and *ready-study.* In the rather late "Of Margaret" he continues the practice, rhyming *hung* with *mothering* and *grass* with *gentleness.* As with Eliot, Ransom often uses rhyme as an aid to his ironic tone.

As I have observed, Ransom is a militant traditionalist in some matters, although to many of his southern contemporaries he was a dangerous modernist. It is well known that he quarreled with his pupil Allen Tate over the merits of T. S. Eliot. To Ransom, Eliot's free verse was undisciplined and fragmentary. It is not surprising, then, to discover that Ransom is no innovator in metrics or stanzaic patterns— though he is not a slave to any tradition. As Bradbury has written, Ransom, like Donne, fails "of keeping of accent"; he thinks nothing of varying his rhythm and the length of his lines when it suits his purpose. Normally he works in an iambic beat and feels most at home in fixed forms such as the quatrain and sonnet, where, despite his variations, the final effect is one of formality and control. Ransom is also a master of the skeltonic line and dipodic nursery line patterns such as those in "Our Two Worthies":

Kneaded it and caked it
And buttered it and baked it . . .

For his lighter fables he often resorts to a loose blank verse or to couplets. His favorite form, however, is his expertly controlled variations of the ballad stanza, which he had begun to master in the early *Poems About God*.

Now for a brief comment on the final stage of Ransom's poetic development. Perhaps there are not enough poems here to make a case for development, yet I feel that a few suggestions might be offered—if it is remembered that there is, obviously, no very sharp break with Ransom's mature style.

It is possible, I think, to detect a decline in power and freshness in *Two Gentlemen in Bonds*, especially in the sonnet sequence built around the contrast of the active mind and the appreciative, contemplative mind. The lines of these sonnets tend to become mannered, too heavily freighted with archaisms and pedantry; and the "story" of the two brothers is rather tedious, perhaps because Ransom cannot interest the reader in his characters as real characters.

Be that as it may, Ransom has published very few poems since his last book—though he has continued to revise his best work for the editions of his selected poems. As Richmond Beatty observed in 1944, "the luxuriant stream of Ransom's poetry has dried up, during the last fifteen years, into a thin and turgid trickle. The incisive wit and brilliant diction . . . has disappeared. The poet, in short, has been swallowed up by the critic."

Of the half dozen or so poems of this late period, only three require comment. "What Ducks Require" seems to be a rather obscure Agrarian fable belonging to the late 20's; two experimental "extended" sonnets have not been reprinted. "Margaret" is a memorable reworking of a Hopkins theme. However, in 1934 Ransom produced three ambitious poems: "Prelude to an Evening," "Painted Head" and "The Address to the Scholars of New England." Although these poems do not represent any new themes, their manner is different: the last two poems especially tend to be more metaphysical, more dense and concentrated in imagery, less accessible to the reader. It is almost as though Ransom had set out to write poems in the fashionable hard manner of the early Tate and Warren—a far cry from the lucidity of *Poems About God*.

At the same time, Ransom abandons rhyme, and his lines move with a more natural conversational flow. These three late poems are written in unrhymed stanzas, in metrics that are unusually free for Ransom. More important, he leaves behind the archaic diction that had often degenerated into mannerism and, except for "Prelude," does not employ his usual

dramatic method. What drama there is in "Prelude" takes place in the husband's mind. All three of these poems are highly intellectual; one cannot help feeling that they are "made" by a learned professor. They are, in short, examples of what the enemies of Ransom have labeled Academic verse. Of course, there are earlier poems—"Armageddon," "Necrological"—that also read very much like set pieces.

A brief look at these three important poems will suggest Ransom's late style. Bradbury has called "Painted Head" "a brilliant metaphysical 'conceit' poem; its theme is based on one of Ransom's obsessions: the war between head and heart, intellect and body. The painting of the head causes the poet to brood over the "dark severance" of mind and body in the twentieth century and represents his "fury against the abstract." The head on the canvas

Stirs up an old illusion of grandeur
By tickling the instinct of heads to be
Absolute and to try decapitation
And to play truant from the body bush.

"The Address to the Scholars of New England" is an occasional poem, a poetic essay unified by the repetition of key words. Ransom's metaphysical wit and irony are much in evidence as he attacks our New England forefathers for their over-simplification of life, for perpetrating Plato's "scandal-mongering" and for keeping their heads in "the always clouds" and "giddying with transcendent clouds." The imagery here is less dense, and as one might expect in a polemical poem, the language tends to become dry and abstract. No doubt "Address" is a brilliant example of verse satire, but one cannot help noting that we are a long way here from such favorites of Ransom's as "Captain Carpenter" and "Bells for John Whiteside's Daughter."

Finally, "Prelude to an Evening" has been often called one of Ransom's best poems. It presents a small family crisis, as so many of his poems do, in a little drama that takes place in a husband's mind as he returns to his wife and family after dealings with "the nations of disorder." He imagines that since he is haunted by the world's evil that he will infect his wife's mind, too, until she will become aware of "unclean spirits" in their home. "Prelude" is one of Ransom's most personal poems; it is one of the two or three poems in which the author appears as himself. Nevertheless, it is rather obscure, so much so that it has been often misinterpreted. Perhaps that is why Ransom recently revised and extended "Prelude," adding five stanzas and giving the poem a "happy ending," wherein the wife does not become victimized by her husband's furies and the husband settles down for an evening of baby-sitting. Ransom realized that the poem might still be baffling; consequently, he added an eleven page explication, explaining that his married couple are really Adam and Eve, and referring to Milton's theology, an article in *ELH* and *The Origin and Development of the Moral Ideas*! As accomplished as this late poem is, one cannot help noting that Ransom's best poems—no doubt all really first-rate poetry—can stand alone without being propped up by prose explications.

Perhaps no summary of the growth of Ransom's style could be more effective than citing what I believe are typical lines from the three stages of development that I have sketched in this brief essay. The following quotations are from "One Who Rejected Christ," "Here Lies a Lady" and "Painted Head."

I'm not like other farmers,
I make my farming pay;
I never go in for sentiment,
And seeing that roses yield no rent
I cut the stuff away.

Sweet Ladies, long may ye bloom, and
and toughly I hope ye may thole,

But was she not lucky? In flowers and lace
and mourning,
In love and great honor we bade God rest
her soul
After six little spaces of chill, and six of
burning.

Beauty is of body.
The flesh contouring shallowly on a head
Is a rock-garden needing body's love
And best bodiness to colorify

The big blue birds sitting and sea-shell
flats
The caves, and on the iron acropolis
To spread the hyacinthine hair and rear
The olive gardens for the nightingales.

As I write this, it is known that Mr. Ransom, after a lapse of nearly twenty years, is writing poetry again. No doubt it is useless to speculate on what his new manner will be—if he further develops his style. But one can certainly expect poems in which one finds a classical control and an intellect of high order. In any event, his new poems will be welcomed by anyone interested in poetic technique. For John Crowe Ransom is one of the greatest stylists America has produced.

Gamaliel Bradford, Psychographer

by EDWARD WAGENKNECHT

When we think of the 1920's in American literature, no doubt it is the poets, novelists, and playwrights who come first to mind. But that remarkable decade was also significant for what it produced in biographical and critical writing, which now, for the first time in living memory, became as interesting to many intelligent readers as creative writing itself.

These interests were not, of course, confined to America. Perhaps the most famous biographer of the time was the Englishman Lytton Strachey, who made his reputation with *Eminent Victorians* in 1918 and clinched it with *Queen Victoria* in 1920. "It is almost as difficult," said Strachey, "to write a good life as to live one"—a statement which could only have been made by a writer who regarded biography as a form of fine art. France had—and, happily, still has—André Maurois. Germany had Emil Ludwig, Austria (a little later), Stefan Zweig. All these men enjoyed an international vogue. But technically none was so interesting or so original as Gamaliel Bradford.

He was born in Boston in 1863, the sixth Gamaliel Bradford in a direct line of descent from William Bradford, of Plymouth Plantation. From boyhood he was passionately interested in literature and aspired to success as a great poet or playwright. Late in life, in August 1929, he published anonymously in *Harper's Magazine* an article called "The Fight for Glory," in which he told the story of the long years through which he struggled for recognition. It is an extraordinary narrative; few men since the Renaissance can have been afflicted by the "last infirmity of noble mind" in so aggravated a form.

Unfortunately he did not have the capacity to be a great poet or playwright, though he published three volumes of verses: *A Pageant of Life* (1904); *A Prophet of Joy* (1920); and *Shadow Verses* (1920), plus thousands of uncollected pieces. The first and the last of those named are lyrics; the other is a novel in verse, lighthearted and gay. In spite of Bradford's intense seriousness, he was something of a connoisseur of humor. He also published three novels: *The Private Tutor* (1904); *Between Two Masters* (1906); and *Matthew Porter* (1908). A fourth, "Her Own Way," was published serially, and a number of others remain in manuscript at Harvard's Houghton Library, along with many volumes of letters and journals. Bradford wrote plays also—in prose and in verse—but only one of these, *Unmade in Heaven* (1917), ever got itself published, and

none, I think, was ever performed. This play, though technically inept, has considerable interest. A devout Catholic girl labors to convert her Protestant lover and succeeds to such an extent that he reaches the conclusion that it is his duty not only to become a Catholic but to enter the priesthood. The character Ned in this play is Bradford's most successful attempt to modernize the Elizabethan Fool, a type he loved above almost everything else in literature; see his comments on it in his portrait of Charles Lamb in *Bare Souls*.

Bradford's literary career was handicapped by his wretched health, which seems to have been both physical and psychosomatic. In his youth he had tuberculosis, of which his mother died while he was very young; in later years, he suffered, among other maladies, from vertigo. At the height of his success, he was never able to work more than two hours a day, and there were times when he would be prostrated for long periods and unable to work at all. His literary career is, in this aspect, a record of such heroic self-discipline as to remind one of Prescott and Parkman. He planned his psychographs with such skill that he was never obliged to make more than one draft; as the sheets came from his typewriter, they went to the publisher, and he did not revise at all. In youth his ill health had made it impossible for him to remain more than part of one term at Harvard—later he was tutored by Professor Marshall Livingston Perrin, of Boston University—but he became a phenomenal reader and linguist, reading prodigiously in both ancient and modern languages. All this was by the clock—fifteen minutes of this or a half-hour of that; his wife used to say she could tell time by what he was doing. He even read detective stories, to which he was devoted, by the clock. He and his wife played their way through the standard piano repertoire by the clock, so much time to play duets every evening after dinner, taking the composers in chronological order and returning to the beginning after they had reached the end. When he was on his deathbed, he begain the study of a new language—Portuguese.

He had many handicaps in his life, but he had two great pieces of good fortune. First, he had money. His father, Gamaliel Bradford V, made a fortune in State Street early in life, after which he retired from business and devoted himself to writing on politics and government. When Boston was in the van of the anti-imperialist movement during the Spanish-

53

American War, he personified the conscience of America; he may well have had more letters in the Boston press than any other man who ever lived in that city. There was no temperamental affinity between him and his son, and neither ever understood the other. But the father left the son his fortune and thus made it possible for him to devote himself to literature, and incidentally to keep alive. The second piece of good fortune was a wonderfully happy marriage. Helen Ford Bradford, who outlived him by more than twenty years, not dying until 1954, when she was nearly ninety, was, if that kind of creature has ever existed on this earth, an ideal wife. She loved him; she respected him; she valued his work; she tolerated all his idiosyncrasies—and she judged them as dispassionately as if they had belonged to somebody she was reading about. When he needed care she gave it to him with tireless devotion; when he was merely indulging himself, she knew how to ignore him. Without her I do not see how he could possibly have survived.

I may here have given a suggestion of morbidness in connection with Gamaliel Bradford; this is not wholly fair to him. Read his *Journal*, edited by Van Wyck Brooks, and published in 1933, and you will get a certain impression of morbidness. You would get more from the unpublished Autobiography. On the other hand, you would get very little from his biographical writing and not much from his *Letters* (1934). He kept this side of his character to himself and, for the most part, let it overflow only into verses or private memoranda. In his home he was pleasant and understanding, in his social intercourse he was charming, and, as the present writer can testify, he would take any trouble and go to any length to encourage young writers. During his later years, he was rarely well enough to go about much, but he and his wife entertained intensively and, as I have already suggested, this was supplemented by a very extensive correspondence. He always took the large view of things, and though there were touches of the New England Brahmin about him—he had his prejudices, and he could be inflexible about them—nobody could approach him without feeling himself in the presence of a man of kindness and benignity and abundant common sense. Speaking for myself, I may say that I have met few men whom I loved as much as I loved him.

Religion was a special case. Temperamentally, Bradford was an intensely religious man. The hunger for God, the knowledge of God, the sense of union with God— he knew that these things alone make life tolerable. But intellectually he was a sceptic. It was not that he ever had any irreligious beliefs or convictions. He resisted strenuously when he was called an agnostic. But his temperament being what it was, he made his religious hungers themselves a source of torment and anxiety to himself. He forgot that while you are wondering whether God exists or not, you must live (a) on the assumption that He does, or (b) on the assumption that He doesn't. If you choose the latter assumption—or if you refuse to choose the first—you make it practically true for yourself. Bradford's doubts led him to give up church, prayer, the reading of the Bible, and religious exercises of all kinds. It was a curiously unintelligent way for so intelligent a man to handle a great problem. Even the existentialists know better than that. But not even this destroyed Bradford's religious feeling; it crops out in practically everything he wrote.

2

Bradford first contributed to *The Atlantic Monthly*—the magazine which made his fame— during the editorship of his friend Bliss Perry, but he did not really arrive until after Ellery Sedgwick had taken over, when he published a series of papers about Robert E. Lee. In 1912 these appeared in book form as *Lee the American*. This was Bradford's first full-fledged exercise in what he called psychography. It at once took its place as a standard book and enjoyed a long vogue, particularly in the South, where enthusiasm for it was motivated at the outset by a sense of wonder that a New Englander could be so sympathetic toward the great Southerner.

Bradford did not really create psychography; it "jes' grew." The principal literary influence upon it was that of the great French critic Sainte-Beuve, whom Bradford adored. But although Sainte-Beuve coined the term psychography — Bradford afterwards coined it independently without remembering that Sainte-Beuve had already used it — he never made it an independent literary form, but merely used it as an adjunct to literary criticism. That was the way Bradford began too, as one may see conveniently by reading through the papers he gathered into *A Naturalist of Souls* (1917, revised 1926). It was his interest in human character—his interest in the particular, which may have begun as a revolt against his father's concern with general concepts—that led him to shift his focus from the writer's work to his personality, until, at last, in the final papers included in the volume, the work drops out altogether or is used only to illuminate the personality, and the full-fledged psychograph has arrived. Metaphysics upset him, and threw his delicate organism off balance; by concentrating on the individual, he could tie himself to reality. He was eminently fair and just in his assessment of different types of human character. He was also infinitely charitable, but his keen insight saved him from sentimentality. The only people he did not judge fairly were those like Henry Adams in whom he discerned something resembling his own shortcomings. He never had any trouble with rascals like Casanova or Aaron Burr, who were altogether unlike himself. He detested Frances Willard, but one would not suspect it from his scrupulously fair portrait of her.

A psychograph is a picture of the soul or the psyche. It should be clear, then, that psychography differs from regular biography in that, instead of telling the story of a man's life, it describes his character. It is exposition, not narrative. Its materials are arranged topically, not chronologically.

Bradford's psychographs are prefixed by an outline of the principal events in the subject's life; this is for orientation. In his later psychographs, he generally gave the second paragraph to a summary of the subject's career. The first paragraph he always used to strike his keynote. Since most of his psychographs were short, intense selectivity was necessary.

He quotes freely, from the subject himself and from the writings of others about him. He used quotations for authority and also for atmosphere. By letting us, as it were, hear the subject's voice, he brought us into his presence. His quotations are short and woven into his text. In his use of quotations, he was greatly superior to Sainte-Beuve, who never mastered the problem of structure, and who, consequently, would sometimes quote a whole letter when only one sentence in it had any bearing on the point under consideration.

In his *Contemporary American Authors*, Fred B. Millett called Bradford a predecessor of the psycho-analytical biographers. This is nonsense. Bradford had no knowledge of psycho-analysis and no sympathy with it. He had no theories about human character. He merely studied and observed the way individuals behave and described it as vividly as possible, using every rhetorical device at his disposal to make it interesting to the reader, and employing evidence, generally in the form of quotations, to tie himself down to the ascertained and ascertainable facts. His real affinities were not with the psycho-analysts but with Plutarch (after whom he named one of his cats), with the character-writers of the seventeenth century, with the great Boston historians, and, above all, with Sainte-Beuve. Such writers as Carlyle, Macaulay, and Robert Louis Stevenson approached him in their biographical essays, but they never achieved psychography because they permitted their analysis of character to get mixed up with other things.

H. L. Mencken, who admired his work greatly, made another mistake about Bradford. Mencken could not confuse him with the psycho-analysts. He hated the psycho-analysts. But he did confuse him with Strachey. "This Bradford," he wrote "is the man who invented the formula of Strachey's *Eminent Victorians*." Because Mencken's name sold books in those days, Houghton Mifflin Company blazoned this over Bradford's book jackets for years. Like Millett's gaffe, it is nonsense nevertheless. There are no affinities of either method or spirit between Bradford and Strachey. However he many have differed from his predecessors in outlook and point of view, Strachey remained a narrative biographer, and he clung to the chronological method.

Lee the American was not Bradford's only unified book, however. He also devoted whole books to Darwin, Samuel Pepys, and D. L. Moody. Perhaps the best way to show that he had no bed of Procrustes into which he forced his subjects, no skeleton-outline to which he compelled them to conform would be to glance at the tables of contents in these four books:

Lee the American

Lee Before the War
The Great Decision
Lee and Davis
Lee and the Confederate Government
Lee and his Army
Lee and Jackson
Lee in Battle
Lee as a General
Lee's Social and Domestic Life
Lee's Spiritual Life
Lee after the War

You would know at a glance that this was not a conventionally-organized biography, but neither does it seem to be a fully-organized psychograph, in which each topic leads to the next and the whole builds up into an integrated picture of the man. At the beginning and at the end there are even remnants of the old chronological method.

Let us look next at *The Soul of Samuel Pepys* (1924):

The Man and the Diary
Pepys and his Office
Pepys and His Money
Pepys and Humanity
Pepys and his Intellect
Pepys and His Wife
Pepys and God

The gain in integration is, I think, immediately evident, and the same thing may be said, with perhaps even greater emphasis, of the other two books:

Darwin (1926)

The Observer
The Thinker
The Discoverer
The Loser
The Lover
The Destroyer
The Scientific Spirit

D. L. Moody, A Worker in Souls (1927)

The Growth of a Soul
Heaven and Hell
Moody the Preacher
Moody and Sankey
Moody the Man of Business
The Molder of Souls

The rest of Bradford's studies in psychography are composite books. Most of his psychographs were originally published in the magazines; later they were gathered into book form. The *Atlantic* was at first his principal outlet; then *Harper's*, but there were few quality magazines of the time in which he did not sometime appear. In the twenties, when his fame was at its height, there was no more prominent magazinist in America. When *The Virginia Quarterly Review* began, the first number opened with his portrait of Dolly Madison.

Bradford's composite books can, in a measure, be arranged in groups. Out of his study for *Lee the American* came two more books about the Civil War: *Confederate Portraits* (1914) and *Union Portraits* (1916). With the *Lee*, these comprise a Civil War trilogy.

There are four books about women. *Portraits of Women* (1916), his first non-American book, concerns largely English and French women of the eighteenth century. *Portraits of American Women* (1919) restored the international balance; except for the presence of Frances Willard in it, it might have been called "Portraits of New England Women." *Wives* (1925) devoted itself to women like Mrs. Benedict Arnold, Mrs. Abraham Lincoln, Mrs. James G. Blaine, and Mrs. Benjamin F. Butler, some of whose husbands Bradford had already written about. In some cases he had found himself becoming more interested in the woman than in her husband. The interesting technical problem, in all these cases, was to reconstruct the woman's soul from what had been written of her husband. His last book about women, *Daughters* of Eve (1930), returned to the European scene and gave him some of the most glamourous subjects of his life, including Ninon de Lenclos, Catherine the Great, George Sand, and Sarah Bernhardt.

American Portraits, 1875-1900 (1922) was planned as the first of a series of books in which Bradford planned to cover American history with a series of psychographs of representative figures, moving backwards in time. He was drawn away from this enterprise by his increasing popularity, which led to offers from publishers of specific and, it was hoped, more profitable jobs. *As God Made Them* (1929) and the posthumous *Biography and the Human Heart* (1932) contain all the rest of the material intended for this series which he was able to write.

The break came with *Damaged Souls* (1923), which was commissioned by, and serialized in, *Harper's Magazine*, and which vies with the *Lee* as Bradford's most popular book, and his own account of its origin goes far to explain the spirit of his work:

> When it was proposed that I should write a series of biographical studies for "Harper's Magazine," the editor first suggested "iconoclastic portraits": "Our idea would be to go back through our national history and select prominent figures who have loomed over-large in their own day and have shone with a false glory—lucky creatures of chance or circumstance who appealed tremendously to the popular imagination of their time. . . . Of course, in dealing with such a gallery we should expect you to proceed ruthlessly and with scant deference to tradition." To this proposal I replied that it made "a fascinating appeal to the worst elements of my nature," and that "nothing would amuse me more than to take empty simulacra down from pedestals where they have enjoyed the secure adoration of ages." At the same time I objected that such a work of destruction was not really worth doing, and that in the end it was likely to do more injury to the critic than to the character criticized. I urged that I did not want "to undermine, to overthrow, to destroy, even the things that deserve it," and I pointed out that "in every character I have portrayed so far it has been my endeavor to find the good rather than the evil, to set the figure firmly on its common human basis, but at the same time to insist that if the human heart were not worth loving, my work would not be worth doing." After reflecting on the matter, I made the counter-proposition, to do "a group of somewhat discredited figures,

and not endeavor in any way to rehabilitate or whitewash, but to bring out their real humanity and show that, after all, they have something of the same strength and weakness as all of us." And I suggested that the series might pass under the title of "Damaged" or "Patched Souls."

From here he went on to *Bare Souls* (1924), which took its title from Sainte-Beuve: "All at once the surface of life is torn apart and we read bare soul." This volume deals with some of the great letterwriters of the world—two of them French, the rest English. Bradford has elsewhere tried to see what he could do about making psychography out of unpromising materials; here he tried to find out whether the psychographic method could rise to the challenge of presenting these superb materials—so rich in the revelation of human character—adequately and successfully.

Not until 1931 did he attempt a psychograph of a living man. He had always maintained that his work could not be done until all evidence was in. Now, however, he was persuaded to produce *The Quick and the Dead,* comprising seven psychographs of which the subjects of four were still alive at the time. And here, for the first time, he used titles. Until now each psychograph had been tagged merely with the name of the subject.

1. The Fury of Living: Theodore Roosevelt
2. Brains Win and Lose: Woodrow Wilson
3. Let There Be Light: Thomas Alva Edison
4. The Wheel of Fortune: Henry Ford
5. The World as Idea: Nikolai Lenin
6. The World as Will: Benito Mussolini
7. The Genius of the Average: Calvin Coolidge

Mussolini found his portrait "simpatico," but Coolidge is said not to have cared for his.

The last of Bradford's books to be composed was *Saints and Sinners,* published in 1932, almost on the day of his death, which occurred on April 11, in Wellesley Hills, Massachusetts, where he had long lived. I remember his writing me, while he was working on it, that if three saints couldn't balance four sinners, he didn't think they were worth much. When he died he was working on Tom Moore and had enough books planned to keep him busy for a long time.

3

How much influence Bradford had upon biographical writing, and how much of that influence remains today, it would be hard to say. Obviously modern biography is more "psychological" than the older biography was, but

it would be dangerous to ascribe this to him; much of it, indeed, derives from tendencies of which he would not approve. Occasionally a biographer will show a tendency toward a topical arrangement of materials; John A. Pollard did that, for example, in 1949, in what is now the standard book on Whittier, *John Greenleaf Whittier, Friend of Man.* Most biographers, however, cling to the chronological method; to the best of my knowledge, I am the only one who uses the Bradford method in all his biographical works. The *Atlantic* continued to publish "Atlantic Portraits" by other hands, but this soon became a somewhat helter-skelter affair. Whether the "Profiles" in *The New Yorker* owe anything to him or not, I have no idea; they are much more journalistic, and their spirit is not his.

All his books are now out of print, and many contemporary readers do not know him. Hardly any of my reviewers show any awareness that I am using his methods. When I myself discuss the method, they argue about it; otherwise they content themselves with pointing out that my book is organized differently from most biographies and let it go at that. As far as method goes, we start from scratch with every book.

"The most unkindest cut of all" occurred in Bradford's own town, where, after his death, a new high school building had been named the Gamaliel Bradford Senior High School. The principal of this institution found himself greatly distressed, a few years ago, by the fact that many Wellesley residents did not know who Bradford was; apparently he thought this placed a heavy strain upon them. It does not seem to have occurred to him that he might have told them; it is possible that he did not know himself. At any rate, he persuaded the powers-that-be—there are few towns where they do not pander to ignorance—to change the name to the Wellesley High School, which, we may be sure, will not cause any trouble to anybody. When, after World War I, Jane Addams was dropped from the D.A.R., she remarked that she had supposed, when she was chosen, that the election was for life, but apparently it was only for good behavior. In Wellesley, however, not even the dead are safe.

My own first direct contact with Gamaliel Bradford came in my early twenties, when I was a student at The University of Chicago. In one of Robert Herrick's courses in advanced composition, I produced a psychograph of the actor Richard Mansfield (afterwards published in *The Sewanee Review),* in which I dutifully and slavishly imitated every feature of Bradford's technique. Herrick thought well enough of it so that I was encouraged to send it to Bradford, who, instead of being offended by it, as he would have had every right to be, wrote me, with really wonderful generosity, that I should probably carry psychography much further than he had been able to do.

This was the beginning of a friendship which ended only with his death. We wrote hundreds of letters to each other, and though I did not then live in the Boston area, I made two lengthy visits to him—one in 1926 and another in 1928. When I wrote *The Man Charles Dickens* (1929), he contributed an introduction and persuaded Houghton Mifflin Company to publish it, and when *Jenny Lind* came out, two years later, both he and Geraldine Farrar reviewed it in the Boston *Herald*. He also tried to get me into the *Atlantic*, but Sedgwick and I did not take kindly to each other, and this came to nothing.

Whether I have fulfilled his prophecy or not depends upon how one reads the word "further." Besides the two works already mentioned, I have published book-length studies of Mark Twain, Longfellow, Theodore Roosevelt, Hawthorne, Washington Irving, Poe, and Harriet Beecher Stowe. Bradford did not make me a writer; that was decided when I read *The Wizard of Oz* at the age of six. The University of Chicago also contributed importantly, especially Robert Herrick, Edith Rickert, and David Allan Robertson. But Bradford did give me a method, and I am sure that none of the works I have mentioned would have existed without him. It is true that I have written other things besides psychography, but I think few of my books have been unaffected by psychography. The chapter on Jane Addams in *Chicago* (1964) is straight psychography, and the sketches in the chapter called "Five Great Chicagoans" are miniature psychographs. I am sure, too, that psychographic influence could be traced in the two *Cavalcades* of the English and American novel.

It is interesting, however, that not until 1964 was I able to produce a composite book. This has not been due to indifference on my part but rather to the general hostility which publishers feel toward this type of publication. And unlike Bradford, who was, as I have said, a great magazinist, except for book reviews, I have always left the magazines pretty much

alone and dealt directly with book publishers. In 1964, thanks to the success of my 1962 publication, *The Movies in the Age of Innocence,* the University of Oklahoma Press undertook a book called *Seven Daughters of the Theater,* comprising studies of Jenny Lind, Sarah Bernhardt, Ellen Terry, Julia Marlowe, Isadora Duncan, Mary Garden, and Marilyn Monroe. Madame Sarah, of course, was one of Bradford's subjects, and I have written book-length studies of four persons of whom he did short psychographs— Mark Twain, Longfellow, Theodore Roosevelt, and Harriet Beecher Stowe. Otherwise we have not overlapped.

Though I still use his methods, and will always use them as long as I write about human beings, I believe I am no longer the slavish imitator I once was. In general, my books are longer than his and based on wider research. Partly because of his limitations of health, he rarely sought out manuscript materials; indeed he did not even try to cover all the materials in print. Strictly speaking, he was less scholar than artist—it was no accident that he would have preferred to do creative writing— and he should be judged by his insight, the astonishing range of his sympathies, and his literary charm. My own books command a somewhat wider variety than that of many writers, but only in the case of Theodore Roosevelt have I deserted the literary-aesthetic field. And Theodore Roosevelt was *sui generis;* we shall not look upon his like again. Indeed, since he *was* (besides being so much else) a writer, it might even be argued that I did not desert my field when I embraced him. Bradford, on the other hand, was equally at home with a man of business or even an adventurer. Nothing human was alien to him. As soon as you get interested in your subject, he would tell me, you will be interested in his work too.

In the advanced courses in American literature which I teach at Boston University, a good many once prominent writers come in for resurrection. Toward most of these the reaction of my students is uncertain and not subject to definition in advance. There are two writers, however, who never fail to awaken enthusiasm. One is Agnes Repplier, and the other is Gamaliel Bradford. I believe that similar exposure elsewhere would produce the same results.

The "Irresistible Lothario":

F. Scott Fitzgerald's Romantic Hero

by FREDERICK J. HOFFMAN

The title of my essay is taken from that paragraph of *Tender Is The Night* which is made up of titles and tags of popular songs. This paragraph has many meanings for a Fitzgerald reader, in and out of this novel. The popular song, the quality of polite excess, the straining for an absolute in a purely "temporary" *milieu:* these are all phases of Fitzgerald's portrayal of the immaturity and the agony that were the 1920s.

Fitzgerald is peculiarly a social and moral historian of that decade. He was four years older than it, so that he was thirty in 1926 (as Nick Carraway is thirty on that hot July afternoon in 1922, in the Savoy Plaza hotel). Thirty is a point of no return. The Fitzgerald world is bright and charming, but it ages quickly. Over the stories and the two novels of the 1930s lies the shadow of Fitzgerald's own "aging." Despite the fact that he was only 41 at the time, a photograph shows him in 1937 to be haggard, exhausted, and full of misgivings: the brilliant smile that had used to dominate the three Fitzgeralds before has here diminished to a tentative hesitant exercise of the lips, withdrawing whatever promise it shows almost as soon as it is offered.

The force with which F. Scott Fitzgerald spent his life (recklessly misspent it, in many respects) is matched by the brilliance of his style, of his passages "of pure gold," and by his own definition of the American promise. It is also, it seems to me, responsible for the creation of his romantic hero, who dominates *The Great Gatsby* and *Tender Is the Night* and several of the short stories, and seemed destined to reappear in the unfinished *The Last Tycoon*. This hero is pre-eminently an American who, perhaps misled by the myths and legends of the American past, wills transcendence of situations by sheer force of human power and illusion. The romantic image is an illusion; it leads to the worst kind of mishap, accident, disaster, tragedy, call it what you will. But there seems a reserve of sympathy for the victim; he has *believed,* and his belief has done him in. He is not *un homme manqué* (as Edumnd Wilson called Dick Diver), but *un homme epuisé* (as Fitzgerald properly named him).

2

Let me suggest some of the more interesting and compelling traits of this American hero, as Fitzgerald defined him. Through an excess of health, ambition, and animal spirits, he begins by thinking himself capable of supernormal deeds, requiring superhuman strength and staying power. His illusion about himself has a certain profane religious power. Chiefly, it enables him to transcend the routine, ordinary *homme moyen sensuel,* to shine forth beyond the disastrously commonplace run-of-the-mill. Aside from all of this, the Fitzgerald hero wills "to be of service," somehow to ingratiate, to acquire friends, to "do good," to heal. But the world, while it is often anxious to be served, ends simply by draining him of all his powers, or by being in some way or other responsible for the exhaustion or death of the romantically "chosen one."

Beyond these characteristics, Fitzgerald tries —not altogether successfully—to associate the hero, by analogy, to the general cultural history of America. In *Gatsby*, we have a feeling that Carraway feels Gatsby to have had a special vision, which is ruined and smashed by the failure of the world to come up to its demands:

> . . . The truth was that Jay Gatsby [that is, the *name*, changed from the prosaic James Gatz] of West Egg, Long Island, sprang from his Platonic conception of himself. He was a son of God— a phrase which, if it means anything, means just that—and he must be about His Father's business, the service of vast, vulgar, and meretricious beauty. . . .

It is not that Gatsby is without fault. Nick has said at least twice that he "disapproved of him from beginning to end." This phrase, if it means anything, suggests that Gatsby is somehow implicated in his own martyrdom. The vulgarity of this "elegant young roughneck" is a part of the condition that destroys him; in that respect, the death is in a small, fractional sense a suicide. For Fitzgerald's romantic hero is himself guilty: because he doesn't understand, or prefers to exploit, or understands only imperfectly, the human relations that are a staple of any morality. Gatsby, for example, is caught on several occasions forcing his romantic will beyond any human capacity of response:

> He wanted nothing less of Daisy than that she should go to Tom and say: "I never loved you." . . .

He broke off and began to walk up and down a desolate path of fruit rinds and discarded favors and crushed flowers.

"I wouldn't ask too much of her," I ventured. "You can't repeat the past."

"Can't repeat the past?" he cried incredulously. "Why of course you can."

He looked around him wildly, as if the past were lurking here in the shadow of his house, just out of reach of his hand.

It is true that Daisy falls short of Gatsby's illusion, as indeed she does of Carraway's moral expectation ("They were careless people," he says of her and Tom, as he closes the book on both of them; "they smashed up things and creatures and then retreated back into their money or their vast carelessness . . ."). Daisy is deceitful, Tom brutally "rich and privileged." But Gatsby's blessed power of transcending the "merely personal" has the unavoidable consequence of making the "merely personal" seem futile and thus any talent for dealing with the nuances of personal relationship somehow gratuitous.

Nevertheless, Gatsby remains the martyred romantic hero. He is dead, in the end, because of what Carraway calls some "foul dust" that "floated in the wake of his dreams." He is the personality "disponible," who is eventually wiped out and—what is worse—all but ignored by the world to which he has dedicated himself.

3

Unlike Hemingway, Fitzgerald never gave up the idea of the self-centered, dedicated hero. His romantic man did not need semi-leftist speculations to justify his acts. His problems were of another sort. The paradox of the Fitzgerald hero comes from 1.) his avowing himself as conditioned for superhuman tasks; 2.) his violating simple limits in order to be "of service"; and 3.) his remaining, in spite of everything, "simply human," and therefore at the disposal of the forces of decline and mortality.

Dick Diver of *Tender Is the Night* is perhaps a more powerfully melancholy hero than even Gatsby. The force of *Tender's* hold on the reader must come partially from the tensions Fitzgerald suffered while writing the book. Even Matthew J. Bruccoli, who, in his book, *The Composition of Tender Is the Night*, vows that he will "set Fitzgerald critics right" about the "biographical fallacy," nevertheless, after many years (months?) of work with 3,500 or more pages of MS, has to admit the force of the personal circumstance that acted as pressure upon the novel.

That novel, despite Bruccoli's assertions, really amounted to very little *until* "personal circumstance" both suggested and forced its theme. The recurrences of schizophrenic mania in Zelda forced him to look to an entirely new view of his hero, as well as of the social malaise he strives vainly to cure.

The young Diver, not long since from Yale and Hopkins and Oxford, appears in Europe (Vienna and Zurich), in 1916 and 1917, ready to "cure the world" by his knowledge, skill and charm.

> Most of us have a favorite, a heroic period, in our lives and that was Dick Diver's. For one thing he had no idea he was charming, that the affection he gave and inspired was anything unusual among healthy people. . . .

Here, and in the chapters following are the characteristics and dimensions of Fitzgerald's romantic hero. He has a great personal endowment, but his ambition forces him to waste it. Almost literally, Dick wishes to "charm the world" into health and happiness.

> Dick got up to Zurich on less [sic] Achilles' heels than would be required to equip a centipede, but with plenty—the illusions of eternal strength and health, and of the essential goodness of people; illusions of a nation, the lies of generations of frontier mothers who had to croon falsely, that there were no wolves outside the cabin door. . . .

Like Gatsby's, Diver's strength of illusion goes beyond the power of any limits to contain. The "courtship" of Nicole Warren (who at 16 had been raped by her father and was now being "repaired" with the aid of the Warren money) begins as an exchange of letters (one needs to note that even here the relationship is somehow more than the required one of patient and doctor); it comes to its first crisis in the garden of the sanitarium, where Nicole plays popular records of the day.

> The thin tunes, holding lost times and future hopes in liaison, twisted upon the Valais night. . . .

And, in the ensuing conversation with the Swiss doctors, the "professional situation," the transference "of the most fortuitous kind," becomes in Dick's mind a "personal situation":

> "I'm half in love with her—the question of marrying her has passed through my mind."

. . . . .

"What! And devote half your life to being doctor and nurse and all—never!"

Partly through Baby Warren's conniving with the Warren millions, partly through Dick's *wanting* it to happen, the marriage to Nicole does occur. One needs to appreciate its complexities: the transference is no ordinary clinical reaction; Nicole has been torn from her father's love and turns to Dick as a father surrogate (he is ten years older than she). In the course of their relations, they are father-daughter, husband-wife, and doctor-patient: an unholy and a ghastly mixture of "personal" with "professional" situations.

We can say that Dick not only suffers the condition, that he wills it to be so. Not only does he want to "be of service" (he could after all have served Nicole by curing her in his role of psychiatrist); he wishes above all to be in a position to charm a sick world into health. The expatriate Americans of *Tender Is the Night* are more than eager to be helped; they are above all dependent upon him, since his is the stronger will. Dick offers himself as martyr to their needs, striving to be at once a leader and the "sole purpose in life" of the entire lot. The desire to love and to be loved is both a crucial flaw in his character and its most ingratiating quality. Dick's tragedy is not just simply that he has ruined his career through yielding to a "personal situation," which he should have "treated" as a professional case, but that he has (like Gatsby) gone far beyond personality itself, striving to act a priestly, or even a godlike role.

He is defeated—by internal weaknesses, by the overwhelming pressure of the Warren money (they have, after all, "bought Nicole a psychiatrist," as Baby Warren had intended), and by draining of resources which occurs as a result of his ambiguous relation to Nicole. It is foolish to test Fitzgerald on the grounds of his use of the psychiatric condition. This is, after all, a major metaphor, as useful as any other, within the limits of Fitzgerald's skill in using it. In its intimate role, it defines the relationship of a man and a woman who are inadvisedly mated. Beyond this, it serves the role of ministering agent to a sick society which hauls and drags its illnesses from country to country, usually landing at some crucial time or other in that great European hospital-state, Switzerland.

4

There is a curiously oblique suggestiveness concerning World War I; Dick, near Amiens, calls the war "a love battle—there was a century of middle-class love spent here." Just after this remark, he says, "All my beautiful lovely safe world blew itself up here with a great gust of high explosive love." These remarks would have to be put down as another of Dr. Diver's "cute remarks," except that there are small explosions of violence throughout the novel, each one coming from a failure of love, or of personal relations. If we can imagine such an explosion of love, leaving the world in pieces, then the psychiatrist is there to pick up the pieces, and Switzerland (a refuge during the War) becomes a suitable "hospital."

The idea is linked to still another conceit: that of the "Achilles heels," the illusions of the American romantic hero who believes he can heal the world by "being good' and accepting others as good, by forcing good will to serve the role of religion *and* psychiatry, against the wilful dependence of others and the cold power a:id privilege of wealth. For Dick is defeated not only by the process of curing Nicole ("The case was settled. Doctor Diver was at liberty."), but by the harsh power of money that somehow allows its possessors to buy their way out of scrapes and disasters, *and* by the willingness of others to use him.

The two major heroes of Fitzgerald's fiction cry out to be used, to be loved; they die as victims of their accessibility to others. The fact that Gatsby's death appeared to Edith Wharton to be a *"fait divers"* of the morning paper testifies really to Mrs. Wharton's poor reading of the novel. Not a stray bullet from the gun of a madman, but a whole series of events somehow maneuvered by Tom Buchanan, is responsible for Gatsby's death. George Wilson, in the absence of any other recourse, has to "believe in" the eyes of Dr. T. J. Eckleburg as the eyes of God. Gatsby is defeated not by his will but because of the "foul dust" that "floated in the wake of his dreams." Diver takes leave of the "bright prayer-rug of a beach" on the French Riviera, as Baby Warren (the "great American Woman, . . . the clean-sweeping irrational temper that had broken the moral back of a race . . .") speaks to Nicole, "That's what he was educated for."

The meaning of these defeats becomes clear in retrospect. Both Gatsby and Diver have "spent themselves," have suffered "emotional bankruptcy." Both are romantic heroes in the sense of having forced themselves and their roles beyond human limitations. They are significant because their quixotic, mistaken, but nevertheless somehow noble gestures are exceptional in a world of indifference, of congenital failure, and of irremediable discontent and unhappiness.

An American Tragedy: Theme and Structure

by SHELDON NORMAN GREBSTEIN

With every passing year it becomes further apparent that there is a greatness in Dreiser which overleaps his defects and his limitations, his bunglings, contradictions, and intrusions. The greatness reached its apogee in *An American Tragedy* which, four decades after its publication in 1925, impresses us more and more as one of the enduring novels of our century. Such distinguished men of letters as Robert Penn Warren pay it homage, and it continues to provoke the most careful and respectful critical commentary, even from those who find Dreiser vulgar or irreverent. Because *An American Tragedy* is so large a novel and so far from a simple one, it might prove instructive to turn our scrutiny once again to this work which has already declared itself more than a curiosity, more than a document of the jazz age (although in part it is that, too), and attempt to explore some of its complexities of theme and structure.

Thematically, *An American Tragedy* is a resonant work which, like all enduring literary creations, reverberates on multiple levels of meaning, at one and the same time bearing individual, social, and universal implication. We need look no farther than the novel's title for an outline of its themes, each word in the title signifying a thematic dimension: "An"— a single but not singular tale; "American"—a tale somehow representative not only of a particular nation but also, as the word increasingly connotes, a social structure, an experience, a life-style; "Tragedy"—a tale which concerns the end of man and its import.

On the individual level, or the simple one-to-one application of the content of a literary work to some aspect of real life within the reader's actual (or potential) experience, Dreiser employed, as is widely known, the records of an actual crime as the basis for his novel. This was the case of Chester Gillette, nephew and employee of a wealthy shirt manufacturer of Cortland (Lycurgus), New York, in which Gillette was convicted for the murder of his pregnant sweetheart, Grace Brown, and executed March 29, 1908, after appeals had delayed the death penalty for almost two years. Although Dreiser's use of this material is of considerable interest, an exhaustive account of the matter is not pertinent here. Suffice it to say that Dreiser relied heavily upon documentary materials, altering fact in two significant areas, however, to better serve the purposes of fiction:

1. The details of the real crime are changed so that the crime in *An American Tragedy* has a stronger element of the accidental. To name only one important difference, in the Gillette case five doctors agreed that drowning was *not* the primary cause of Grace Brown's death; the murder weapon was allegedly a tennis racket carried into the boat by Gillette and later found with all its strings broken.

2. More important, Clyde Griffiths only partly resembles Chester Gillette. He is less athletic and physically effectual (Gillette's photographs show him a bull-necked, deep-chested young man—also, Gillette admitted during the trial that he had initiated sexual relations with Grace Brown by force); less poised and self-contained (if contemporary newspaper accounts can be believed, Gillette did not lose his nerve under stress of indictment and trial); less well-equipped intellectually (Gillette had attended Oberlin for two years and seems to have been quick-witted, or at least glib). Finally, in contrast to Clyde's passion for Sondra, it is doubtful that Gillette was enamoured of any one girl in the wealthier class to which, like Clyde, he had gained access.

Much of what is different from the novel's Clyde Griffiths and life's Chester Gillette was supplied by Dreiser himself, from the raw materials of his own youth. The moving from place to place; the shame at the poverty and ineffectuality of the parents, especially the father; the sister who was made pregnant and then deserted; the young Dreiser's burning sexual hungers frustrated yet intensified by parental thou-shalt-nots and his own fears of inadequacy; the lust for beauty which expressed itself in a fascination with fine things, money, prestige, and which became inextricably interwoven with Dreiser's sexual appetites; the pervasive guilt for all desires and deeds not consonant with the iron doctrines of the devoutly Catholic father—all this was Dreiser and was to become Clyde Griffiths. This transubstantiation does much to explain the peculiar poignancy of Clyde's characterization.

The total effect of Dreiser's alterations of Chester Gillette, conjoined with the projection of his own experience, is cumulatively much stronger than the individual changes themselves would seem to suggest. They result in a character who is far weaker than one might expect a murderer to be, yet who is more sympathetically and credibly motivated because he kills, or plans to kill, not only for money but for beauty and love. As Dreiser himself remarked in a letter protesting the diluted and cheapened film version which had been made of his novel, Clyde's affair with Roberta is not wholly sordid: "As they [the film's producers] picture it, there is nothing idyllic about it, and there should be—there must be. Until Sondra comes into his life, Clyde is content, more or less happy in his love life with Roberta." We recall, too, that as Clyde languishes in the death house for nearly two years the one element of his past he does not repudiate, the one element in the whole complex of factors leading to his fate which he continues to affirm and which sustains him almost to the end, is the vision of Sondra's beauty and the thrilling memory of her kisses. For better or worse he loves her more than he has loved anyone and to the limit of his capacity to love, and if his discrimination can be questioned, the fact of his feelings cannot. It is a fact which recommends Clyde to the reader's heart, if not to his approving judgment.

Just as the individual or personal thematic level of *An American Tragedy* is hardly simplistic, so its social content has at least two dimensions.

First, the novel is the fictional but not fictitious treatment of an all too common situation in American life, that in which some desperate young man kills his poor (and usually pregnant) sweetheart in order to marry his way up the social scale. It might be called the tragedy of the aspiring young man, the pregnant working girl, and the debutante. Although Dreiser chose the Gillette-Brown murder case as the basis for his story, he had dozens of similar episodes at his disposal. As a boy Dreiser had immersed himself in potboiling fiction, one of whose staples was the poor-boy-gets-rich-girl theme, and he had early concluded, both from his reading and experience that money, not achievement, was the chief American ideal. Moreover, as a young reporter in various cities Dreiser encountered at first hand similar cases, some of them involving murder. And when, Helen Dreiser tells us, many years later he was formulating plans for the book first titled "Mirage" and then "An American Tragedy," he studied fifteen such incidents before finally deciding on the Gillette case. Not only did the Gillette case conform to his thoughts, it had been so well publicized that it was still being discussed into the 1920's and its records were readily accessible.

To Dreiser, then, the story of Chester Gillette and others like him became symbolic of certain dominant forces in American life, and in the characters and events of *An American Tragedy* he dramatized trends that had been true for generations: the worship of the goal of success, together with the refusal to condone the methods and consequences it engendered; the excitation and prurient display of sexuality in all forms of entertainment, billboards, magazines, popular literature, yet the stern legal repression of all but the narrowest forms of sexual expression (in marriage for the purpose of procreation only); the pretense of democratic egalitarianism, yet the existence of rigid class stratification; the absurd idealization of women; the stifling influence of intrinsically false but powerfully institutionalized religious creeds—these were elements which for Dreiser had tarnished the once-luminous American Dream. And all this shapes the social purpose of *An American Tragedy*. In addition to its depiction of these broad issues, (and much of Dreiser's triumph in *An American Tragedy* is that he depicts rather than editorializes), the novel indicts the legal system which could condemn and slaughter a youth whose real sin was weakness and real crime that of illicit sexual pleasure. The trial itself is vividly dramatized, with Dreiser demonstrating persuasively how Clyde becomes as much a victim of rigged evidence, political ambition, and public opinion as of "Justice;" *e. g.*, at one point in the proceedings a spectator speaks out in the voice of the people when he interjects: "Why don't they kill the God-damned bastard and be done with him?" Throughout, Dreiser is remarkably objective, but at moments toward the conclusion of his narrative, unable to restrain himself, he drops the guise of novelist and speaks with missionary fervor directly to the reader about the brutality of prisons, the death house, and by implication, the concept of justice which could tolerate such practices. Some critics would find this a flaw in the novel; nevertheless, there is probably no more trenchant argument against capital punishment in American literature.

Despite the weight of its social burden, *An American Tragedy* is much more than a tract, much more than a problem novel. Rather, it is a chronicle of American life. In the handling of his material Dreiser once again simply but effectively transformed history into art by means of a skillful manipulation of time. His main stratagem was to move the time of the action forward about ten years, or just enough to make the book's composition and publication parallel the events it narrates. That is, unlike its documentary source the story begins sometime during the 'teens and ends in the '20's, rather than in the period before 1910, when the Zeitgeist belonged to the 19th century, not the 20th. Thus, as F. O. Matthiessen has noted, the novel occurs in and conveys a generalized atmosphere of the era following the end of the first World War, the historic moment parent to much of what we are now living. Although *An American Tragedy* is perhaps the most sober book of the decade, its cast nevertheless includes a number of authentic sheiks and flappers, of both high and low class, who dash around in automobiles, carry hip flasks, dance to jazz music, and neck—or worse. Even that elite group of young people of Lycurgus who comprise the Olympian company to which Clyde aspires display a freedom from parental restraint and a mobility unknown before the war. Certainly Hortense Briggs, one of the novel's minor triumphs of characterization and a girl best described in the parlance of the time as a tease and a gold-digger, could not have existed before 1920 as an accepted member of society.

In this respect it could even be said that *An American Tragedy* tells another part of the story Fitzgerald recorded in *The Great Gatsby*. The analogy need not be carried too far, but Clyde Griffiths and Jay Gatsby have kinship, as do Sondra Finchley and Daisy Buchanan. Clyde and Gatsby pursue the same dream, the dream of an orgiastic future embodied in a beautiful girl with a voice like the sound of money; both pursue it passionately but illicitly, and with similarly disastrous results. There the comparison of the two books should probably end, but clearly it is more than a coincidence that two novels so superficially different yet thematically so alike should be published in the same year and should come to the same mordaunt conclusions about American life.

It has already been remarked how *An American Tragedy* functions on the individual and social levels; it remains to be seen how the book fulfills the third and most profound thematic dimension—the universal—or, in brief, how it functions as tragedy. Here Dreiser has fused an individual but representative instance and a social milieu into the larger saga of what happens to any man whose desires exceed both his capacity to satisfy them and his ability to avoid retribution, since satisfaction can only come at the expense of others. On this level Dreiser is no longer a meliorist concerned with changing certain attitudes toward poverty or sex or crime. Rather, he is a tragedian, a tragic ironist, who confronts the problem of human destiny and demonstrates what can happen in a cosmos indifferent to human suffering but inhabited by humans who persist in finding meaning in their suffering. In *An American Tragedy* he gives us a synthesis of the two basic tragic situations of western literature, the tragedy of frustrated love and the tragedy of thwarted ambition, as played by a proletarian hero and as written by a compassionate agnostic.

The source of Clyde's anguish (and, we may conjecture, Dreiser's as well) is that he belongs neither to the old theistic world, with its assurance of certain certainties, however harsh, nor in the new existential one, in which man (like Mersault, also a condemned criminal, in Camus's *The Stranger*) can stoically accept and even find a sense of happiness in the benign indifference of the universe. Man's law has declared Clyde guilty but few of the men who judge him have been so fiercely afflicted by the same desires. Belknap, Clyde's lawyer, is one of the few who can be honestly sympathetic because he, too, had once gotten a girl into trouble. Like one of Dreiser's earlier characters, the hero of the play *The Hand of the Potter*, Clyde could well cry out as his only defense, "I didn't make myself, did I?" Consequently, Clyde can feel none of the guilt whose admission his fellows wish to exact from him, and although just before his execution he signs a Christian testimonial-warning to errant youth, he does so only to repay his mother and the Reverend McMillan for the love and spiritual labor they have lavished upon him. It is grimly ironic that Clyde goes to his death still unconvinced in his heart of his guilt, while the Reverend McMillan, closest to him at the end, leaves the death house both convinced of Clyde's guilt and shaken in his belief in the efficacy of his own Christian mission.

Although in his refusal to confirm Clyde's guilt, or to confirm the fact of human guilt at all, Dreiser has risked the approval of much of his audience—for most of us believe that without guilt tragedy can have no moral value and consequently result in no catharsis—his tough-mindedness and his refusal to compromise his position invoke our admiration. If he has rejected the Christian or moralistic solution to man's dilemma, the promise of redemption and salvation through suffering, he refuses equally to take comfort from the science-inspired creeds of Naturalism or Determinism, which imply that all problems, including evil, are soluble once we learn enough about them. Instead, Dreiser persists in employing as his tragic formula that which has never been quite compatible to western man: the tragedy of humans overwhelmed by an omnipotent external fate. Accordingly, he does not permit Clyde even that dignity which is the agnostic, humanistic substitute for redemption. In his very weakness Clyde Griffiths becomes a metaphor of human frailty, and in his refusal to accept guilt he signifies the futility of human thought and endeavor in the context of life's essential meaninglessness. The result could easily have been stark nihilism, yet somehow, perhaps because of the indefinable quality of what has been called Dreiser's brooding pity,

Clyde's story is meaningful and poignant.

Purists in tragedy might argue that Clyde's fate is not tragic because his weakness does not permit sufficient struggle. Dreiser provides the basis for a reply. The death house is populated with others wiser and stronger than Clyde, *e.g.*, Nicholson, the lawyer, who has had all the advantages Clyde lacked; these are men of different races, religions, backgrounds—a Negro, an Oriental, Italians, a Jew, Irish—and all share the same fate. Obviously the death house is another of Dreiser's metaphors of the human condition. It is the place, the metaphor implies, where all men, wise or stupid, weak or strong, meet because all are condemned to a common fate not because they have sinned but because they are men. To their credit, most of them—including Clyde—leave life more nobly than they have lived it.

To assert, then, as a number of critics have recently, that Dreiser's treatment of tragedy is inferior because of some supposed flaw in his tragic vision, his employment of inadequate heroes, his denial of free will, is neither to comprehend Dreiser's position fully nor to judge it fairly on its own terms, but really to disagree with it. Granting Dreiser his premises and placing him in the appropriate tradition of tragedy, one can only say that one prefers some other tradition, not that Dreiser fails. It is also likely that Dreiser's hostile critics have confused his world-view with his workmanship, attributing to one a defect of the other, for if Dreiser falls short he does so as a stylist rather than a tragedian (I speak here, of course, specifically about *An American Tragedy*). That is, we have always had difficulty distinguishing between the tragic situation and the writer's treatment of it and his mode of utterance. To western audiences, consequently, the most splendid and moving tragedies are those most splendidly and movingly written, whether the idiom be Shakespeare's high rhetoric or Hemingway's colloquial cadences, and in Dreiser we find neither the soaring magnificence nor purged intensity of language which strikes the reader as the proper vehicle for tragedy.

Here, too, there is the tendency toward an unjust appraisal of *An American Tragedy;* for although Dreiser fails to overwhelm us with his eloquence, he persuades us by means of his novel's exceedingly durable and tight structure and by his use of ironic parallels, juxtapositions, and foreshadowings, which effectively emphasize the tragic irony of its theme.

Structurally, *An American Tragedy* is by far the most carefully planned of Dreiser's novels, each "Book" of the novel's three-part division is deliberately matched to a major aspect of its situations and themes. Although the three "books" vary in length, they achieve considerable symmetry, the first two dealing with cause and the third with effect. Further, Books I and II together comprise about two-thirds of the novel, with Roberta's death occuring almost exactly at the two-thirds mark. To use an analogy from drama, Book I is like the first act of a three-act play. It is relatively short, quick in movement and action, and it sets out the main lines of characterization as well as the basis for the conflict. (Note: in Dreiser's original manuscript Book I was considerably longer, containing nine chapters detailing Clyde's boyhood and offering additional documentation for his sense of inferiority). In Book II the conflict between sex and ambition is established, intensified by complications which produce a crisis (Roberta's pregnancy) and which result in a climax, the "murder." Book III provides a long dénouement, the trial, imprisonment, and execution, in which matters are settled but, as we have already observed, not resolved. That is, *An American Tragedy* is an open-ended drama. Within this general framework Clyde's tragic career may be described as an arc rather than a rise and fall. Just at the midpoint of his climb, when he has become a member of the smart set, has accompanied Sondra home for a midnight snack and declared his love for her, and she responds —a scene which occurs almost exactly midway in the novel—Roberta tells Clyde she is pregnant. For a time his momentum continues to carry him forward to greater social prestige and romantic success with Sondra, but to the observer, if not to Clyde himself, it is clear that the only possible movement is downward.

This deliberateness in structure carries over into Dreiser's use of various devices for ironic emphasis, devices thickly but not obtrusively deployed throughout the novel. By far the most obvious is the similarity of scene with which the novel begins and ends. Despite the passage of twelve years, the disgrace of a daughter and the execution of a son, the Griffiths continue to loft their prayers and hymns to a just and merciful God against the tall, indifferent walls of a commercial city, as a symbolic darkness descends. Everything Mother Griffiths has learned can be summed up in the dime for ice cream she gives Esta's illegitimate child, Clyde's replacement in the group of street evangelists; it is her way of forestalling another American tragedy. And the door through which the group disappears into the mission house reminds us of the door through which Clyde had passed to the electric chair. Another such parallel concludes both Book I and Book II. At the close of Book I Clyde flees, in darkness, from an accident in which a girl has been killed; at the end of Book II Clyde flees, once more in darkness, from the scene of a second girl's death. A somewhat similar device is Dreiser's detailed reproduction of religious mottoes and fragments of scripture at just those moments when the bitter facts of life are most shockingly apparent, especially in Books I and III. Note, for example, the heavy irony in the last few pages of Chapter xvii of Book III, where each stage of Mother Griffiths' anguish at hearing of Clyde's indictment for murder is interlined with fragments from the Psalms.

There are still other ironic techniques, only a few of which will be set down here. One of the more subtle is Dreiser's use of season and weather. Clyde's job at the Green-Davidson Hotel, a crucial experience in the shaping of his desires for sex, money, and position, begins in the fall (a better season for endings than beginnings; that, too, is intentional). Likewise, Clyde's sexual intimacy with Roberta begins in the fall, and his trial for murder takes place in the fall. Winter is an even gloomier Dreiserian season, for Clyde runs away from Kansas City in the winter, Roberta announces her pregnancy to Clyde in the winter, the judge passes sentence on Clyde in the winter, and Clyde's execution is carried out in the winter—and in darkness.

Finally, Dreiser stages a series of suggestive word-plays and scene-parallels which serve both to foreshadow and intensify the action. Just after coming to Lycurgus Clyde admires the Griffiths' stately home, which has as its lawn decorations a fountain in which a boy holds a swan (would Clyde have let Sondra drown?), and an arrangement of statuary in which dogs pursue a fleeing stag. Soon after this Clyde finds himself in the company of an all-too-willing girl named Rita (whom he has

met at a church social), and in his efforts to remain on his feet and avoid risky sexual entanglements he dances with her to a tune called "The Love Boat." When, a few months later the lonely and now less cautious Clyde encounters Roberta on the shores of a nearby lake, he persuades her to come into his canoe, assuring her, "You won't be in any danger. . . . It's perfectly safe. . . . It won't tip over." Shortly after this, when they meet on the street (in darkness) for their first rendezvous, Clyde says presciently, "We have so little time." Later still, just after Roberta has determined that Clyde must either arrange an abortion or marry her, Dreiser shifts focus momentarily to Sondra, whose romantic daydreams of Clyde include fancied episodes in which she and Clyde are alone in a canoe on some remote, idyllic lake. And after Roberta's death, when an inwardly hysterical Clyde has rejoined the gay vacation group at Twelfth Lake, Sondra says to a boy steering a boat in which she, Clyde, and others are riding, "O, say, what do you want to do? Drown us all?"

Is it now not obvious that any judgment of *An American Tragedy* which has been made solely or largely on the basis of its "style" (always the same word) must be a narrow and capricious judgment? This is too big, too significant, too serious a book to permit an assessment of the writer's diction and command of sentence structure to stand as the last word; the strength and dimensions of its architecture tower over whatever defects may appear in the facing. In any case, *An American Tragedy* has already survived virtually a half-century of critical winnowing. It seems safe to predict that it will continue to grow in our esteem, and that in time it will join that all-too-small group of permanent books we call American classics.

Sinclair Lewis and the Hollow Center

by MAURICE KRAMER

Mark Schorer's definitive biography of Sinclair Lewis has been quite naturally and rightly criticized for being too massive. But its concern with minutiae is also in perfect keeping with its subject, who was (as Schorer makes absolutely clear) a master of mimicry who could not resist this gift and who in fact found it a vital substitute for self-analysis. Lewis's novels abound in details not only because his realistic technique called for them but also because he himself was pleased by them. The reader is also considerably pleased when, in a fine novel like *Babbitt*, the details create satirically revealing images of American character; but often, when Lewis's own pleasure becomes merely a complacency over his abilities of recall and research, the result is undeniable tedium.

This is the problem that Lewis presents to critics: how can he be both so good in spots and so generally bad? The biography offers some assistance in its picture of the painfully insecure boy who drove himself to become a good fellow, a Yale man, a successful writer, a public figure who supplied, in the Twenties, a good deal of conscience to a nation of confused moralities. But if there was public success, there was also private failure, notably in Lewis's two marriages; and the continuing insecurity, the continuing pain are revealed in his steady drinking, his clowning and his tantrums, and the pathetic loneliness which led him to find a young mistress in his last years (and which is readily seen, too, in the admirable photograph by Man Ray). Noting the many faces, assumed and hidden, of Lewis, Schorer says, "there must have been not two but six or eight or ten or two hundred selves and, because they could never be one, a large hole in the center."

Such a man might very well exist as a reflector of his society. But Lewis could not be simply "other-directed," a mere Babbitt. He was, for one thing, the fiercely energetic recorder of what he saw. But more importantly, his upbringing in a Midwest dominated by Progressive idealism, coupled with his sense of being always just outside the circles of success, made him a figure somewhat old-fashioned in the Twenties. He still remembered some promises of American life, "promises," to quote Schorer again, "of a society that from his beginning would have not only tolerated but also treasured *him*. That is the personal basis," says Schorer, of the social viewpoint of the novels.

Generalized, it becomes an idealization of an older America, the America of mid-nineteenth century, an America vast and formless but overflowing with the potentialities for and the constant expression of a wide, casually human freedom, the individual life lived in honest and perhaps eccentric effort (all the better), the social life lived in a spirit that first of all tolerates variety. . . .

The source of Lewis's satire lies in the American defection from the American potentiality for individual freedom. When he scolded America it was because Americans would not be free, and he attacked all the means by which they betrayed themselves: economic system, intellectual rigidity, theological dogma, legal repression, class convention, materialism, social timidity, hypocrisy, affection, complacency and pomposity.

This is the basis of Lewis's attitude, and it is distinctly negative. He saw his society with a terribly sharp sight, but what he saw were glossy surfaces that he knew to be surfaces. Unable to find a center in himself, he found only emptiness again in the society to which he eagerly sought to attach himself. There is, then, no real depth in Lewis's work. It would be distortion to say, for example, that he raged with frustration against his society; the tone of his satire is rather that of gleeful parody.

What kind of society would, after all, treasure this homely, tense, capricious and critical man? The midwest of the mid-nineteenth century? Sherwood Anderson praises it warmly in *Poor White* but indicates that its individualistic culture was never more than potential and that the potentiality had been destroyed by the massive industrialization of the 1880's and '90's. Vachel Lindsay remembers its last vigorous rising in "Bryan, Bryan, Bryan, Bryan," but he has to invoke a fanciful, adolescent mood to do so. When Lewis seeks to find the positive basis for his criticism in a society that probably never existed except as an idea, that by his own testimony existed only as a corrupted idea in the Twenties, he gives up his claim to seriousness.

Yet this is just what he tries to do. *Dodsworth* is the key novel in this respect, the one in which Lewis tries to work out his idea of what is good in the United States after having depicted what is bad in four powerfully satiric novels (*Main Street, Babbitt, Arrowsmith* and *Elmer Gantry*). Lewis's difficulty in turning about is evident in almost every aspect of the novel. In the satires the knavish fools are often articulate—Babbitt the orator, Chum Frink the poet. But th, hero of *Dodsworth* is just enough not a Babbitt to know that he has never thought for himself, and this negative honesty becomes both his basic trait and his basic virtue. There is very little that is positive in Sam Dodsworth, despite Lewis's frequent assertions of his inventiveness as an engineer.

Admittedly Dodsworth has great handicaps to overcome. He has been needled into a state of cultural inferiority by his pretentious wife, and she leads him into a snobbish European society that can only confirm his sense of the good fellowship of American vulgarity. It is only through some expatriate American businessmen that Dodsworth comes to recognize a certain superiority in the European way of life— a greater calmness and privacy as well as a more sophisticated interest in the object of living. This, however vague itself, leaves a very thin line of defense for Dodsworth the good American. To a Berliner's pronouncement that Europe is "the last refuge, in a Fordized world, of personal dignity," Dodsworth can only reply that America is young and that there are a "whale of a lot of Americans who are going slow and quiet, and who are thinking. . . ."

Through his European experiences Dodsworth learns that his slowness and quietness are virtues, virtues which America is losing. Lewis goes so far as to suggest that Americans can even relearn the virtue of proper vulgarity in Europe. The Europeans, declares Edith Cortright, "love earth and sun and wind and rain."

> That's the strength of Europe—not its so-called 'culture,' its galleries and neat voices and knowledge of languages, but its nearness to earth. And that's the weakness of America—not its noisiness and its cruelty and its cinema vulgarity but the way in which it erects steel-and-glass skyscrapers and miraculous cement-and-glass factories and tiled kitchens and wireless antennae and popular magazines to insulate it from the good vulgarity of the earth.

Europe can teach the American, if he avoids the trap of cultural snobbery, to return to the earth like Anteus in order to renew his strength, his creative spirit—to find again what Lewis would call the pioneering spirit. For Lewis's positive position is, finally, to offer the possibility that the roots and virtues of the United States are in its "tradition of pioneers pushing to the westward . . . a religious procession, sleeping always in danger, never resting, and opening a new home for a hundred million people."

After all of Dodsworth's debates and fresh experiences, Lewis seems to reach a conclusion here. But it is regrettably vague despite (probably because of) the painstaking honesty of the argument. Having reached his conclusion, Lewis does not know what to do with Dodsworth, except negatively to keep him out of the hands of his wife. There is much talk of building beautiful native houses, of making something new, but it is all tentative, featureless. Even Mrs. Cortright, shortly after her criticism of skyscrapers, blithers about skyscrapers being "the first really new thing in architecture since the Gothic cathedral, and perhaps just as beautiful."

The confusion of Lewis's viewpoint, of his very self, is evident here. Though he understood that real individuality would have to shake loose from mass produced conformity, he himself could not give up the monuments of modernity—or even its gadgets. They constituted his style, and he had no real desire to do away with them, or at least no power to do away with them. He knows, as he says in *Main Street,* that the days of pioneering are deader than Camelot in the Midwest of the Twenties, and he bases his satire on that knowledge; but he writes only of the indubitable, bland facts of the present. *Dodsworth* seems, when the novels are read in sequence, a crucial attempt to inform modern America of its old values. But its vague ending prefigures a group of lumbering and flatly drawn heroes in the later novels. *Ann Vickers,* the novel which follows *Dodsworth,* returns for the most part to journalistic issues, presented in great surface detail, but without quite the satiric bite of *Elmer Gantry* or *Arrowsmith,* as though Lewis knew that he had pushed his talent to its furthest reaches and that the rest would be mere work.

Lewis only barely meets the test of having an identifiable style, one integrated with his subject matter. As suggested in the last paragraph, it is a style that attends to objects. Lewis is always at his best when describing. In writing of personal relationships (and he is very much concerned, in particular, with marital relationships), he tends to flatness, an insistent weighing of motives, temptations and morals. Though Lewis is an old-fashioned narrator, an admirer of Edith Wharton, his style not only lacks subtlety but almost recoils from it, is certainly suspicious of it.

Lewis is, in fact, as wary of abstraction as was his fellow Midwesterner, Ernest Hemingway, and apparently for some of the same reasons. He can sense the modern presence of the pioneering spirit only in the type of the capable individualist, the man who knows how to control the objects of manufacture and nature

68

among which he lives. Such types have little use for speculative thought, of course. Yet the difference between Lewis and Hemingway is certainly more informative than this similarity. For Hemingway made out of his manly ideal a highly personalized and formal style, both in his writing and in his life, and that Lewis was never able to do.

The crux of Lewis's weakness as a novelist lies exactly in this difference. Where Hemingway, for all his commitment to virility, committed himself at least equally to his art, Lewis's notion of manliness kept him suspicious of art itself. Lewis did not much like his fellow novelists; he was always more at ease with journalists. Too much style, he thought, would be phony. One perceives at once the limitation of intelligence, the real commitment to middle class common sense as the ultimate truth of things. Though Lewis can write, like Hemingway, of the "healing" powers of nature, he cannot realize those powers in practice or in style. What he can realize, however, with brilliant lucidity and bite, is the corruption of those powers among the Babbittry. The fact is that Lewis is dull when being positive but delightful when being negative. *Babbitt* is his masterpiece. The description of the hopeless hero's flight to the Maine woods makes one realize how both typically American and wonderfully romantic is Hemingway's very serious account of Nick Adam's retreat in "The Big Two-Hearted River." Nor is Lewis wholly cynical. The scenes of Babbitt emerging from his cabin in flapping new khakis and of the Indian guide relating his dream of making money in a little store are the most striking, but there is also a sympathetic view of the hustling buisnessman easing temporarily out of his strains.

It is probably this ability to sympathize that makes Lewis the great chronicler of Babbitt. All of Lewis's weaknesses of thought, style and viewpoint turn to strengths in this full portrait of the unthinking American loudmouth. It is doubtful that anyone of greater sensitivity could have dwelt with such care on such a subject, and it is unlikely that anyone less fascinated by surfaces could have recounted not only the objects of Babbitt's life but also his very speeches in elaborate detail. Moreover, there is enough of Babbitt in Lewis himself to enable him to perceive that, beneath the ignorance, dishonesty and cruelty which make Babbitt so terrible to others, are the loneliness and the boredom which make him so terrible to himself.

This makes it altogether fitting, too, that there should be nothing positive in the novel at all, except for the admirations of skyscrapers and Maine scenes which Babbitt and Lewis share. The socialist lawyer, Seneca Doane, sums up Lewis's theme, as follows:

> The real villains of the piece are the clean, kind, industrious Family Men who use every known brand of trickery and cruelty to insure the prosperity of their cubs. The worst thing about these fellows is that they're so good and, in their work at least, so intelligent. You can't hate them properly, and yet their standardized minds are the enemy.

But Doane prefers to live in Zenith, the city run by the manipulators of these standardized minds, for the thoughtless reason that it has "a future so unknown" that it excites his imagination. This vagueness, this refusal to think the evidence through to real conclusions, links Doane to Babbitt (they are, in fact, personal friends). None of Lewis's characters gets beyond this point of development, because Lewis himself never does.

Lewis must have been aware that one conclusion would have been despair, and in this respect he may be compared with another younger novelist of the Twenties, Scott Fitzgerald, who was also a Midwesterner with Eastern ambitions and failures. Like Lewis, Fitzgerald had a mind full of conventional American rag-tags, "the tawdry souvenirs of his boyhood," to quote from a description of Dick Diver in *Tender is the Night*. "Yet," the passage goes on, "in that somewhat littered Five-and-Ten, he had managed to keep alive the low painful fire of intelligence." The clear prose of *The Crack-Up* testifies to the maintenance of a similar flame in Fitzgerald himself. Lewis, at his best, is never so quiet and precise; he is noisy, busily displaying the objects (or lengthily mimicking the speeches) that will constitute his subjects. So in his novels, and apparently in his life too, there are many striking accidents, but never the complete crack-up that seems often to threaten; neither is there any firm core at the center of his art.

Sherwood Anderson and the Lyric Story

by SISTER M. JOSELYN, O.S.B.

At this date, not much remains to be done by way of appointing Sherwood Anderson a place among American writers; in fact he himself succinctly indicated his own position when he remarked in the *Memoirs* that "For all my egotism, I know I am but a minor figure." There is little disagreement, either, about the work on which Anderson's reputation rests— *Winesburg,* "Death in the Woods," a few stories from *The Triumph of the Egg.* When we come to estimate the accomplishment represented by *Winesburg,* however, things are not quite so clear. There are those who wish, still, to view the collection as a frame-story, but they then must reckon with the difficulty of seeming to reduce all the stories to the dead level of equivalent exhibits. Those on the other hand who want to read *Winesburg* as an initiation novel about George Willard have to face the problem of resting their case upon a character who in the end remains the thinnest figment. To choose to relegate Anderson and *Winesburg* to the limbo of regionalism is no longer acceptable.

Perhaps the sanest way is to view *Winesburg,* an uneven collection, as a special kind of amalgam of naturalism and lyricism. Every reader, whether approvingly or not, acknowledges the lyric intensity of the best Anderson stories. To Herbert Gold, Anderson is "one of the purest, most intense poets of loneliness," while Irving Howe (who has also called Anderson a "pre-poet") holds that no other American writer "has yet been able to realize that strain of lyrical and nostalgic feeling which in Anderson's best work reminds one of another and greater poet of tenderness, Turgenev." Robert Gorham Davis ascribes the "great impression" made by *Winesburg* to its "freshness and lyric intensity." It is Paul Rosenfeld, however, who has seen most clearly that Anderson's lyricism is a method as much as an effect, for to this reader, Anderson's narratives "really are lyrics with epic characteristics, lyrics narrative of event."

In analyzing the elements that go into Anderson's lyricism, Rosenfeld notes the "legendary tone, the repetitions of slow rhythms and the loose joints" of the American tale, as well as the personal feeling that rises from the region between Anderson's "conscious and unconscious minds." But Rosenfeld places greatest stress on the purely verbal aspects of Anderson's poetic quality, for

> Anderson's inclusion among the authors of the lyric story . . . flows first of all

from the fact that, using the language of actuality, he nonetheless invariably wrings sonority and cadence from it; unobtrusively indeed, without transcending the easy pitch of familiar prose. . . . He sustains tones broadly with assonances and with repeated or echoing words and phrases. He creates accent-patterns and even stanza-like paragraphs with the periodic repetition or alternation of features such as syllables, sounds, words, phrases, entire periods . . . . (Introduction to *The Sherwood Anderson Reader,* pp. xiv-xv.)

Many readers of Anderson will see these assertions as a part of Rosenfeld's special pleading and will doubtless be more inclined to share Irving Howe's belief that amidst the "chaos of his creative life Anderson had to cast around for a device with which to establish some minimum of order in his work" and found it "in the undulations of his verbal rhythms . . . ." Indeed, it is precisely in those pieces where he was "most at sea imaginatively" that "the rhythm is most insistently established."

Rosenfeld, I think it can be shown, is on much stronger ground when contending that Anderson's stories are—in other ways—"lyrics with epic characteristics," and in holding that

> As for his own specimens of the lyric story-kind, they have 'inner form' like Gertrude Stein's, but their rhythms are livelier, longer, more self-completive than those of the somnolent lady-Buddha of the *rue de Fleurus.* While wanting the suavity of expression in Turgenev's lyric tales, Anderson's share the warmly singing tone of the Russian's, surpass them of course in point of tension, and have the Andersonian qualities of subtlety of attack and humorous and acute feeling, perceptions of the essential in the singular, glamour over the commonplace, boldness of image . . . Wonderfully they 'stay by us.' (*Sherwood Anderson Reader,* p. xix.)

What, precisely, is the "inner form" of Anderson's stories and how can they be said to be "lyrics with epic characteristics"?

In the first place it must be noted that the best Anderson stories always contain and lead up to a *revelation,* epiphany, or state of realized experience. Robert Morse Lovett has said that Anderson's stories "reach outward into the unknown," while Granville Hicks asserts that "Surfaces, deeds, even words scarcely concern him; everything is bent to the task of revelation." To Herbert Gold, "The experience of epiphany is characteristic of great literature, and the lyric tales of Anderson give this wonderful rapt coming-forth, time and time again." Irving Howe — uncomplimentarily — notes that Anderson "wrote best when he had no need to develop situations or show change and interaction—," but Anderson's own ideal of art is expressed precisely in his idealization of "the tale of perfect balance," with all its "elements . . . understood, an infinite number of minute adjustments perfectly made . . . ."

Summaries of Anderson stories reveal even less than is usually the case about the significance of the narratives; obviously in Anderson what is at stake is not histories, biographies, gossip, or even tales. From Anderson's best work one does derive an unmistakable sense of authentic experience being worked out from within, in the manner of the great Russians—Turgenev and Chekhov—with their unparalleled suggestiveness and extreme economy of means. Like the Russians, Anderson does not "import his poetry into the work—he allows only the poetry that is *there*" (Herbert Gold). The significance of an Anderson story has very little to do with the "facts" that are related but it has something to do with the arrangement of those facts and with the relationship of these "epic" elements to other, more properly poetic strains.

Anderson's abandonment of pure naturalism involved him in a movement away from structures dependent upon sequential action or gradually increased intensity and toward an arrangement of events which would better dramatize the centrifugal, diffused, resonant effect his materials called for. The halting, tentative, digressive style, and the circular, hovering or "Chinese box" approach to "what happened" thus do not so much demonstrate Anderson's affectation of the manner of oral tale-telling as they illustrate his understanding that the "epic" base of the story must be manipulated in such a way that weight is thrown upon the significance of the happenings as it reveals itself to the central consciousness and to the reader, rather than upon the events themselves. This is, of course, essentially a "poetic" strategy.

Moreover, as Jon Lawry has demonstrated in his reading of "Death in the Woods," the narrative strategy, by which the story is not really "told" to any assumed audience, makes it possible that "its process of growth and contact is discovered by the audience, through the act itself rather than through the narrator's relation of the act," for "The audience is invited to enter as individuals into a process almost identical with that of the narrator and to reach with him for contact with another life." This narrative method makes it possible for the "unacknowledged audience" to "share directly not only the narrator's responses but his act of discovering and creating those responses"—and this is precisely the "method" of the post-symbolist lyric. It is also the technique by which in Anderson fantasy is most controlled, or, "if not exactly controlled, simplified, given a single lyrical line," and ambivalent—if not contradictory—emotions enfolded within one action.

Before turning to an analysis of stories by Anderson which illustrate the lyrical effects we have been describing, we may mention briefly other marks of the poetic character of his narration: non-realistic, ritualistic dialogue, the use of symbols to embody and dramatize themes, and the exploitation of suggestiveness, "the art of leaving out." In thinking of the whole of Anderson's achievement it is well to bear in mind that he began his writing career "under the influence and patronage of the realists at the time when realism was being modified by symbolism" (Robert Morss Lovett).

The first story of *Winesburg*, "Hands," affords a vivid illustration of one of the ways in which Anderson manipulates his story-line in such a way as to evoke a maximum resonance from the events narrated. Normal time sequence is almost obliterated as Anderson penetrates with the reader further and further into the mysterious recesses of Wing Biddlebaum's mind. The tragedy of Wing Biddlebaum is of course presented by means of the things that happened to him—not even the lyric story can totally dispense with the "epic" elements essential for the narrative genres—but the events of Biddlebaum's life are presented neither straightforwardly nor in a conventional flashback sequence. Rather, Anderson uses a kind of box-within-box structure as he takes us into the interior mystery of his character by means of a series of vignettes in which Biddlebaum is revealed first through the eyes of the townspeople and the casual berry-pickers who pass his house, then through the eyes of George Willard (whom Anderson cunningly utilizes as both the confidant the plot requires and as an objective correlative for all that Biddlebaum seeks), and finally through the protagonist's own sense of himself. But these sections flow so smoothly through the story-teller's hands, and are so completely suffused with Wing Biddlebaum's consciousness, that we are not aware of any awkward juncture between sections. In this structure, the first event in Biddlebaum's "chronological" life becomes the last in the record of his emotional life, because the beating of the schoolmaster was the one event which both precipitated and contained the entire mystery of the man. With the presentation of this event, also, Anderson has brought his story to its maximum level of universalization, for without resorting to allegory but by remaining wholly within the confines of realism Anderson has made us feel that we are all Wing Biddlebaum and that we are also the men who cast him out of the village half dead, and that Biddlebaum's situation enfolds within it the entire condition of man. The last section of the story is a beautifully falling cadence; coming after the event of the beating, it simply shows us Wing Biddlebaum as he now is, as we have made him, as we are:

> When the rumble of the evening train that took away the express cars loaded with the day's harvest of berries had passed and restored the silence of the summer night, he went again to walk upon the veranda. In the darkness he could not see the hands . . . . Although he still hungered for the presence of the boy, who was the medium through which he expressed his love of man, the hunger became again a part of his loneliness and his waiting. Lighting a lamp, Wing Biddlebaum . . . prepared to undress for the night. A few stray white bread crumbs lay on the cleanly washed floor by the table; putting the lamp upon a low stool he began to pick up the crumbs, carrying them to his mouth one by one with unbelievable rapidity.

Anderson's exploitation of the symbolic aspect of the eating of bread, and of the hands themselves, requires no commentary.

Other kinds of dislocation of the narrative line appear in "Adventure," in "The Thinker," and in "Sophistication." In the first story, a report of the exterior events of Alice Hindman's life is counterpointed by an account of the development of her inward, emotional life. The patterns move in opposite directions, for while Alice's outward existence appears to run steadily downhill into dull meaninglessness, her inward life climbs with increasing intensity toward a climax of desperation and hysteria. A review of only the story's outward events would seem to confirm the frequent accusation that Anderson is given to assembling large, undifferentiated narrative masses out of which he is unable to bring order or illumination, yet when he is at his best, Anderson's unfolding of inner life— even when it is not so strongly cross-grained as in "Adventure"—does provide a sufficient makeweight for outward event, and in fact the out-

come toward which the narrative strives is precisely an evocation of the *quality* of the relationship between inner and outward event. In Anderson, this evocation is essentially poetic or musical. And while restraint is not a trait usually ascribed to Anderson, it is this virtue of tact which rules such sections of his narrative as the conclusion of "Adventure," in which Alice Hindman, recalling herself from the wild scene in the street, goes weeping to bed with the words,

> "What is the matter with me? I will do something dreadful if I am not careful," she thought, and turning her face to the wall, began trying to force herself to face bravely the fact that many people must live and die alone, even in Winesburg.

In "Sophistication," the "epic" elements are arranged in such a way that George Willard's restlessness and puzzlement are dramatized— rather than merely reported—through the structure itself with its jerky, spasmodic focusing and refocusing. Anderson, moreover, demonstrates a high degree of cunning in not attempting any sort of philosophic resolution of George's dilemmas but by providing instead a rather quiet culminating scene in which all the contradictory aspects of George's and Helen's consciousness are caught up in a symbolic action (is it ludicrous to see a resemblance to Yeat's use of the great-rooted blossomer?):

> It was so they went down the hill . . . . Once, running swiftly forward, Helen tripped George and he fell. He squirmed and shouted. Shaking with laughter, he rolled down the hill. Helen ran after him. For just a moment she stopped in the darkness. . . . when the bottom of the hill was reached and she came up to the boy, she took his arm and walked beside him in dignified silence.

Other symbol-like devices appearing in the story are the cornfields, the dry leaves and trees, the stallion, and the grandstand. Anderson's conducting of the narrative is too loose and diffuse for these objects to form a genuine symbolic pattern, but their presence does add power to the lyric suggestiveness of the narrative.

Structure in "The Thinker" is much more complex. As in "Hands," the problem here is to develop for the reader the sense of a particular personality, in this case one not nearly so unusual as Wing Biddlebaum, and that of a much younger man. Anderson begins the story by describing in his rambling, tentative manner Seth Richmond's house, the circumstances of his mother's widowhood, and her present feeling for the boy. A quarter of the story elapses. before we hear any words from Seth himself, but with his return from the runaway trip we are moved directly into his consciousness and from then on the story is told from Seth's point of view. At the same time, the eerie disjointedness of experience is conveyed directly with (for Anderson) surprisingly little editorializing as we follow the young man through his brief visit with George Willard, his eavesdropping on the quarreling hotel men, his meeting with old Turk in the street, and his unsatisfactory encounter with Helen. At almost exactly midpoint in the story comes the devastating self-revelatory comment that Seth "was not what the men of the town, and even his mother, thought him to be," for "No great underlying purpose lay back of his habitual silence, and he had no definite plan for his life." Observing from afar the sullen, furious baker with the empty milk bottle in his hand, Seth "wished that he himself might become thoroughly stirred by something . . . ."

For the elucidation of Seth's identity, Anderson has ranged around the central silence and dumbness of the young man various "talkers," including Turk Smollett with his "absurdly boyish mind," the half dangerous old wood chopper "who hurries along the middle of the road with his wheelbarrow and its nicely balanced dozen long boards." Seth knew that

> when Turk got into Main Street he would become the center of a whirlwind of cries and comments, that in truth the old man was going far out of his way in order to pass through Main Street and exhibit his skill in wheeling the boards. "If George Willard were here, he'd have something to say," thought Seth.

Along with the windy political quarrelers briefly overheard in the hotel lobby is grouped the emptily ebullient George Willard who announces, "I know what I'm going to do. I'm going to fall in love. I've been sitting here and thinking it over and I'm going to do it." The climax comes as Seth, equally disgusted and bored with George's prattle and his own silence, seeks out Helen White, who utters almost no words during their walk together.

The central meaning of the boy's encounter with all these persons is conveyed in two interpolations. In the first, during the silent walk with Helen, Seth remembers the moment the day before in a field where he had heard "A soft humming noise" and looking down "had seen the bees everywhere all about him in the long grass":

> He stood in a mass of weeds that grew waist-high in the field that ran away from the hillside. The weeds were abloom with tiny purple blossoms and gave forth an overpowering fragrance.

Now imagining himself with Helen in that field, Seth thought he would lie "perfectly still, looking at her and listening to the army of bees that sang . . . above his head." But a little later, as the distant thunder moves closer and the spot where they are sitting is momentarily illuminated by lightning, "The garden that had been so mysterious and vast, a place that . . . might have become the background for strange and wonderful adventures, now seemed no more than an ordinary Winesburg back yard, quite definite and limited in its outlines." Unable either to go forward into a meaningful existence or to preserve his integrity by a return to innocence, Seth Richmond can only stand, after Helen's departure, "staring, perplexed and puzzled . . . as he had been perplexed and puzzled by all the life of the town out of which she had come." Again, it is through the arrangement of actions and by a quiet exploitation of the symbolic aspects of objects and events that Anderson succeeds in bringing before us a full-dimensioned protagonist fraught with the burdens and fleeting joys resembling our own.

It is in the *Winesburg* stories such as "The Thinker," "Adventure," "Hands," "Sophistication," and "The Untold Lie" that Anderson manages to reinforce a certain surface fidelity with what Ernest Boyd has called the "deeper realism which sees beyond and beneath the exterior world to the hidden reality which is the essence of things." By combining in a special manner the story's "epic" elements with characteristic lyric devices, Anderson is able, at least on occasion, to reach the "something totally private, untouchable, beyond appearance and action, in all of us" and thus exemplifies his own belief that "To live is to create new forms: with the body in living children; in new and more beautiful forms carved out of materials; in the creation of a world of the fancy; in scholarship; in clear and lucid thought. . . ."

Rhetoric and Vision in Mencken's Satire:
The "Medieval" Mob

by M. K. SINGLETON

Henry Louis Mencken achieved celebrity during the 1920's as an enemy of sumptuary legislation, academic pussy-footing, "Victorianism," Wilsonian idealism, Harding "normalcy," Coolidge paltriness, and most cultural manifestations of gentility, Christianity, and Democracy. His vogue as iconoclast led some to call the decade following the First World War "the Age of H. L. Mencken." Catering to a mood of fashionable disillusionment, he took the side of the modernists—the so-called "civilized minority"—against the pressures of an increasingly standardized and arrogant Babbittry.

At present, however, most of Mencken's immense output has been shelved as strident and dated, and close study of his rhetoric is lacking. To be sure, Mencken has certain modest claims to historical importance. In a period when the more genteel makers of literary opinion brought to their craft only "church membership and an honest face," Mencken's support for such emerging authors as Theodore Dreiser and Sinclair Lewis was as timely as it was unmodulated; and his great contribution to lexicography, *The American Language*, with its several revisions and supplements, is still consulted. Likewise unforgotten is his swashbuckling editorial conduct, with the help of George Jean Nathan, of *The Smart Set* and *The American Mercury;* these two reviews, popular with urban sophisticates, made such engaging sport of the "booboisie" that satire became one of the parlor diversions of the self-consciously "emancipated." That satire today, for many critics, is a *genre* ranking well below comedy and only slightly above topical journalistic scavenging is unfortunate, because with satire Mencken was able, as Jim Tully observed in 1927, to teach "a million thinking people the value of fundamentals."

Nevertheless, if Mencken is to be established as an accomplished stylist in satire, criticism of him must become both wider and deeper than it has been for a number of years. Much recent discussion of his work adds up to little more than a scolding of him for his anti-New Deal politics. More potentially fruitful lines of approach are anticipated by early tributes to his prose: in 1926, Edmund Wilson discerned that the writing style of his Baltimore colleague gave "a certain literary satisfaction" based on "most attractive eighteenth century qualities of lucidity, order and force." And F. Scott Fitzgerald, also writing in 1926, hailed Mencken's

invective as equal to that of Jonathan Swift, and as "the most forceful prose style now written in English." The word *force,* so frequently met in statements about his style, shows the respect of Mencken's contemporaries for the power of bluntness, but of the sort of invective created by Juvenalian indignation Mencken is relatively free. After all, he was not, even by implication, attempting to correct vice; and even his famous name-calling is conducted with an almost Horatian mellowness. A major reason for his *force* has been hitherto undefined: his recurrent and extensive use of "medieval" figures of speech and diction to define his satiric panorama. Any inquiry into his mastery of satiric form must take account of this part of the satiric landscape and its use in some of his *Prejudices.*

A surprisingly pervasive body of metaphor in the *Prejudices* is drawn from "medieval" tropes —or, more precisely, from the stereotyped language used by Enlightenment and progressivist nineteenth-century authors to describe the benighted era of the "Dark Ages." Although Mencken had next to no knowledge of, or interest in, the actualities of medieval history, he had a good familiarity with Mark Twain's several books exploiting medieval settings to elaborate Twain's anti-clerical, progressivist hostility to survivals of European "feudalism;" and Mencken borrowed from Twain the "Dark Ages" diction and phraseology that Twain, in turn, had lifted from such liberal historians of the nineteenth century as W. H. Lecky and Jules Michelete. With such quaint, archaic, or otherwise historical epithets drawn from Twain's medieval tableaux did Mencken embroider his own tapestries: *peasantry, yeomanry, Berserker, knave, paladin,* and *Vandal.* Denounced in such essays as "Roosevelt: An Autopsy," "On Being an American," and "Chiropractic" are such follies as *sorcery, demonology, credulity, superstition, mountebankery, medieval despotism, charlatanery* — all in their modern guise, of course, but still freighted with derogatory "Dark Ages" connotations. Individuals are also likened to personages from the Middle Ages: Theodore Roosevelt, feeling mettlesome, swells into a "national Barbarossa," and when he denounces a political enemy, it is with "the wildest interdicts of a medieval pope;" Jackson, with his "merry men," breaks down the barriers against popular democracy; Wilson serves the "holy crusade" of Prohibition as its "Peter the Hermit;" and Harding, in the eyes of the credulous, becomes a "Charlemagne." Generalized types are also satirized in a pseudo-medieval frame: the prairie demagogue, aspiring to dictatorship, is likened to "that Pepin the Short who found himself mayor of the palace and made himself King of the Franks." Genteel literary critics meet in "ponderous conclave," issue "bulls," and, if New Humanists, are "of the apostolic succession." Evangelical Methodism is burlesqued as "the Only True Christianity," its "secular arm" is the Ku Klux Klan, and its issues "excommunications" in large number, because, to the "rabble of peasants" all discussion of ideas must take the form "of a pursuit and scotching of demons;" after all, "anything strange is to be combatted," "is of the Devil," and one "cannot think of a heresy without thinking of a heretic to be caught, condemned and burned." William Jennings Bryan, despite his defeat with Free Silver and his temporary set-back at the Scopes trial, is "a protean harlequin" still able to lead the "motley horde" (or "fabulous mob") of Fundamentalists because the "mysticism of the mediaeval peasantry gets into the communal view" of its heroes. Indeed, the more one reads Mencken, the more one is willing to accept his personal admission of a "mediaeval but unashamed taste for the bizarre and indelicate."

At times Mencken rolls up scathing catalogues of his countrymen and their follies, catalogues reminiscent of the hundreds of now-amusing ancient "catch-all" ordinances passed during the Middle Ages against sturdy beggars, fornicators, actors, goliards, harlots, buffoons, jugglers, rogues, minstrels, and mountebanks; and other compilations recall the delightfully indignant compilations by Burton in his *Anatomy of Melancholy*. In a number of his surveys of boobus americanus, Mencken sets forth mock-medieval compendia of "the most timorous, sniveling, poltroonish, ignominious mob of serfs and goose-steppers ever gathered under one flag in Christendom since the end of the Middle Ages," a mob whose daily measure of communal follies includes "unending processions of governmental extortions and chicaneries, of commercial brigandages and throat-slittings, of theological buffooneries, of aesthetic ribaldries, of legal swindles and harlotries, of miscellaneous rogueries, villanies, imbecilities, grotesqueries, and extravagances . . . steadily enriched with an almost fabulous daring." By such listings, Mencken stressed the multitudinous nature of folly by images which define vast and unremittingly panoramic nonsense. (At times the burgeoning mobs of gaping peasants resemble the numerous credulous and childish folk depicted so comically in Dan Beard's

illustrations for the first edition of Twain's *A Connecticut Yankee in King Arthur's Court*). Mencken's mobs, mobile in choice of error, but fixed in susceptibility to it, proliferate ridiculously: the incurable optimists and reformers, for example, are a host: "Thousands of poor dolts keep on trying to square the circle; other thousands keep pegging away at perpetual motion." Despite the fact that these "Dark Ages" metaphors in themselves are nothing more than rubber-stamps, Mencken's use of them for his ridicule of the "mediaevalism at home" (as he called it) imparts a sort of metaphoric unity to the satiric landscape, yet it also gives a comically disheveled air to his essays by showing, as do some of the teeming scenes in Rabelais' *Gargantua and Pantagruel*, the undignified scramblings of the nether herd.

At times, though, Mencken employed medieval figures of speech in a somewhat more delicate way than indicated above, skewering the rustics rather than clubbing them. In his brilliant essay "The Husbandman," he runs through several kinds of mocking comparisons; initially the farmer is burlesqued by a lavish rehearsal of the immense praise he commonly receives. First given are assorted "Common Man" tributes; next advanced are comparisons of the farmer with classical personages, such as the Gracchi and high priests at the altar of Ceres; then the satirist, after waggishly pretending to have lost sight of his subject ("submerged in rhetorical vaseline, so that it is hard to tell which end of him is made in the image of God and which is mere hoof") moves from heavily Biblical tributes (*Laborantem agricolam oportet primum de fructibus percipere*) into a scathing denunciation grounded in reductive animal tropes ("simian," "mammal," etc.). Finally Mencken utilizes his stock of "medieval" metaphor by envisioning the American intelligentsia as "beleagured in a few walled towns" by a swarm of errant Fundamentalists armed with dung-forks and determined to put God into the Constitution. The satirist warns the city dweller—the aristocrat in his castle—that, if the rural religionists triumph, "then *Eoanthropus* will triumph finally over *Homo sapiens*. If [they do triumph], then the humble swineherd will drive us all into his pen." This climactic sentence, with its very ambiguous use of *humble*, is utterly contemptuous: the swineherd is truly "lowly," but certainly not "deferential"; in fact, he is outrageously "pushy," without any of the virtues of humility (cf. St. Thomas Aquinas on the proper attitude of swineherds). This key sentence is clearly an embodiment of the farmer for cautionary purposes because his "Dark Ages" barnyard theology is dangerously anachronistic to the besieged aristocrats peering down in alarm from the crenelated ramparts of their towns. Mencken's phraseology suggests the lineaments of rustics painted by Pieter Bruegel: Bruegel's canvases of lumpish Flemish peasants, heavy in their leathern aprons and stupidity, happy in their sparse and coarse possessions, were painted for the amusement of the wealthy burgher. Bruegel's anti-pastoral paintings, with their hundreds of dense, lumbering, and happy oafs, share the fundamental haughtiness of Mencken's essays; and both imply an approach quite different from that, say, of Gay's *Beggar's Opera*. Gay's work was intended, as William Empson points out (*Some Versions of Pastoral*), to describe the lives of "simple" low people for an audience of wealthy and refined persons in a way so as to make it appear that " 'this is true about everyone' and then 'this is specially true about us' "—a sleight-of-hand transfer of associations highly flattering to both classes—and starkly antithetical to Mencken's terms of approach. Mencken's readers, he assumed, were aristocratic in temperament, skeptic in thought, able to remember with nostalgia the native exuberances of the nineteenth-century German-American saloon, yet sophisticated about Continental elegances. The Baltimore author tried to be of service to this community of superior men by, on the one hand, encouraging their willingness to "dance with arms and legs" in the Dionysian and Libertarian fashion, and, on the other hand, by helping these free spirits, scoffers, and bibuli to resist what Nietzsche called *Herdenmoral:* the jealous effort of the congenitally inferior democratic man to reduce to his own frumpy level, by the enactment of "Puritan" legislation, the happier, superior, individualistic, "first-caste" man.

Certainly Mencken did not write primarily to "stir up the animals," as is frequently charged. His essays were intended for the amusement and instruction of his cronies and the intelligent minority. Although his work features, on occasion, a number of "constructive" suggestions, these were intended for the sophisticates besieged in their "walled towns," or, more specifically, for mellow and civilized professional men such as Mencken's friends in the Saturday Night Club, which met for many years in Baltimore. When his written opinions fell into the hands of the *chandala,* the author could be mildly interested in the ensuing howls; but, as he sardonically admitted, *The Saturday Evening Post* was appropriately edited for "just folks," and to attempt to snare its ample following would have been, in its way, as immoral an interference with "divine will" (by which he meant "natural selection") as if

chiropractors were prevented from freely ministering to the "botched."

Seen in perspective, the "medieval" phase of the satiric landscape is only a part of a thoroughly eclectic vision. Mencken's assumptions about life were drawn from several quarters. Many of his general attitudes were grounded on "Augustan" or "eighteenth-century" viewpoints. For example, his preferences in architecture were based on his esteem for "the principles which went into the English dwelling-house of the Eighteenth Century," so, as he expressed it, he simply borrowed them "with a clear conscience." Of the merits of the Enlightenment, he had little doubt: "It got rid of religion. It lifted music to first place among the arts. It introduced urbanity into manners, and made even war relatively gracious and decent." And important for Mencken's materialistic, even mechanistic, view of nature, was the eighteenth century's encouragement of science, which it turned "to the service of man, and elevated . . . above metaphysics for all time." Moreover, he often expressed pleas for normative agreement among gentlemen on matters of the "fundamental decencies," "sound sense," and honor, dignity, and decorum. In his description of the vision which inspired the Founding Fathers of the Republic, Mencken set forth something of his own values: "the Fathers, too, had a Vision. . . . What they dreamed of and fought for was a civilization based on a body of simple, equitable and reasonable laws—a code designed to break the chains of lingering medievalism, and set the individual free." Onto this background of "Augustan" or Enlightenment attitudes, he projected more particular ideas derived from such nineteenth-century writers as Nietzsche, Spencer, Darwin, Huxley, Twain, and Shaw. His immense respect for biology and medicine as sciences, his hunkerous *laissez faire* social philosophy, and his bellicose tone were adapted from these thinkers in his pantheon.

As for the twentieth century, it provided him, especially during the 1920's, with responsive readers. In justification of his right to lecture these readers, Mencken clearly felt that, as the most efficient spokesman for two great and enlightened centuries, he had a secure mandate to criticize any resurgence of the "Dark Ages." That his purview was simplified and eclectic was immaterial to him; but that many thinkers of the twentieth century would have thoughts and second-thoughts of their own about the concept of progress, eventually became bewildering to the Sage of Baltimore. By 1932, his Libertarianism, so heady to the "scofflaws" of the 1920's, appeared to the younger set of the 1930's as too generalized and too nostalgic for their needs. Most of the intellectuals during the grim 1930's saw Mencken's yen for Libertarianism as similar to Don Quixote's love of chivalry: at best, laughable antiquarianism; at worst, political reaction. But for many old-timers—and a growing number of youthful fans —Mencken's exhortation to forget our "brum-magen Grails for one week. . . . Let us have a Common Decency Week" is, though perhaps "generalized," worth remembering whenever public esteem for the fundamental decencies has worn perilously thin.

Willa Cather and the Decline of Greatness

by JOHN H. RANDALL III

The decade of the Twenties was Willa Cather's most productive period. In it she published a volume of short stories and no less than five novels, and the end of the decade saw her working on a further volume of short stories and yet another novel. Moreover, in the 1920's her reputation was at its highest. With the possible exception of Edith Wharton, she was admired—even revered—more than any other of the elder American writers then living. And yet, for all her success, by the early Twenties she had reached a point where she could no longer accept the world of her contemporaries. Her entire career had been a search for fulfillment through beauty, and almost as soon as she had established herself and received critical acclaim, she declared the search to be impossible. The goal of the comely life brought her into open hostility against modern America; she became convinced that self-realization and even survival could be obtained only at a tremendous price: alienation from that culture of which she no longer felt a part.

This is a familiar predicament for the modern artist; in fact, it has been *the* problem since the Second World War. But writers of the Forties and Fifties have conceived the problem in different terms from those of Willa Cather. They see it as a search for identity, a way of remaining human and withstanding the erosions of the "faceless corporate world" with which modern commerce and industry surround us. She saw it as a decline of greatness: the modern world's difficulty in producing heroic individuals whom we can admire and emulate. The two are aspects of one problem, for if we do not find heroic individuals to admire, how can we define our own best selves?

Willa Cather had not always felt disenchantment with American life and character. Unlike the writers of the Forties and Fifties, she had once had a sense of belonging to her culture and then lost it. In *O Pioneers!* and *My Ántonia*, written when the century was in its teens, she had celebrated the life of the pioneer farmers of the Great Plains where she had grown up. Then, so it seemed to her, the dominant people who set the tone for her society had been people of character with whom she could identify. As she once wrote,

> With these old men and women, the attainment of material prosperity was a moral victory, because it was wrung

from hard conditions, was the result of a struggle that tested character.

They lived an active moral life from which material reward and enjoyment of the beauty of nature issued naturally as the result of effort; no conflict existed among the three, which formed a unified life organically related to the land. But these pioneers had had their day of labor and accomplishment in the 1880's and '90's; their society was agrarian, preindustrial. Their children faced no such tremendous physical and moral challenge as had their parents; they had only to maintain what their parents had created. Moreover, unlike their parents, they were heirs of the industrial revolution, which, for Willa Cather, deluded people into thinking they could get something for nothing, without effort. So she wrote,

> The generation now in the driver's seat hates to make anything, wants to live and die in an automobile, scudding past those acres where the old men used to follow the long corn-rows up and down. They want to buy everything ready-made: clothes, food, education, music, pleasure.

What they want, in effect, is a ready-made life. But a ready-made life is a contradiction of terms; life must be earned, not granted; hence the gadgets of an industrial civilization wean men away from knowledge of their own identities, which can be obtained only through effort and hard work. This was the stage which Willa Cather felt America had reached after the First World War. Where would it go from there? Willa Cather herself posed the question when she asked, "Will the third generation . . . will it be fooled? Will it believe that to live easily is to live happily?"

Judging from the fiction she wrote in the Twenties, her answer was a sorrowful "Yes." The widening gulf between her ideals and those of her contemporaries can be seen in four novels she wrote in the Twenties: *One of Ours* (1922), *A Lost Lady* (1923), *The Professor's House* (1925), and *Death Comes for the Archbishop* (1927). In them one can trace the growing alienation, the increasing conviction that the heroic life of individual greatness was no longer possible, which led her in the last novel to a permanent break with the present as subject matter, a decision that the modern world was not for her.

One of Ours tells of Claude Wheeler, a

Nebraska farm boy whose search for something splendid in life is repeatedly frustrated until America enters the First World War; then he enlists in the Army, becomes an officer in the AEF, and dies fighting gloriously in France. Claude belongs to the generation following that of the original settlers, and his Middle West is very different from the one Alexandra Bergson and Ántonia Cuzak knew. He has a hardheaded Yankee father given to playing practical jokes upon his dreamy son, and a brother Bayliss who has left the farm to open a business in town selling agricultural machinery. Bayliss, who has given up producing for a life of buying and selling, shows how far the children of the pioneers have fallen away from the pioneer ideal. Mean, small-spirited, and stingy, he has utter contempt for all human activity other than money-making; when Claude tells him of a friend who wants to study abroad and become a professor, he asks, "What's the matter with him? Does he have poor health?" Since this is the kind of talk Claude has grown up hearing, it is no wonder that his aspirations toward something better are vague. Unfortunately, everything else in his environment seems equally designed to frustrate him. He loves learning and had hoped to attend the state university, but, instead, to please his mother, he enters a small denominational college from which he eventually has to withdraw for lack of funds. When he tries to fulfill himself in marriage, his wife turns out to be a cold pietistic woman who is more interested in traveling around the country attending temperance lectures than in taking care of her husband. Eventually she takes an indefinite leave of absence from him to nurse a sick missionary sister in China. Clearly neither the intellectual nor religious atmosphere nor the life of personal emotions as lived on the Great Plains can satisfy Claude or help him define himself as a man.

Then comes World War I. At first Claude has doubts that the transatlantic cousins of the peaceful German farmers he knows in Nebraska could possibly have committed the atrocities attributed to them, but gradually he (along with Willa Cather) develops a war mentality, and he enlists in the fight to save France and civilization from German barbarism. The Army supplies what Nebraska had failed to provide: fellowship in a group of men not dedicated to selfish profit but to a noble cause. At last he finds heroic individuals he can emulate, and becomes a hero himself. He also discovers artistic companionship and the graciousness of French culture with the violinist David Gerhardt and Mlle. Olive de Courcy, friends whom but for the Army he never would have met.

Unfortunately, once Willa Cather starts describing the Army she falls victim to sentimentality of the sort popular in 1917-18 but not since. The war for her is "the big show," and she can say of an airman shot down in flames:

That was one of the things about this war; it took a little fellow from a little town, gave him an air and a swagger, a life like a movie-film,—and then a death like the rebel angels.

And although Willa Cather grants Claude a hero's death in a holy war, she makes it clear that afterward the mechanized ugliness and commercialization which had so oppressed him in Nebraska were bound to take over the whole country. Claude's mother reflects:

It seemed as if the flood of meanness and greed had been held back just long enough for the boys to go over, and then swept down and engulfed everything that was left at home. When she can see nothing that has come out of it all but evil, she reads Claude's letters over again and reassures herself; for him the call was clear, the cause was glorious. . . . Perhaps it was as well to see that vision; and then to see no more.

In a society that expects all its members to maximize their wealth, the person who aspires to do something fine is an outsider. Not only does society provide no place for him; it virtually forces him to the wall. Noble aspiration is incompatible with self-aggrandizement. In *A Lost Lady* Willa Cather identifies these two views with successive generations and thus writes a social allegory of the decline of the Middle West from its days of pioneer greatness. The novel chronicles the growth of cultural awareness in Niel Herbert, who watches Captain Forrester, the aging and crippled railroad builder, give way to the up-and-coming young shyster lawyer, Ivy Peters. Years before the story starts, the Captain had picked out a garden site on the Sweet Water to build a great house on, and then married a beautiful young wife who made their home famous for hospitality from Omaha to Denver. Marian Forrester represents the civilization of the Old West, her husband the pioneer virtues on which it was based. But Niel, charmed by the lady's graciousness, soon discovers that all is not well. Mrs. Forrester, twenty-five years her husband's junior, is having a love affair which Niel inadvertently discovers. Meanwhile the Captain is in Denver liquidating a bank failure, choosing financial ruin for himself so that his creditors may be paid off one hundred cents on a dollar. Soon after he becomes physically helpless due to a stroke, and Ivy Peters begins to take over. He rents the Forrester estate, drains the beautiful marshland to put it into wheat, and exults in the Captain's downfall. Deprived of her husband's strength, Marian goes to pieces. She takes to brandy, cannot keep the townspeople from invading her house, and after the Captain's death becomes Ivy Peters's mistress. Niel, in disgust, turns against her and the whole world of his boyhood; but years later, after a successful career in the East, he realizes what her charm had taught him and is glad "that she had had a hand in breaking him in to life." A friend tells him that she had remarried a rich Englishman living in Buenos Aires, and, although everything about her now was artificial except her laugh, "she was well cared for to the very end."

Like *One of Ours*, *A Lost Lady* explains Willa Cather's alienation from modern culture, this time in symbolic form and with far greater success. The Captain's generation created the West; that of Ivy Peters merely exploited it. With an eye for beauty, the pioneers heroically created a civilization; with an eye for profit, their successors destroyed all beauty and debauched civilization as Ivy debauched Marian Forrester:

> Now all the vast territory they had won was to be at the mercy of men like Ivy Peters, who had never dared anything, never risked anything. . . . The space, the colour, the princely carelessness of the pioneer they would destroy and cut up into profitable bits, as the match factory splinters the primeval forest.

Niel Herbert learned about the beauty of life from Marian Forrester, but it was the Captain's absolute probity which made it possible; and his old-fashioned sense of personal responsibility ruined him in the Denver bank failure when the other bank officers, less scrupulous and more modern, refused to follow his example in paying off the entire amount of their indebtedness. Ivy Peters, of a later and even less scrupulous generation, has no probity at all and destroys beauty. In a world dominated by him Niel would find nothing admirable to emulate; yet it is precisely his standards which have come to prevail.

The climax of Willa Cather's quarrel with the present comes in *The Professor's House*. So many resemblances exist between author and protagonist that it is hard to escape an autobiographical inference. Professor St. Peter and Miss Cather are the same age, fifty-two; after years of effort both have won international fame and a prize by writing a great work on the American past—in the Professor's case, a history of *The Spanish Adventurers in North America;* in spite of their success both reach a point of such acute exasperation with the materialistic money-grubbing and status-seeking of the American Twenties that they feel driven to a blanket rejection of the age in which they live.

The Professor has had two great loves in his life—his wife and his work. He has also had a great friendship with a brilliant student, Tom Outland, who before coming to college had discovered the remains of the cliff dwellers on Blue Mesa. This astounding archeological discovery had inspired the Professor to finish the last four volumes of his work. But Tom had been killed during the Great War, and his fiancée, one of St. Peter's daughters, had married an amiable young man who exploits not only the Professor's fame and social standing but also the commercial possibilities of an aeronautical discovery Tom had made while working under a physics professor. Equally at home with the beauty of past civilizations and contemporary scientific fact, Tom was a whole man who represented the older America. But American history killed Tom's kind, and its successors are people like the Professor's son-in-law, who seize on Tom's discoveries to achieve status and wealth for themselves.

The Professor, at fifty-two, can no longer take pleasure in anything. He is depressed at the emptiness of his life after the completion of his great work; estranged from his family, who he feels have become increasingly worldly; estranged from his society, which no longer follows the ideals of men like Tom Outland; estranged even from his university, which is less and less interested in things of the mind and more and more in danger of becoming a trade school. His revulsion against the life around him is so extreme that he loses the desire to live, and when a leaky gas stove in his study nearly asphyxiates him, he doesn't lift a hand to save himself. He is saved from death at the last minute only by the intervention of a pious German Catholic seamstress, who teaches him that it is possible to live without delight and that one must face the ultimate realities alone.

The middle third of the novel, "Tom Outland's Story," is a flashback which describes Tom's discovery of an abandoned city of cliff dwellers on the mysterious Blue Mesa. Little as it seems related to the rest of the novel at first reading, actually this supplies the book's meaning and serves as its source of value, for the relics of the cliff dwellers reveal an ancient and traditional civilization in which beauty was a part of everyday life, as it is not in twentieth-century America. The cliff dwellers had "built themselves into the mesa and humanized it." Their dwellings are grouped around a central tower, forming an artistic whole; and every artifact found on the mesa displays an equal sense of form; even the household utensils combine to a remarkable degree the useful with the beautiful. To Tom, the composition, symmetry, and organic form of the cliff city suggests the balanced, orderly lives of the people who once had inhabited it: they must have made of their everyday lives something approaching the order and harmony of a work of art. This stands in sharp contrast to the chaos and ugliness of Professor St. Peter's America. The Professor, an historian, looks to history for values for the present day. Tom Outland's discovery of the Blue Mesa reveals to the Professor that there once existed in America the possibility of beauty in day-to-day living which is precisely what his own life lacks. Tom had been able to draw on the American past for values to sustain him in the present, to fortify him against the drabness of his commercial surroundings, and permit him to remain a whole man. He is able to pass on something of this feeling to the Professor and enable him to finish his great work. The two of them have achieved greatness, not by imitating heroic individuals around them, but by emulating an heroic group in the past.

But the cliff dwellers are no longer leading their comely life amid beautiful surroundings; they have disappeared completely. What happened to them? Tom Outland's friend Father Duchene has a theory about this: he believes "they were, perhaps, too far advanced for their time and environment." Having raised themselves from savagery to high civilization, they "possibly declined in the arts of war." Then, when they had left the mesa to go down to their summer camp, they were probably wiped out by some roving Indian tribe who exterminated them for their belongings or for sheer love of slaughter. It is in keeping with Willa Cather's growing alienation from her own time that she makes the hypothetical hostile Indian tribe into a symbol of the destroying present wreaking havoc on the civilized past. She became increasingly convinced that superior groups, as well as heroic individuals, are disliked by their inferior neighbors, that the more they perfect the arts of civilization, the less time they spend on self-defense, so that they become increasingly vulnerable to extermination by their more brutal neighbors. Since this is what she describes as happening to the Middle West in *A Lost Lady*, to all of America in *One of Ours*, and to the entire Western world after the First World War in *The Professor's House*, it would seem that the following of tradition in order to maintain value in the present doesn't always work. In spite of the consolation of the Blue Mesa, the Professor almost dies; tradition is not always efficacious or viable, since sometimes values are destroyed altogether. This bleakly pessimistic strain in Willa Cather's thinking was to dominate for the rest of her life and issue in the conviction that anything of beauty and worth was bound in time to be destroyed by a brutally hostile and uncomprehending world. So strong was this feeling that, with the minor and partial exception of *My Mortal Enemy*, *The Professor's House* was her last full-length treatment of the contemporary scene. Starting with *Death Comes for the Archbishop*, she turned to historical novels and fictionalized reminiscences of her childhood; and as each of them ends with the approach of modernity, we are given the feeling of living on into the new Dark Ages.

Ernest Hemingway and the Rhetoric of Escape

by ROBERT O. STEPHENS

When in *The Sun Also Rises* Hemingway depicts the American writer Bill Gorton telling Jake Barnes what their homeland thinks of a newspaperman who refuses to return home, he presents a scene epitomizing a key movement in twentieth century literature: "You're an expatriate. You've lost touch with the soil. You get precious. Fake European standards have ruined you. You drink yourself to death. You become obsessed by sex. You are an expatriate, see? You hang around cafes." Like these two men, Hemingway's protagonists from first to last serve as prime commentators on the tendency of the spiritually dislocated of the age to seek their salvation by escaping from the horrors of the age. In this essay I should like to explore the responses of Hemingway's people to their times, particularly as they are depicted in his uniquely suitable idiom. This escape motif appears in virtually all Hemingway's stories and novels. The most intense presentation, however, appears in those works of the twenties and early thirties—*In Our Time* (1925), *The Sun Also Rises* (1926), *Men Without Women* (1927), *A Farewell to Arms* (1929), and *Winner Take Nothing* (1933).

All these narratives show that escape means more than alienation of the artist from his homeland. It is a significant contribution of Hemingway to world literature that he has explored the possibilities and implications of escape more than has any other writer, including Henry James. Because of his explorations we can get a clear rationale of escape that is true for his time and for all times the literary tradition speaks for. As a narrative motif, escape quickly identifies the issues of the conflict. It is one of three possible responses to an intolerable situation, the other two being resignation and struggle to change the predicament. Protagonists choose escape when the menace of the world seems too great and the stature of man too small to challenge the order of things and when man is still too rebellious or too horrified to accept things as they are. Such was the predicament of the apocalypse-minded Christians of the first century, such was the mind of the Leatherstockings and Huckleberry Finns of nineteenth century American literature, and such is the mind of Hemingway's heroes of the twentieth century.

Implicit also in this response is the pattern the escapist must follow through the three stages of rejection, avoidance, and quest for new values or a new situation. This process emphasizes directly perceived experience rather than abstract teachings about experience. The protagonist is an agent of action rather than speculation. He rejects the initial situation because it is too menacing to his body or his pride. He escapes *from* that situation by acts of avoidance—physical flight or emotional withdrawal. He escapes *to* another situation to find more tolerable experience. Escape must thus be understood as a technique or process, not an end in itself.

Hemingway's people live in a pragmatic world where independently existing values no longer prevail. Their values are tied to actions, to the deeds themselves which are moral or immoral, not to any outside ethical frame of reference. Thus Jake Barnes describes his relationship to the world: "Perhaps as you went along you did learn something. I did not care what it was all about. All I wanted to know was how to live in it. Maybe if you found out how to live in it you learned from that what it was all about." The exiles' research in the vanities, then, as Robert Penn Warren notes (*Kenyon Review*, 1947), is not a random sampling of sensations but a disciplined quest for pragmatic values derived from the basic, sensational level of perception. Having recognized the invalidity or irrelevance of abstract traditional values, as Frederic Henry does in *A Farewell to Arms*, they occupy themselves with concrete details of moment-to-moment living. Their future they make sensation by sensation, syllable by syllable.

In *The Sun Also Rises*, which I should like to use as the focal point of my examination, one of the key distinctions in characters is that between the truly questing escapist and the pseudo-expatriate. The true expatriates, or the insiders of the escape experience, are self-directed; they share a common experience that they recognize without speaking about it. They are in rebellion against the values of their homelands and live in Paris to be free of conventions that hamper their quests. Their belief in the validity of the immediate and individual action frees them of claims by the outside world. They form a minority society always in flux. Wherever their individual quests take them, they deny the previous experience or locale by occupying themselves with only the present action. Thus Brett Ashley takes a succession of lovers in her quest for the one who can give back to her a sense of spiritual integrity she has lost. Similarly the insider savors the individual drink, the individual meal, the individual scene as the basis of value. Jake Barnes notes this about Count Mippipopolous when he says of the dinner he shares in the Bois with Brett and the Count: "It was a good dinner. Food had an excellent place in the count's values. So did wine. The count was in fine form during the meal. So was Brett. It was a good party."

Another criterion of the insiders is their awareness of *nada*, the knowledge that not only social values but also personal beliefs in one's immortality—emotional beliefs, not just abstract recognition of the fact of death—have been seriously damaged by the war. Jake has his nighttime terrors when he must keep a light to ward off the irrational fears of darkness associated with his wounding. Brett's actions reflect her inner torture, which Jake notes when he says, "She was afraid of so many things." Count Mippipopolous qualifies through his participation in seven wars and four revolutions, during which he has received his illusion-destroying arrow wounds. Bill Gorton admits he is "daunted" sometimes, and Harvey Stone knows horrors that make him hide in his room "like a cat." The outsiders are those like Robert Cohn, Mrs. Braddocks, Robert Prentiss, the artist Zizi, the bal musette homosexuals, and the Paris and Pamplona tourists who are unhaunted by *nada*, have no real cause for rebellion against their societies, and are messy and undisciplined as they imitate without comprehension the actions of the insiders.

These intellectual and emotional wounds are the basis of the expatriates' rhetoric. Part of their code is that they must not talk directly about their knowledge of *nada*, though it is implied in every word. Robert Cohn's failure to observe this causes the others to scorn his "damned suffering" when his illusions are shattered at Pamplona. This is what Brett means when she tells Jake, after renouncing the young matador Romero, "Don't let's ever talk about it. Please don't let's ever talk about it." But there are ways they talk about their predicament indirectly. By extremely simple language loaded with hidden connotations, by various ironies, by personal symbols, and by allusions, they carry on the business of their quest. It is presumably the only language they can use and still be true to the exigencies of their search.

Both Jake Barnes and Count Mippipopolous comment on the ostensibly simple rhetoric of the insiders. Jake links Brett's language with the ultra-simple, sensuous, and even primitive language of the Eskimo or the Cherokee:

What rot, I could hear Brett say it. What rot! When you were with English you got into the habit of using English ex-

pressions in your thinking. The English spoken language—the upper classes anyway—must have fewer words than the Eskimo. Of course I didn't know anything about the Eskimo. Maybe Eskimo was a fine language. Say the Cherokee. I didn't know anything about Cherokee either. The English talked with inflected phrases. One phrase to mean everything. I liked them, though. I like the way they talked.

It is this implied relationship between speaker and listener that carries the inflected meaning past the simple word and elliptical syntax. The count also notes that much remains unstated in Brett's talk. When he complains that she never finishes her sentences, she points out that she leaves them for the listener to finish as he likes. The count calls it "a very interesting system." As to those shorthand words *fine, nice,* and *grand,* Harry Levin in his study of Hemingway's style (*Kenyon Review,* 1951) shows that the fictitional characters use the terms as agreed-upon counters of evaluation, not attempts at description.

Jake Barnes finds the simple language adequate to convey the immediacy of his sensuous perceptions. At San Sebastian after his upsetting experiences at the Pamplona fiesta, he goes through a series of simplified, ritualistic actions to regain control of his feelings. These actions constitute a series of individual perceptions linked by the arbitrary control of a mind that chooses to see and feel these sensations as the calming ones he needs. Concrete, separate, monosyllabic, the statements are close to the elemental language he noted in Brett; now they combine description with evaluation:

After lunch I went up to my room, read a while, and went to sleep. When I woke, it was half past four. I found my swimming suit, wrapped it with a comb in a towel, and went downstairs and walked up the street to the Concha. The tide was about halfway out. The beach was smooth and firm, and the sand yellow. I went to a bathing-cabin, undressed, put on my suit, and walked across the smooth sand to the sea. The sand was warm under bare feet. There were quite a few people in the water and on the beach. . . . I waded out. The water was cold. As a roller came I dove, swam out under water, and came to the surface with all the chill gone. I swam out to the raft, pulled myself up, and lay on the planks.

Irony is a second device used by the expatriates to say more by saying less. Not only does irony reflect their distrust of language, it also serves as an index to their awareness of a contradictory and chaotic world. This mode of perception and statement appears particularly in the incongruous dinner between the emasculated Jake and the prostitute Georgette. As Jake inwardly mocks himself for his act, he notes without comment the discrepancies of their predicament. His summary of their dinner conversation is all terse understatement: "We would probably have gone on and discussed the war and agreed it was in reality a calamity for civilization, and perhaps would have been better avoided." Similarly, the English fisherman Wilson-Harris hints by understatement at his knowledge of *nada* and his authority for belonging to the insiders: "I've not had much fun since the war." Jake uses even more effectively the ironic pause of the enthymeme or truncated syllogism to indicate his disappointment at the dinner with Georgette: "She grinned and I saw why she made a point of not laughing. With her mouth closed she was a rather pretty girl." But perhaps the most sustained use of irony occurs in the talks between Jake and Bill at the Burguete inn and during their fishing trip to the Irati. At those times Bill Gorton, a fully initiated though temporary expatriate, reminds Jake that "Irony and Pity" are the watchwords of the insiders.

A third way the escapists say something without saying it overtly is to attach private and special meanings to ordinary words. That this manner of statement has its beginnings in their way of feeling can be seen in the passage of Jake's narration after Brett misses their meeting at the Crillon. Riding in a taxi to the Dome cafe, he notes: "The Boulevard Raspail always made dull riding. It was like a certain stretch on the P.L.M. between Fontainebleau and Montereau that always made me feel bored and dead and dull until it was over. I suppose it is some association of ideas that makes those dead places in a journey." This is the mind also of Frederic Henry in *A Farewell to Arms* when he confesses a special affection for the name "Archbishop Ireland" because it reminds him of "island" and escape from the war. In *The Sun Also Rises* the expatriates make a special meaning for the word "steer" after they see the unloading of the bulls at Pamplona and Mike Campbell goads Robert Cohn with the term: "I would have thought you'd love being a steer, Robert . . . They lead such a quiet life. They never say anything and they're always hanging around so." Jake and Bill see much meaning for the word "utilize" in their talk at the Irati. For them it signifies their quest for pragmatic and sensuous values, and they use it to mark the significance of their eating and drinking: "Let us utilize the fowls of the air. Let us utilize the product of the vine. Will you utilize a little, brother?" They pass the term on to Wilson-Harris, and Jake notes that by the time to return to Pamplona, the Englishman certifies his initiation by using the term.

Perhaps the key device of the escapists' rhetoric is allusion. Because of their knowledge of something too obscene to say openly, they speak obliquely. They say a name and imply the qualities that go with the name, or mention an attribute and suggest the unspeakable name. Allusion is the key to the code language of the expatriates. During their "Irony and Pity" talk at Burguete, Bill tells Jake the degree of the insiders' acceptance of the phrase by saying "It's just like the Fratellinis used to be." Thus Jake understands the acridly comic possibilities of the phrase by Bill's mention of the cabaret clown act. The conversations at the inn and at the fishing stream are filled with such allusions —hints of the Freudian-Krafft-Ebing fad and mockery of Kipling's psychological innocence ("The Colonel's Lady and Judy O'Grady are Lesbians under their skin"), the Dayton evolution trial and Bryan's fundamentalism ("I reverse the order. For Bryan's sake. As a tribute to the Great Commoner. First the chicken; then the egg"), and the prohibition-Catholic dispute ("I went to Notre Dame with Wayne B. Wheeler"). Some of the allusions reflect the most personal preoccupations of the speakers. Bill speaks analogously of Henry James's rumored sexual injury to speak of Jake's when he says: "That's the sort of thing that can't be spoken of. That's what you ought to work up into a mystery. Like Henry's bicycle."

Allusion works still another way through Jake's narration. He involves the readers as an insider to the extent that he cites actions and scenes familiar to the initiated and implies the reader's understanding, as though he were across the table at the Select. When he describes the walk he and Bill take back from Madame Lecomte's restaurant, he mentions the landmarks they pass as though they are totally familiar and need only to be mentioned to be evoked. "We crossed the bridge and walked up the Rue du Cardinal Lemoine. It was steep walking, and we went all the way to the Place Contrescarpe." He links allusion with the quest for sensate values and implies a common understanding about the qualities of specific drinks. He records ordering and drinking his Jack Rose, his Anis del Mono, or his *vieux marc* without apparent need of characterizing it.

Hemingway's rhetoric of escape has, however, another major manifestation besides that of the language of the insiders. Like the expatriates, Hemingway the novelist must find a proper idiom for his theme. He finds it in the pattern of escape, which serves as a structural guide for all levels of his novel. The pattern of rejection, avoidance, and quest is a repeated one when seen along the whole range of Hemingway's writing. Numerous critics have noted that the novelist's heroes embody a continuum of experience, so that later heroes incorporate the experience of earlier ones. Colonel Robert Cantwell of *Across the River and into the Trees* (1950) most clearly exemplifies this pattern. At fifty, he has lived through his initiation by wounding as have Nick Adams and Frederic Henry, sampled the expatriate life known to Jake Barnes, and witnessed the loss of Spain as has Robert Jordan. What is also noticeable about these protagonists is that each carries out a cycle of the escape pattern and in his quest for new values goes on to another predicament which he rejects and avoids in order to turn to another situation and enter another cycle. This pattern represents the process of learning for the cumulative hero. Nick Adams rejects provincial Michigan to escape to war, but in war he experiences further horror and escapes to make his separate peace. Frederic Henry carries out the latter part of that pattern with more emphatic feelings. Jake Barnes begins where Nick Adams and Frederic Henry leave off, and he, at first turning to the expatriate life, finds it discredited at the chaotic fiesta of Pamplona, then turns to the ever smaller society of aficionados. This cycle is then followed through by Hemingway himself as narrator in *Death in the Afternoon*. And the pattern goes on through all the protagonists' careers.

Seen as an abstract design this pattern suggests a traveling circle—philosophically a vicious circle if one fails to note the development from one protagonist to another. This tendency is at least one of the reasons for the critical labeling of Hemingway as a writer of despair. This circular design can also be seen as the aesthetic plan in each work. Particularly does it describe *The Sun Also Rises*. When Jake Barnes rides with Lady Brett in the Madrileño taxi in Book III, he is ostensibly back where he started—riding stoically with Brett in the Parisian taxi of Book I. He has, however, outgrown his bohemian friends and is emotionally ready to seek the values of the matador Romero, the only one in the book who overtly escapes the futility of the expatriate circle.

That this circular design serves as the rhetorical basis of Hemingway's statement can be seen on several levels of organization in the book. The epigraph to the novel suggests that although one generation considers itself uniquely lost, it is part of a succession of generations on the earth: "The sun also riseth, and the sun goeth down, and hasteth to the place where he arose . . . The wind goeth toward the south, and turneth about unto the north; it whirleth about continually, and the wind returneth again according to his circuits. . . ."

On the paragraph level this pattern prevails. The Hemingway paragraph, particularly when Jake Barnes rises to comment through narration on the theme, is the well-rounded paragraph with the final sentence that turns back on the rest of the paragraph. The comment at the beginning of the Pamplona festival serves as an example:

> The fiesta was really started. It kept up day and night for seven days. The dancing kept up, the drinking kept up, the noise went on. The things that happened could only have happened during a fiesta. Everything became quite unreal finally and it seemed as though nothing could have any consequences. It seemed out of place to think of consequences during the fiesta. All during the fiesta you had the feeling, even when it was quiet, that you had to shout any remark to make it heard. It was the same feeling about any action. It was a fiesta and it went on for seven days.

This paragraph style derives from Hemingway's apprentice period when the total composition was paragraph length. The sketches of *In Our Time* all gain their ironic, deadpan forcefulness by this device. Chapter III, for example, foreshadows the pattern in the novel:

> We were in a garden at Mons. Young Buckley came in with his patrol from across the river. The first German I saw climbed up over the garden wall. We waited till he got one leg over and then potted him. He had so much equipment on and looked awfully surprised and fell down into the garden. Then three more came over further down the wall. We shot them. They all came just like that.

And so do the paragraphs.

The relationship between the sentences of the paragraph and the circular design is best seen in the device of accretion through repetition. As F. J. Hoffman points out in his study *The Twenties*, Hemingway's prose gives evidence of his having observed Gertrude Stein's rule to maintain a continuum of perception by "beginning again and again" and by using all the perceptions that convey immediacy. Thus the almost arbitrary separateness of each sentence as a perception is at least partially counterbalanced by the aesthetic progress through accretion of ideas and perceptions. During one of Jake's nighttime terrors the subject and manner of the moment-by-moment sequence are integrated through the traveling circle sentence. Key words like *thinking* and *jumping* recur in a kind of incremental repetition to suggest both continuity and "beginning again and again.":

> I lay awake thinking and my mind jumping around. Then I couldn't keep away from it, and I started to think about Brett and all the rest of it went away. I was thinking about Brett and my mind started jumping around and started to go on in sort of smooth waves. Then all of a sudden I started to cry. Then after a while it was better and I lay in bed and listened to the heavy trams go by and way down the street, and then I went to sleep.

Here the continuity is aided by overt connectives. In the fiesta paragraph earlier the continuity is achieved with only implied connectives. In both cases the circular design haunts the passage.

In both act and idiom Hemingway thus clarifies the escapist mind of his twentieth century heroes and readers. In *Exile's Return* Malcolm Cowley, himself an expatriate as well as chronicler of the times, attests to the degree of truth that the "lost generation" found in Hemingway's novel: "young men tried to get as imperturbably drunk as the hero, young women of good families took a succession of lovers in the same heartbroken fashion as the heroine, they all talked like Hemingway characters and the name was fixed." Perhaps the greatest achievement of Hemingway's rhetoric of escape then was to make all his readers potentially insiders to the great dark secret.

Implications of Form in *The Sun Also Rises*

by WILLIAM L. VANCE

Part of the achievement of Ernest Hemingway in *The Sun Also Rises* is in the creation of a plot that is both naturalistic and Aristotelian. It suggests the random episodic and circular realism of the former while achieving the dramatic unity and interest of the latter. The philosophical and ethical implications of the compound form are ambiguous, but not, I think, incoherent; they are true to a modern sense of the human situation in a way that implications of the older forms singly are not.

The episodic and circular aspects of the structure, which are the more obvious, are the more commonly observed. There is no beginning and no end; title and epigraph forewarn us to expect no meaning in the form beyond this futile circularity; at the close Jake and Brett ride off into the night whispering vanities like those they whispered chapters and months before and, presumably, like those that, by easy but redundant extension of the book, they could be whispering chapters and years later on. Nothing has happened. Nothing except essentially repetitive episodes of life: drinking and bull-fight watching for all, sex for some, and fishing for the rest. And talk and self-torture. There is no conscious human ordering of these events; they occur according to inner impulses, outer stimuli, and the season. Compulsion and reaction are all; and God, if he exists, does not show his hand in the matter. Seen thus in its naturalistic shape, the book's unity would seem to depend on character, symbol, and theme.

But its unity is nevertheless predominantly a unity of action. In this it is Aristotelian, and from this the book gains a cumulative dramatic interest which stems, as it must, from characters in action, in successive encounters and altering relationships with each other. In the previous view, one might begin at any point on a circle and travel around it as long or as short a distance as necessary to show the random, non-sequential character of the whole. But the starting point of *The Sun Also Rises* is not random; which is to say the book has a beginning. It also has a middle and an end. The action comprises one complete and coherent round, and thus raises questions of meaning that a really discontinuous episodic form, with an arbitrary concluding point, could not.

The action begins with Robert Cohn. The symbolically impotent and necessarily static love affair between Jake Barnes and Lady Brett Ashley exists as a constant, having begun long before the novel opens, and continuing throughout the book and beyond its ending. They try not to see each other, and when they do, they try not to talk about it. Brett is going to marry "This drunkard," Mike Campbell—perhaps; the outcome of that relationship is as uncertain at the end as at the beginning. Jake finds some pleasure in Parisian life, which cannot, however, compensate for his frustrated love for Brett, and which at least once takes the perverted form of picking up a *poule* to whom he must confess his "sickness," and who observes, "Everybody's sick. I'm sick, too." Whatever games they play, everybody's miserable at bottom. That is constant. But this time the particular shape the misery takes is the shape of Robert Cohn, and what he does.

His importance is emphasized by Hemingway—or by Jake (in most questions of the shaping of the narrative, they are interchangeable)—by the long exposition of his character and background in Chapter I. Of the three main characters, he is the only one so treated; expositions of Brett and Jake are absorbed within the narrative and are rendered more dramatically. If it were not for Robert's importance as the active agent in the plot, this primary and stylistically unique exposition would seem disproportionately long, and superfluous in detail. We learn more of his family background, education, and efforts at career and marriage than we ever learn of Brett, and more than there is, evidently, to learn of Jake. Moreover, Robert's organic connection with a psychologically continuous past is pointed up by the distinctive expository method, which would have been inappropriate to characters like Brett and Jake whose lives have been severed, who live in and from the present only, that is, episodically.

The second chapter is more "scenic" (in Henry James' sense) than the first, but it only emphasizes through Robert's immediate presence and direct statement his frustrations and romantic illusions, the underlying motivations causing him to lend a sequential character to the events that follow. The ensuing episodes themselves—or others virtually like them—would have occurred without Cohn, with only that inherent meaning previously described; but what gives them in addition a meaningful sequence and unity is the action of Robert Cohn.

He falls in love with Brett, and goes with her to San Sebastian. To Brett herself and to the others this constitutes an episode only, with no necessary antecedent or consequence; but to Robert it is a beginning: it must mean something and lead somewhere. It must mean love and happiness and children. A naturalistic plot is "like life" in just the way Brett and Jake see life; but Robert sees life in another way. That he expects life to have meaning and sequence and consequence is a part of his gaucherie, but it is this contrary view that Jake and Hemingway superimpose on the naturalistic *tranches de vie* to give their narrative form.

The impression of Cohn given in the first two chapters is unsympathetic, and the precipitate manner in which he falls in love in the third chapter is rendered satirically ("He looked a great deal as his compatriot must have looked when he saw the promised land.") In Chapter V, while questioning Jake about Brett, he appears ridiculous in his idealizing of her: to him, she must be not only "remarkably attractive," which she is to everyone, but also "absolutely fine and straight," a woman of "quality" and "breeding" who wouldn't "marry anybody she didn't love" even though Jake says "She's done it twice." In other words, she is the kind of woman he, Robert Cohn, *deserves*, in consequence of his lovable character (gazing at Brett earlier, "he had a look of eager, deserving expectation"; she is "promised" him as Israel was Moses).

This person is to be the principal agent of the significant action of the book, and concern by the narrator that he may not be taken seriously enough becomes evident. In Chapter VI, and despite the already comparatively extensive characterization given him, Jake must say: "Somehow I feel I have not shown Robert Cohn clearly." And he attempts to make him less unsympathetic, attributing to him in fact a "nice, boyish sort of cheerfulness" and normalcy that make him rather more attractive than the cynical sophisticates who reject him. His view of life is at least worth considering as an option to theirs.

The rest of Book I is devoted to the rendering of the quality of the lives of the others, and to a nasty public scene between Robert and Frances, his mistress to whom (characteristically) he feels an "obligation" and who, partly by this very scene, drives him free. Book I concludes, and the action definitely begins, with Robert's going away with Brett. Again, to her this is to be an episode. To Jake she says, "I'm going away from you, and then Michael's coming back." That is all. There is no thought that the antecedent "going away" from Jake and with Robert will at all alter the fact or character of Michael's "coming back"—possibly to marry her.

And so it develops, at least as far as Brett is concerned. In Book II she comes back, Michael comes back, and perhaps they are going to get married. The stay at San Sebastian should make no difference to any of the three men. To Michael, it doesn't, until later it has consequences: for the reason it doesn't matter is that it should have none. But, Brett is surprised to discover, it does offend Jake when he finds out. Openly sarcastic to her ("Congratulations," he says), his feelings are characteristically mixed:

> I was blind, unforgivingly jealous of what had happened to him. The fact that I took it as a matter of course did not alter that any. I certainly did hate him.

But the greatest difference it makes is, of course, to Robert himself. He, Jake, and Bill Gorton have planned a fishing trip to Spain, to be followed by the fiesta at Pamplona. Brett and Mike ask to be included, but it occurs to her that the situation might be "rough" on Robert Cohn, since she would be with Mike. It is something that she should realize this much; but when Cohn is informed that she and Mike will be going along, his being "keen about it" strikes her and Jake as "rather odd." "He's wonderful," they say.

To Robert Cohn, Brett's joining him (for so he sees it) on the trip to Spain is just what rightly follows from their beginning at San Sebastian. This is a development in their love affair. He writes to her suggesting that he meet her in San Sebastian again, on the way to Spain. But getting no answer, he awaits her—shaved, shampooed, and nervous—in Pamplona. She doesn't arrive. Fearing a misunderstanding, he now feels he must forego the fishing episode altogether—it cannot mean anything in itself to him as it does to Jake and Bill—in order to meet Brett when she does arrive, acting according to the romantic principle that gives continuity to his acts.

In the plot of the novel, the eleventh and twelfth chapters—the fishing episode—exist in a truly episodic fashion, that is, as an interlude which by its very inclusion points up the meaningful sequence of the action linking the other "episodes" and depending upon Robert Cohn for its progression. His very absence from this one is what to a considerable degree gives it its distinctive character. It makes the case, in itself and without Cohn there as a whipping-boy from the opposition, for the impotent Jake's necessarily episodic view of life, in showing that it is not valueless. Some episodes in life, evidently, can be of such character, in their identification with the earth that "abideth forever"—the earth that itself has no beginning, middle, or end—that a sense of sequence and development within the span of an individual life becomes inessential. It shows too, that the absence of sequence need not reduce every episode to the same level of futility: the circle is drawn over hills and valleys, not on a plateau.

The interlude ends, and the action resumes, with telegrams from Brett and from Robert which lead to a regrouping in Pamplona. Comically and naively, Robert is playing the escort to Brett and Mike:

> "I brought them up here," Cohn said.
> "What rot," Brett said. "We'd have gotten here earlier if you hadn't come."
> "You'd never have gotten here."
> "What rot! . . . "
> "Did you get good fishing?" Mike asked. "We wanted to join you."
> "It wasn't bad. We missed you."
> "I wanted to come," Cohn said, "but I thought I ought to bring them."
> "You bring us. What rot."

Robert's sense of obligation again. Love and gratitude for past favors evoke it. To Brett this is "rot," and Robert is a nuisance. He persists in being one as the fiesta proceeds, and the person most irritated by this is of course Mike: "Is Robert Cohn going to follow Brett around like a steer all the time?" To Robert he says: "Don't sit there looking like a bloody funeral. What if Brett did sleep with you? She's slept with lots of other people." And to Jake: "Brett's gone off with men. But . . . they didn't come and hang about afterward." To which Brett adds: "Damned good chaps. . . . Michael and I understand each other." This non-sequential view of life is what Robert cannot understand. Michael becomes belligerent, but a fight is avoided, and later, when he is to meet Robert again, he asks, "How should I meet Cohn?" The answer is: "Just act as though nothing had happened." That is the motto of the episodic world.

But Cohn persists. "He could not stop looking at Brett. It seemed to make him happy. It must have been pleasant for him to see her looking so lovely, and know he had been away with her and that everyone knew it. They could not take that away from him." Jake here attributes to Cohn his own way of seeing things: that an experience can be self-contained and possessed in inviolate separateness forever (in the next chapter he says of a passage in Turgenieff: "I would always have it.") But an episode is unsatisfactory to Cohn except as part of a larger whole, and his continuing pursuit of Brett leads to the climax of the book. He follows her and Jake to church, he sits with Brett and Mike at the bull-ring. He cannot believe there will be no third act wedding climaxing his love affair with Brett. So he is there when Mike, drunken and maddened by Brett's newly developed attraction to the bullfighter Romero, needs a victim. But Mike's attacking *him* seems to imply that he is a rival, that in fact his affair is progressing: "His face had the sallow, yellow look it got when he was insulted, but somehow he seemed to be enjoying it. The childish, drunken heroics of it. It was his affair with a lady of title." Mike challenges him. "He stood waiting, . . . proudly and firmly waiting for the assault, ready to do battle for his lady love." But the chivalric opportunity is lost again. The others maneuver Mike away. All Cohn can do is volunteer to sit with Brett. " 'O, don't!', Brett said. 'For God's sake, go off somewhere.' " And so, obedient, he goes. Brett and Jake agree that he has "behaved very badly" all along, and that "He had a chance to behave so well." This, of course, by their episodic conception of behavior. But Brett does not miss his point of view. She has on a previous occasion obliquely said that love interferes with the values of even episodic people, and now she says, "You know I do know how he feels. He can't believe it didn't mean anything." Seeing him later waiting in the shadow of an arcade, she says, "Poor devil! . . . I hate his damned suffering." But she does not feel responsible, because she refuses to believe that her own behavior implied anything in itself and she certainly intended nothing by it; the fault then, is in him who draws inferences.

It takes more than words to convince Robert Cohn. It takes another action from which, if he drew the same inferences, he could only conclude the error of those he applied to himself. The decisive action is Brett's going off with Romero, motivated both by his attractiveness and her disgust with the behavior of Robert and Mike. Brett's being with Mike has signified nothing to Cohn, since Mike had simply been there first, and Brett could break with him. Cohn's egotism, emphasized from the beginning, prevents him from seeing the truth about Brett from the fact of her going off with him while "engaged" to Mike; that seemed only natural. But Brett's leaving them both for Romero is very clear in its meaning, and in response Robert can only resort to physical violence (also prepared for on the very first page). He beats up Jake, for arranging the assignation, then he beats up Romero, and tries to take Brett away. This finishes him with everyone, and is the climax of his affair with Brett: this is what came of it all. "I'm going away in the morning," he says.

"I just couldn't stand it about Brett. I've been through hell, Jake. It's been simply hell. When I met her down here Brett treated me as though I were a perfect stranger. I just couldn't stand it. We lived together at San Sebastian."

To him it is incomprehensible. "We lived together at San Sebastian." It seemed such an absolute proof. And then to be treated as a stranger! As though to assure himself that something endures, that something links the episodes together, he tries to patch up his friendship with Jake. "You were the only friend I had, and I loved Brett so. . . . Please forgive me, Jake. . . . You'll shake hands, won't you?" But he says, "Now everything's gone. Everything." So Jake was wrong. They *could* take it away from him. To a man for whom the meaning and beauty of an episode depends upon the way it fits into a romantic whole, the incompletion of the whole nullifies the episode.

By her affair with Romero Brett has rid herself of Robert, and from this point the action falls toward the denouement, that is, it comes full circle. The morning after, Jake observes: "It was the first time I had seen her in the old happy, careless way since before she went off with Cohn." In the brief Book III, there remains only the necessity of Brett's ending her new episode with Romero; she ends it, ironically, because he expects it to lead somewhere: to marriage and children, to be something more than an episode. But Brett knows herself at least this well, to know that the attempt would have been ruinous for Romero. She is now what she is—a woman of episodic character—however much she may believe that with Jake she could have been different. Out of the whole sequence, so strangely linked together by the illusions of Robert Cohn, for Brett there is only one gain: the riddance of that very man. "I'm all right again. He's wiped out that damned Cohn." To which Jake says, "Good." They are back where they started.

Hemingway's superimposing of a pyramidal plot upon a circular and episodic naturalistic one gives his book a greater unity than the latter alone could have provided. At the same time a meaningful thematic emphasis is made by the tension that exists between the two plot forms, because they inherently suggest differing views of life which are in varying degrees held by the characters themselves, as the preceding analysis has shown. The two forms are unified into a third distinct but ambiguous form through the point of view of the narrator. Jake Barnes is of necessity an episodic man (in that his life must lack the integrity of conventional social fulfillment or religious commitment), but his entire interest in telling the story of Robert Cohn— who is, after all, only one out of several lovers of Brett, all of whom he must resent—depends upon Cohn's *not* holding the episodic view. Jake's emotional duplicity is what impressionistically unifies the circular and pyramidal forms. Although Cohn, who in the naiveté of his romantic expectations acts out a pathetic three-part drama of love and loss, is of insufficient stature to sustain his role on a heroic level even in his own eyes, his story is further blunted and rendered absurd by the incongruous naturalistic (anti-romantic) frame of reference, by the unresponsiveness of the other characters, and by the complicated attitude of Jake ("I was . . . jealous . . . I took it as a matter of course.") The pyramid of Cohn's affair can be discerned only through the dead sea waters of Jake's own love for Brett. Although Robert links the separate episodes of this particular round together, in the end they only merge, in effect, into one: the Robert Cohn Episode, to be followed by innumerable others.

The peculiar plot of *The Sun Also Rises* thus avoids an implicit dogmatism of form to be found in abstracted conceptions of traditional forms. The linear episodic plot implies a lack of coherent sequence to events but also implies freedom, variety, and unconditioned potentialities in the experiences of the unifying character, as can be seen from *Moll Flanders* to *Augie March;* it may be modified, as in the middle part of *Huckleberry Finn*, by the recurrence and intensification of a situation (Huck's alliance with Jim) which stimulates moral growth and discovery in that character; or, through virtual repetition of pattern it may suggest circularity and thus either futility (as, in isolation, this aspect of *Sun* does) or, if united with natural or religious imagery, a positive cyclical recurrence (birth, death, resurrection), as in *My Antonia*. The pyramidal plot affirms meaningful sequence—even necessity—of events *developing* in response to deliberate actions of characters and having an inevitable ethical consequence: the best examples in American literature are probably *The Scarlet Letter* and *The Great Gatsby*. Gatsby and his story have significant points in common with Robert Cohn and his, but are allowed to dominate the book, with the episodic characters and their world subordinated to Gatsby's attempt to fulfill *his* romantic expectations. There is in *Gatsby* also a finer and purer irony in the point of view of the narrator (Nick fortunately does not love his cousin Daisy), so that Gatsby's dream seems beautiful as well as childish, and his fate even more tragic than pathetic and absurd. In comparison with *The*

Great Gatsby, which truly (if through irony) affirms the possibility of a romantically integrated life, *The Sun Also Rises* seems more assertive of the naturalistic circle of futile discontinuity, more like Chekov's *Three Sisters.* And so it is; my point is simply that while Robert is used to give unity to a series of happenings which still persists in presenting itself as episodic and circular and futile (partly because, as opposed to Gatsby's case, Robert's failure nullifies his whole attempt, and partly because the episodes are given at least equal development in their own discontinuous character), nevertheless the mere existence within the book of a conception of sequence, and its artistic exploitation throughout, in effect present it as an option.

One might argue that the manner in which it is presented, with Robert Cohn as its representative and his puling end as its outcome, renders it rather emphatically *not* as a "live" option, and perhaps even goes further toward negating it than its absolute exclusion would have done. My answer to this is that the assumptions Cohn represents can survive a bad representative of them and his particular fate. Such an assumption, for instance, as that one person acting in relation to another is responsible to a degree for the inferences the other draws from his acts. If one can say that Cohn ought not to have concluded anything from Brett's sleeping with him, one can also say that Brett ought to have discovered beforehand what kind of conclusions Cohn was likely to draw from her sleeping with him; but the egotism of the self-consciously sophisticated (like Daisy: "God, I'm sophisticated!"; and Brett: "We've all been around. . .") allows them to believe that anyone not equally so can suffer the consequences of associating with them ("I hate his damned suffering.") Romantic ethical idealism is at the heart of Hemingway's work: it is the loss of that idealism which is regretted, and it is there to be contemplated by the reader even if it is rendered in terms of characters who as a result of their several wounds have abjured it as inefficacious, or through those like Robert whose particular attempts to act by it fail. The cynicism, bitterness, and self-pity of the point of view of those who have given up hardly recommend it to the reader either, even if he acknowledges it as more "realistic" and as having compensations in the practice of the "code" and in the self-contained sensual pleasures of Paris and Spain. Whatever truth and viability there is in the point of view of the episodic

characters would have been more assertive if Robert Cohn had not been there to present— however feebly— a challenge to their position and to evoke the streaks of meanness and false superiority in Jake and Brett.

Further comparisons emphasize this point. The experiences of Augie March are just as discontinuous but contain an element of joy wholly absent from *The Sun Also Rises,* and thus represent the episodic option more attractively, just as Gatsby shows the other view in its more beautiful if still naive potentials. But if Augie suggests an episodic life more joyous and hopeful, we can see that naturalistic plots can also be made more assertive of pessimism and despair. The design of *Sister Carrie,* for instance: here again is a book in which clear, unifying lines of development are submerged within an episodic world. It is made to *seem* to have the random quality of life itself, as *Sun* is, but the lines of development hidden in it, in contrast, themselves demonstrate a thesis about the "vagaries of fortune." Carrie rises, Hurstwood declines, and Drouet swaggers through on an even level; and not from any moral causes or free choices, but because of incomprehensible forces of determinism. Or consider Frank Norris's *McTeague* (weak as it is, probably our purest example of the *roman experimental,* where all is tightly sequential but deterministic): take this beast with latent capacities for sex and violence, put him in this environment, add one tiny blonde female (who herself is thus subjected to experiment), add one quantity of gold, take away a dental license, and see what happens. This "experiment" is carried out in part through "episodes" of great verisimilitude, each of which contributes to the general realism while playing its part in the dogmatic design by providing behavioristic evidence of environmental and physiological forces.

In contrast to any of the other novels I have mentioned, how tentative and even regretful of its implications, how unassertive for all its clarity, seems the unique form of *The Sun Also Rises.* It attains its high degree of artistic unity, and yet remains true to the essential fragmenting skepticism of its time and of its author, to their distrust of absolutes. A nonsequential style handled thus is not asserting *non sequitur* as final truth, or a dogmatic agnosticism like Dreiser's. It rather tells only what it sees, while suggesting what romantic arteries of continuity it *wishes* might be shown to exist. ("Isn't it pretty to think so?")

Hemingway as Moral Thinker:
A Look at Two Novels

by PAUL RAMSEY

Hemingway was not, in one real sense, a moral thinker at all. He was a writer, a maker of books. To be sure, he thought. He thought what words to use, in what order. He was a thinker in the sense that a bricklayer is: a bricklayer thinks where to lay the bricks. But that is not what we normally mean by "thinker."

In another sense he was not a thinker at all, in that he revered action and often despised thought. He had a very low opinion of "literary" people: he admired soldiers, bullfighters, athletes, hunters. He wanted his books somehow to *be* action, to escape thought. He wished to present reality cleanly, as reality is, without decoration, almost without interposition of words. Words could get in the way of things; reality could falsify the direct response to things. His style is stripped, bare, plain of gesture, firmly conscious of plainness. Had he been thoroughly consistent, he might have put words aside altogether, as he did when he hunted lions and fought wars.

He felt uncomfortable in the presence of ideas. "You'll lose it if you talk about it," one character says. Another says with strong contempt, "A theory, like another." Ideas and the words that represent them are unable to express reality. That idea is in fact one of the ideas most often expressed in his work.

How then can he be called a moral thinker? He can because he was. He seldom engaged in ethical abstractions, but his ideas none the less passionately emerge, in the sympathy or lack of sympathy felt for characters, in his very choice of structures of action, in the slant and power of his imagery and his prose style.

I shall look at those ideas mostly in two novels: *The Sun Also Rises* and *For Whom the Bell Tolls*. First I would like to examine a brief and famous passage in which Hemingway catches some of his most essential views in an image.

The narrator of *A Farewell to Arms*, near the tragic end of the book, remembers seeing ants perish in a campfire. The ants scamper to no avail, some perish early, some later. They suffer and die, and do not understand their pain. Yet it is their nature to fight for being, for survival. In the long run they have no chance. Nothing outside of their world—the burning log —really helps or hinders them. The man does throw some water on the log, but it only steams them. Such, Hemingway is suggesting, is reality. Such is human life.

What sort of reality is that? A reality based on chance or fate, lacking purpose, painful, destructive, inexorable, completely unconcerned for the individual consciousness. It is a world without God or, at the most, a world to which God is indifferent. It is a world without real value. It is a world Hemingway's heroes face, a world in which they must decide how they are to behave, a world in which they must decide what it is to behave well or badly.

The Sun Also Rises and *For Whom the Bell Tolls* seem very different from each other. The first seems pessimistic, the second optimistic. In the first the most important characters desperately drift, in the second they fight for a social cause. But the books are at heart very much alike.

If one turns an unsympathetic eye on *The Sun Also Rises* and applies ordinary moral standards to it, one can be harsh. The book treats sympathetically adultery, drunkenness, self-centeredness, snobbery, self-pity, social irresponsibility, cynicism, atheism, and even anti-Semitism. Robert Cohn is disliked by the others not only for his unattractive qualities but also just because he is Jewish and some very unpleasant things about his being Jewish are said. There is also one example of corrupting the young, when Brett Ashley seduces the nineteen-year-old matador, and something very like pandering when Jake Barnes helps her arrange the seduction. Even though all he does is to introduce them, he does so knowing full well what she is after.

Is such a view of the book fair? No, though it is not entirely unfair either. The cynicism follows from the view of reality I have sketched. The religious scepticism of most of the characters is qualified by the narrator Jake Barnes's sentimental and backsliding Catholicism and his feeling that perhaps there is real meaning in religion. Also Jake Barnes is stauncher than his friends: he endures hardships of war and love more stoically; he presumably does his newspaper work efficiently, though he does not seem very interested in it; his drinking, though heavy, is not top-heavy. The book also suggests strongly that the right sexual relationship is fidelity between people in love. Brett Ashley is largely excused for her promiscuity, because she has led a hard life and because Jake Barnes' war wound makes him unable to satisfy her. Neither she nor the narrator approves her conduct, and at the end she feels better for giving up the young matador, achieving some responsibility to individuals if not to society.

The social irresponsibility of the book is the direct fruit of the extreme individualism of Hemingway. He hardly even sees society as real, except as a threat. The individual is, and the individual is all. Society is just individuals. But individual value is very real: friendship, courage, dignity, and tender sexual love are beautifully praised in the book, even when they are known by their absence.

The narrator reveals something permanent and central in Hemingway when he says that nobody ever lives his life all the way up except bullfighters. In that remark cluster some attitudes which Hemingway is never to leave. The best life is the most intensely active. Man should achieve as much reality as possible, and the greatest reality is individual feeling, especially when interlaced with or threatened by the presence of physical pain or the presence of death. Such activity calls for strong self-discipline, a rightness of means, a sense of honor, and consequent moral restraint. The restraint is, however, for the sake of individual richness of experience, not for some ideal outside the self. The standard is private.

The characters are then individuals reaching out into a moral dark. It is a very dark dark. Their moral position is, finally, impossible. One cannot really, in the long run, believe in one's own values unless one believes that the values are really valuable. But if they are merely one's own values, they are not valuable: they correspond to no reality. One cannot base moral opinions on a view of things which makes all moral opinions false. Modern thinkers try and try and try; but it cannot be done.

The moral and ontological attitudes of *The Sun Also Rises* may be roughly summed up as follows: (1) pessimism—the world and society work against the individual and will in the long run defeat him; (2) stoicism—individuals must bear the harshness of life with a proud dignity; (3) something very like and very unlike traditional hedonism—the book implies that, since death destroys all, one should lead his life as intensely as possible, with an intensity which includes pain as well as pleasure, in order to achieve the most reality, the fullest existence; (4) radical individualism—society exists only as a hostile and indifferent "they" and the individual must hack out his own path; (5) the greatest values are friendship, dignity, and tender sexual love—these are the only basis for genuine community and communities so founded are tragically brief, certain to be split by death, apt at any time to be split by discord. Accompanying these attitudes is an excellent (and highly moral) literary ideal: to present reality as firmly and clearly, and honestly, as possible.

Those views of the book are, I would argue, at once metaphysical and inconsistent. For one cannot consistently hold that the according to one's self to reality, the honest facing of "fact," is genuinely valuable, and at the same time hold that all morality is essentially private armor. Morality is metaphysical or an illusion, and Hemingway does no worse, and in some ways better, than professional philosophers who have tried to bridge the unbridgeable gap.

Nor does Hemingway leave those views. *For Whom the Bell Tolls* seems to depart from them to reach social idealism, but I am not convinced that the journey is a long one. Robert Jordan voluntarily goes from America to Spain to fight for the communists. Yet he offers few arguments, he admits knowing little about communism, and he even says that he is fighting for his belief that all people should be left alone, a view not possible to square with the planned society the communists labor for. Neither he nor Hemingway is very interested in social theory. The reason is, I suggest, that Robert Jordan is Jake Barnes behind a thin veneer, or perhaps we can say he is a "bullfighter," a hero following out a code of personal conduct punctiliously and honorably. His duty does not cohere with abstract or social ideals; it is rather a means of achieving personal dignity and unity.

This is true, underneath, from the beginning. It becomes extremely clear later in the book. At first Jordan feels a sense of exaltation at belonging to the cause. He hates fascist atrocities, wants to save the Spanish people from them. Later he becomes largely disillusioned, and the exaltation vanishes. He sees grim atrocities committed by the communists; he sees petty and malicious bickering and intrigues; he has reason to fear for the future of the peasant. Yet his duty stays firm. It is no longer duty *to* anything; it is something *he* needs to keep himself intact against the stern facts of life and death.

The attitudes toward religion are very close to those in *The Sun Also Rises*. The book is mostly sceptical, with some tentative religious patches. The patches are different from those of the earlier book. Instead of the Catholicism there are gypsy mysteries and the semimystical bond of love between Robert and Maria. But the fundamental attitudes are similar to what they were in *The Sun Also Rises*. Anselmo, a sympathetic character, says that he clearly misses God but that a man must be responsible to himself. Jordan speaks of the consolation of religion when death is near, but adds that he prefers to face death "straight." We are back to the log and the ants and modern pessimism. Man, lonely, against a senseless world.

93

The love between Robert Jordan and Maria is impressive and tender, yet somehow—even in the most famous scene—less impressive, less convincing than the tender and tragic love in *A Farewell to Arms* or the wildly frustrated and intense love of *The Sun Also Rises*. I feel in the great claims made there for love a desperateness. Perhaps Robert Jordan does not believe what he says to Maria about the transcendental bond of their love. Perhaps he is merely cheering her up because, though he faces death straight, he does not wish her to. But I cannot help feeling that he at least says what Hemingway would have liked to believe and could not.

The attitudes for *For Whom the Bell Tolls* may be summed up as very much like those of *The Sun Also Rises:* pessimism (behind the optimism of the social hope); individualism (despite the social idealism offered, then put aside), stoicism, a hedonism which includes the value of facing pain, the temporary and fragile values of friendship, love, personal courage and dignity. The attitudes have changed little. Nor do I believe that they change much in later works. They are the ideals of a lonely individual in a world he does not understand, that he does not believe can in any real measure be understood.

An idol is a limited reality set up as the greatest reality. Hemingway's work can justly be called idolatrous. All literary art in some sense must be: writers are people; people are fallible and contingent beings. But, even relatively, Hemingway's limits are severe. And I would like to say plainly that I believe his work has done moral harm: it has encouraged self-pity, self-indulgence, sexual and social and religious irresponsibility. But that is not to say that his attitudes are worthless. They are valuable precisely to the degree to which they achieve and fit reality. For to call them meta-physically confused, as I have, is to imply that they have some serious truth within them. In Hemingway's work they can lead to discipline, order, beauty, and dignity, and should be respected.

And Hemingway is a better artist than moralist. His view of art is essentially moral. I do not believe that that view is consonant with his ontological assumptions, but I am glad that he held it. He believed that art should be honest before the facts, not fake. His view of the "facts" is limited: his work misses much of reality. But what is seen is seen often with superb precision and energetic beauty, the style clean, the eye precisely on the object. He knew something of the facts of human personality, especially its dignity and loneliness in times of trial. His best work is a valuable and intense image of human life. Of his age, self-consciously of a generation, he achieved much that is universal, much of composed and dignified strength. He was a very good writer. I suspect that in one sense he was a truly great writer. He was a great descriptive writer.

For one holding his views, the physical universe should be as senseless as human society. But, for him, it was not. Nature was to him worthy of enormous and awed respect. He treated it as though it were created, though most of the time he did not believe that it was. It is the physical facts which come most powerfully alive in his work, whether the facts of action, or of cities, or of landscapes. He found the physical world good and rendered it with a splendid artistic discipline that conveyed and reflected the truth of that goodness. To have done so was a morally good thing to do. It expressed knowledge. It expressed love. Love and knowledge are the touchstones of genuine morality and quite near the essence of the redemptive power of art.

Faulkner, Hemingway, and the 1920's

by WILLIAM VAN O'CONNOR

William Faulkner was a poor student, and left high school after the tenth grade for a job in his grandfather's bank. He read widely, wrote poetry, painted pictures, and sketched. He was a friend of Phil Stone, a young lawyer who had attended Yale and who knew quite a lot about the then new writers, such as T. S. Eliot, Conrad Aiken, Eugene O'Neill, Sherwood Anderson, and many others.

Because he was only five-feet-five in height, Faulkner was turned down by the United States Army. He joined the Royal Flying Corps in Toronto, Canada, as a cadet. This gave him some of the material he would use in his first novel, *Soldier's Pay*. As a veteran, he was allowed to enroll at the University of Mississippi, where he studied English, Spanish, and French. He was in residence for one academic year. He took a job in New York, in a bookstore, where he met a Miss Prall, who would shortly be married to Sherwood Anderson. The job did not last long, and Faulkner was soon back in Oxford. With the help of Phil Stone, he published a volume of poetry, *The Marble Faun*.

There have been a number of studies of Faulkner's reading, reviews and comments from this period of his life — his apprenticeship. Clearly the young Faulkner was no yokel. He may not have had a critic's mind, but he had a craftsman's sense of what he, with his talents, could use or find meaningful. Stone later said Faulkner was not interested in books on aesthetics or criticism; he was interested in fiction, in poetry, and drama. He kept up with *Poetry, The Dial, The Little Review, The Egoist,* and much besides. His early reviews for *The Mississippian* have been collected in *William Faulkner: Early Poetry and Prose,* by Carvel Collins. His *Times Picayune* sketches about the artists' quarter in New Orleans have also been reprinted. A small Wisconsin publisher long ago issued some of his *Double Dealer* poems and manifestoes.

Faulkner's sensitivity to the sort of writing he could use appears early. In 1921, he wrote, "In the fog generated by mental puberty of American versifiers while writing inferior Keats or sobbing over the Middle West, appears one rift of heaven sent blue—the poems by Conrad Aiken. He, alone of the entire yelping pack, seems to have a definite goal in mind. . . ." He deplored "Mr. Vachel Lindsay with his tin pan and iron spoon, Mr. Kreymborg with his lithographic water coloring, and Mr. Carl Sandburg with his sentimental Chicago propaganda."

T.S. Eliot seems to have moved him—at least to plagiarism—more than any other contemporary poet. Many of Faulkner's poems are obviously borrowed from Eliot. *Mosquitoes,* his second novel, has many Eliotic phrases. One is "Spring and the cruelest month were gone. The cruel months. . . ." Another is

> The Raven bleak and Philomel
> Amid the bleeding trees were fixed,
> His hoarse cry and hers were mixed
> And through the dark their droppings fell

Mr. Talliafero is a J. Alfred Prufrock type, and, in fact, Faulkner rather frequently refers to Prufrock. In *Pylon,* his most waste land-like novel, he models The Reporter, his central character, on J. Alfred Prufrock. In *Sartoris* he had his woodlands "splashed with dogwood and judas trees," and he has "a dying fall." There are, in later books, such phrases as "a thousand indecisions," and "tell me what you're thinking about, tell me."

Keats became a lasting influence. Faulkner sees Darl Bundren and Jewell struggling "like two figures in a Greek frieze." Hightower sees his life "like a classic and serene vase, where the spirit could be born anew and sheltered from the harsh glare of living. . . . " In *The Bear* it is Keats on beauty and truth who points to the story's central meaning.

The titles, quotations and allusions Faulkner takes from Shakespeare and the Bible are many. As a Southerner, living in a kind of theocracy, Faulkner knew the Bible, even though he attacked the churches and righteous Christians who hid their viciousness in pious phrases.

Although young and overflowing with cynicism, Faulkner recognized that Conrad "wrote of the eternal verities." He read and reread *The Nigger of the Narcissus,* "Falk," "The End of the Tether," "Youth," *Heart of Darkness, Victory* and *Lord Jim.* Internal evidence makes it clear that *Absalom, Absalom!* is structurally indebted to *Lord Jim* and, especially, to *Chance.* In fact, Faulkner's methods of narration are a development out of Conrad. And Faulkner's images are often borrowed from him: "The world was becoming dimensionless, the tall bearded cypresses drew nearer one to another across the wallowing river with the soulless implacability of pagan gods, gazing down upon this mahogany-and-brass intruder with inscrutable unalarm." If Marlowe and Stein could have known Faulkner, they'd have said, "He is one of us."

The influence of Joyce was also considerable,

especially in *Mosquitoes, The Sound and the Fury,* and *As I Lay Dying.* Faulkner has also acknowledged Dickens, especially the meaningful exaggerations and distortions. He later justified his Snopes creations by saying they were not realistic—they were his own sort of Dickensian characters. There are other writers, including Russian novelists too, who influenced the young Faulkner.

In 1925, Faulkner went to New Orleans, intending to work on a freighter, thereby paying his way to Europe. But in New Orleans he got to know Sherwood Anderson and other writers. He contributed to the *Times Picayune* and wrote for the *Double Dealer,* a "little magazine" that published Hart Crane, Hemingway, and others. During this period he wrote *Soldier's Pay.*

Even before going to New Orleans, Faulkner had been impressed by Sherwood Anderson. Faulkner would later say that Anderson had made modern American writing possible—he had opened the way for writers like Hemingway and himself. And he long regretted his early satirizing of the older writer in *Sherwood Anderson and Other Creoles.*

In a review published in the spring of 1925, Faulkner called "I'm a Fool" the best American short story. And he praises the descriptions in *Winesburg, Ohio:* "behind all of them [the characters—there is] a ground of fecund earth and corn in the green spring and the slow full hot summer and the rigorous masculine winter."

Faulkner and Anderson were temperamentally unsuited to each other, and often quarreled, but Faulkner, even in the last years of his life, continued to praise Anderson and to ask that he be given his proper recognition.

Faulkner and a painter named William Spratling did ship out of New Orleans on a freighter, and toured Italy and France, mostly on foot. In Paris, Faulkner later recorded, he sought out the cafe where he had heard he could see Joyce. Faulkner entered, looked at Joyce, and left. Back in New York, he found his first novel published. It was favorably received, but made no great impact.

In Pascagoula, Mississippi, he wrote a second novel, *Mosquitoes* based on his New Orleans experiences. Dawson Fairchild, one of the chief characters, is based on Sherwood Anderson. Anderson and Faulkner had "worked up" a number of "tall tales," highly exaggerated and bizarre stories, and a couple of them are incorporated in the novel.

Another literary "influence" on Faulkner—one would hesitate to call it a debt—from the 1920's was Ernest Hemingway. Like Scott Fitzgerald, Faulkner was troubled by Hemingway's early success and great eminence—and later Heming-way was troubled by Faulkner's eminence.

On several occasions William Faulkner referred to the fiction written by Ernest Hemingway. Usually he made the point that Hemingway early discovered what he could do as an artist—and was satisfied to repeat himself. Considering that Hemingway's success came before Faulkner's and for a period his reputation greatly overshadowed Faulkner's, such expressions might appear at least injudicious.

Injudicious or not, they were just. Almost all of the Hemingway critics agree that the Hemingway characters and situations recur in novel after novel. Faulkner, especially during his middle period, was a restless and a tireless experimenter, attempting to define his own "world." It would be understandable if he sometimes felt a little jealous of Hemingway's popularity.

In July, 1936, Professor Harry Burns spent some days visiting Hemingway at Key West. He recalls that Hemingway praised Faulkner very highly, saying he deserved more attention and acclaim than he was getting. Burns, Hemingway, and Hemingway's wife drove from Florida to New Orleans, and Burns also recalls that Hemingway, in passing through Mississippi, kept putting both arms up in the air and declaiming, "This is the Faulkner country!" In 1952, after Faulkner had been given the Nobel Prize, Hemingway tended, in a later conversation wth Burns, to minimize Faulkner's gifts. Hemingway, of course, would receive the Nobel Prize in 1954.

In the light of the lives of the two men, one dead in 1961 by his own hand, the other a year later, after continuing to write and to publish at something like his old pace if with something less than the old fire, it may be useful to take a look at their rather one-sided relationship. Faulkner, born in 1897, was a year older than Hemingway, but was slower at finding himself as an artist. *The Sound and the Fury* and *A Farewell to Arms* were both published in 1929. But *The Sun Also Rises* had been published in 1926, the same year as *Soldier's Pay. Mosquitoes* (1927) and *Sartoris* (1929) would intervene before Faulkner would hit his stride.

During his stay in New Orleans in the early months of 1925, Faulkner undoubtedly heard Sherwood Anderson talk about Hemingway. Anderson and Hemingway had known each other since the winter of 1920-21. And in the literary circles that supported the little magazines Hemingway early developed a good reputation as a writer doing something quite new. In 1923 the *Little Review* carried several of his stories. The same year the Dijon Press of Robert McAlmon published *Three Stories* and *Ten Poems.* Other stories appeared in Ford

Madox Ford's *Transatlantic.* Two editions of *In Our Time* appeared, one in 1923, and the other in New York in 1925. One may assume that Faulkner in writing *Soldier's Pay* knew the Hemingway stance, and the Hemingway *dramatis personae.*

Throughout these early years Faulkner was trying to free himself from Hemingway. As late as 1939, with *The Wild Palms,* he is carrying on his own "dialogue" with Hemingway. An understanding of that book is crucial if one is to understand the relationships of the two men, the two "contenders," as Hemingway would have said, for the championship. But first a look at the early works.

Soldier's Pay, in large part, reads like a pastiche of *The Sun Also Rises.* Joe Gilligan and Margaret Powers are ineffective variations on Jake Barnes and Lady Brett. Faulkner seems always on the verge of treating them satirically. He appears not to have believed in them. On the other hand he had not found what the Southern town—this one in Georgia—signified for him. He is trying to see people in the post World War I society as Hemingway did, as divided into "initiates," like Gilligan and Margaret, and "messy" types, like Cecily Saunders and some of her associates. But none of these characters are a part of Faulkner's own vision—they are all borrowed.

With *Mosquitoes* something of the same air of being initiated is maintained, but the novel shifts from one focus to another, and was essentially Faulkner's "Hemingway world," not the "world" Faulkner himself was trying to discover. Bayard Sartoris is a Southern "initiate," except that he doesn't understand the Hemingway code. He feels the old Southern world once had glamor and romance. But the universe is dying, and the Player (God as chess player) had tired of the old romances. Bayard feels empty, bleak, hopeless—and seeks his own death. Although there are many beautiful and moving scenes having to do with the lives of the "red neck" McCallums and the terribly poor Negro family, Faulkner continues to mistake the nature of his subject. Bayard tries to see a "solution" in his family's past, whereas the solution was in the present, in the lives of the patient McCallums and the long-suffering Negroes. Bayard rejected the universe, and was rejected by it. The McCallums and the poor Negroes accept whatever they have to accept—and thereby overcome it.

Acceptance would be one of the chief doctrines in *The Sound and the Fury, As I Lay Dying, Light in August,* and *The Hamlet.* Dilsey is a great *accepter.* She endures. *As I Lay Dying* is about what a man has to accept if he would get on top of life, and make it

meaningful. *Light in August* is about the peace of the human heart. Joe Christmas rejects, but Lena Grove and Byron Bunch accept. And Reverend Gail Hightower learns to accept too. In doing so each achieves peace. In *The Hamlet* Faulkner presents the ancient doctrine of comedy: after suffering for his own foolishness and weaknesses, man picks up the pieces and begins over again.

With these works back of him, Faulkner wrote *The Wild Palms,* which we have called his "dialogue" with Hemingway. Several people have pointed out the similarities between the love story part of *The Wild Palms* and *A Farewell to Arms.* One of the more recent is H. Edward Richardson, in "The 'Hemingwaves' in Faulkner's 'Wild Palms' " (*Modern Fiction Studies,* Winter, 1958-9). The commentary is useful in pointing up the borrowings, but does not make clear what Faulkner was really trying to say.

The love story of *The Wild Palms* has many parallels with *A Farewell to Arms.* Henry Wilbourne, a young intern, falls in love with Charlotte, married and the mother of two children. Charlotte, the more dedicated of the two, urges their absolute commitment to love. She believes that society destroys love. They live in Chicago, on a lake in northern Wisconsin, at a mine in Utah. They know cold and poverty, but nothing is allowed to interfere with their love. Charlotte becomes pregnant, and urges Wilbourne to perform an abortion. For a time he refuses but then does perform it. They return to the Gulf Coast. Charlotte hemorrhages, and dies. Wilbourne is arrested, tried, and sent to prison.

Lieutenant Frederick Henry and Catherine Barkley also resign from society. Like Faulkner's couple, Henry and Catherine feel the world is blind to the needs of lovers. The idyll of love enjoyed by Hemingway's characters is more peaceful than the "idyll" of Faulkner's lovers, but both women die, one from abortion, the other after childbirth.

In both stories the men say that if society catches "you out of step once" (Wilbourne) or "off base" (Henry) it destroys you. When near death both women are on fire from pain, and say "Don't touch me." In both stories the men are reluctantly allowed to see the corpses of their lovers. In *The Wild Palms* defeat is symbolized by the palms, jeering and visible in the wind; in *A Farewell to Arms* it is the rain.

As Mr. Richardson points out, there is a passage, during the Chicago interlude, in which the character named McCord says, "Yah, . . . Set, ye armourous sons, in a sea of heming-waves." He is a bluff newspaperman, and sounds like a Hemingway character or like

Hemingway himself. Outdoorsy, he belongs to the country associated with Nick Adams' fishing and hunting adventures in Michigan. At one point Wilbourne says he has learned something about love from McCord, and adds, "Give me a blessing." " 'Take my curse,' McCord said."

Most commentaries on *The Wild Palms* and *A Farewell to Arms* state that Hemingway's love story is more poignant and touching than Faulkner's—and it is. But Faulkner's *all-for-love* is not "loaded" to the extent that Hemingway's is. Charlotte's love is at the expense of her husband, her children, her own life, and Wilbourne's career and peace of mind. She is not in love with Wilbourne; she is in love with love. Love is her way of giving intensity to her life. Like Hemingway initiates she finds the *meaning* in sex and love. In a sense, Wilbourne is her victim.

Faulkner is not saying he accepts the doctrine that society destroys love. On the contrary, he is saying that an excessive commitment to love is itself destructive.

In commenting about the two story strands in *The Wild Palms*, Faulkner said that when he finished the first chapter of the love story he felt something was missing. "So I wrote on the Old Man story until *The Wild Palms* rose back to pitch."

"Old Man" is a criticism of the love story. The tall convict accepts his obligations and goes to almost ridiculous lengths to satisfy his sense of duty. He fights the river in flood, subdues snakes and alligators, avoids bullets intended for him, and voluntarily returns to prison after anguishing adventures. In his bunk, he enjoys watching the smoke from his cigar curl upward in the twilight. He asks only "permission to endure and endure to buy air, to feel sun," to feel the earth under his feet. Like Dilsey or Byron Bunch, the tall convict is one of Faulkner's *accepters*. Like another Faulkner character, he does not believe "life is supposed to be easy on folks." Nor would he try to divide the world into the sophisticated, knowing "initiates" and the "messy ones." He knows, although he would not know how to say it, "love no more exists just at one spot and in one moment and in one body out of all the earth and all time . . . than sunlight does."

The "Hemingway world," with the sleepless man, tricked by the universe, emphasizes defeat and rejection. After his initial attempt to understand the "lost generation" stance, Faulkner moved toward an "acceptance." He moved from characters like Gilligan and Bayard Sartoris to Byron Bunch and the "Tall Convict." In the process, he carried on a kind of dialogue with the eminent personage of Hemingway. It is an interesting dialogue because it has something to do with their own lives and a great deal to do with their literary legacies.

When Faulkner was twenty-eight years old and just beginning to write fiction, Sherwood Anderson warned him that he had almost too much talent, that it might use him and prevent his development. That Faulkner did not allow this to happen is now quite clear. A writer's contemporaries are frequently mistaken, or so posterity feels, in the men they single out for acclaim. Faulkner's contemporaries have been a little slow to place him in the line of greatness, which suggests that they had first to learn in what ways he has used that originality to quicken the permanent truths. Genius being rare, we may assume that posterity will neither forget nor neglect him.

ABOUT THE CONTRIBUTORS

SISTER M. JOSELYN BALDESHWILER, Order of St. Benedict, holds an M.A. from the University of Minnesota and a Ph.D. from Fordham. She has published critical articles in COLLEGE ENGLISH, RENASCENCE, SOUTH DAKOTA REVIEW, and STUDIES IN SHORT FICTION. Her work has appeared in two University of Nebraska Press volumes: *Literature and Society,* and *Myth and Symbol.* She has done book-length translations from French for several publishers. Sister Joselyn is Chairman of the English department at the College of St. Scholastica, in Duluth, Minnesota, and recently was awarded an AAUW Post-Doctoral Fellowship to work on her forthcoming book on the lyric short story.

RICHARD CALHOUN has taught at Davidson College and teaches now at Clemson University. He is currently on leave as Research Fellow in the Humanities at Duke University and the University of North Carolina. His articles on literary criticism and modern poetry have appeared in various journals. He earned his A.B. at Peabody College, his M.A. at Johns Hopkins University, and his Ph.D. at the University of North Carolina.

FREDERIC I. CARPENTER is a Research Associate in English at the University of California (Berkeley). He was educated at Harvard and the University of Chicago, and has taught at both those universities. He has published several books: *Emerson and Asia; Emerson Handbook; American Literature and the Dream; Robinson Jeffers;* and *Eugene O'Neill.* Much of the material included in his Jeffers essay in this volume is drawn from his lengthy correspondence with Jeffers.

FRANK DOGGETT is an unusual high school principal, at Duncan U. Fletcher Senior High School, Neptune Beach, Florida, whose critical articles have appeared in dozens of scholarly journals, such as THE SEWANEE REVIEW, THE EMORY UNIVERSITY QUARTERLY, THE EXPLICATOR, THE NEW ENGLAND QUARTERLY, CRITICISM, COLLEGE ENGLISH, CHICAGO REVIEW, and the JOURNAL OF ENGLISH LITERARY HISTORY. His book on Wallace Stevens, *Stevens' Poetry of Thought,* has received high critical praise in manuscript and is now being considered by Johns Hopkins University Press, for publication.

MALCOLM S. GLASS took his A.B. at Stetson University, his M.A. at Vanderbilt University, and has done work toward his Ph.D. while teaching English at Austin Peay State College,

in Tennessee. He is a widely published young poet, and his work has appeared in many of the "little" magazines and academic journals.

SHELDON GREBSTEIN is the author of *Monkey Trial, Sinclair Lewis, John O'Hara,* is editing a collection of critical essays to be called *Types of Contemporary Criticism,* and recently contracted to write a book on Ernest Hemingway. He has published many critical articles in such journals as NEW ENGLAND QUARTERLY, ENGLISH JOURNAL, WESTERN HUMANITIES REVIEW, THE HUMANIST, and MIDCONTINENT AMERICAN STUDIES JOURNAL. His book reviews have appeared in AMERICAN LITERATURE and SOUTHERN FOLKLORE QUARTERLY. He was educated at the University of Southern California, Columbia University, and Michigan State University. He has taught at the University of Kentucky, the University of South Florida, and is now at Harpur College.

MAX HALPEREN took his B.S. at City College of New York, his M.A. and Ph.D. at Florida State University, and is now an Associate Professor of English at North Carolina State University, Raleigh, N. C. His critical articles have appeared in TRACE, FLORIDA STATE UNIVERSITY STUDIES, and THE EXPLICATOR. He is a poet, whose work has appeared in various magazines, and is co-Editor (with Guy Owen) of SOUTHERN POETRY REVIEW.

FREDERICK J. HOFFMAN, a widely known American scholar, has produced such books as *Freudianism and the Literary Mind, The Twenties, William Faulkner,* and *The Mortal No: Death and the Modern Imagination.* Educated at Stanford University, the University of Minnesota, and Ohio State University, he has taught at Pasadena Junior College, the University of Chicago, Ohio State University, and the University of California (Riverside). In the fall of 1965 he will assume the post of Distinguished Professor of English at the University of Wisconsin.

SY KAHN is a well known contemporary poet who received his A.B. degree from the University of Pennsylvania, his M.A. from the University of Connecticut, and his Ph.D. from the University of Wisconsin. He has published two books of poetry: *Our Separate Darkness* and *Triptych;* dozens of poems and critical articles in magazines and journals; and his explication of Crane's *The Monster,* published in *Essays in Modern American Literature,* attracted a good deal of critical praise. He teaches now at Raymond College, in California, and has taught at the University of Connecticut, the University of Wisconsin, Beloit College, the University of South Florida, and the University of Salonika, Greece, where he was Fulbright Lecturer. He recently received a Borestone Mountain Poetry Award for a best poem published in the United States during 1964.

MAURICE KRAMER took his A.B. and M.A. degrees at the University of Pennsylvania, and his Ph.D. at Harvard University. He has taught at Harvard and Rutgers, and is now at Brooklyn College, where he teaches modern American literature. His criticism has appeared in various scholarly journals.

HILTON LANDRY has written (with Maurice Kramer) a concordance to the poems of Hart Crane; is editing the papers and letters of Elinor Wylie; has published a book, *Interpretations in Shakespeare's Sonnets;* and his essays on Shakespeare, Blake, Gogol, and many others have appeared in various scholarly journals. He has received a grant from the American Philosophical Society, and the Society for Religion in Higher Education has awarded him a Cross-Disciplinary Post Doctoral Fellowship. He was educated at Harvard College and Harvard University, and teaches now at the University of California (Davis).

RICHARD E. LANGFORD was educated at the University of Florida and Stetson University; he served as General Editor of *Essays in Modern American Literature,* the initial publication of Stetson University Press, and his essay, "Eugene O'Neill: The Mask of Illusion," appeared in that volume. With Guy Owen and William E. Taylor, he has edited several editions of *IMPETUS,* a poetry journal (now entitled SOUTHERN POETRY REVIEW). His account of his 10,000 mile voyage aboard the brigantine *Albatross,* a school ship, won him a READER'S DIGEST First Person Award in October, 1961. He teaches American literature at Stetson University.

GUY OWEN is a poet, novelist, editor, and teacher who is currently a Professor of English at North Carolina State University, Raleigh, N. C. With Richard E. Langford and William E. Taylor he edited *Essays in Modern American Literature,* and his essay, "Imagery and Meaning in *The Great Gatsby,*" was included in that volume. While teaching at Stetson University he started (with William E. Taylor) IMPETUS, a poetry journal, and edited that publication for several years; that annual is now called SOUTHERN POETRY REVIEW, and is edited by Guy Owen and Max Halperen, in

Raleigh, N. C. Owen and William E. Taylor collected and published an anthology of verse entitled *Southern Poetry Today,* in 1962. Professor Owen's first novel, *Season of Fear,* was published by Random House in 1960; his second, *The Ballad of the Flim Flam Man,* was published by Macmillan in 1965 and is now being filmed by Twentieth Century-Fox. He has published poems, articles, essays, reviews, short stories, etc. in dozens of magazines and journals and was awarded the Henry Bellamann Foundation Award for fiction in 1965. His three degrees are all from the University of North Carolina.

PAUL RAMSEY is a widely published poet whose work has appeared in many periodicals and anthologies, such as THE PARIS REVIEW, THE HUDSON REVIEW, QUARTERLY REVIEW OF LITERATURE, THE TRANSATLANTIC REVIEW, IMPETUS, and others. His book of criticism, *The Lively and the Just,* was published in 1962, and his new book of poems, *In An Ordinary Place,* will be published in September, 1965, by the Southern Poetry Review Press, University of North Carolina (Raleigh). His A.B. and his M.A. are from University of North Carolina (Chapel Hill) and his Ph.D. is from the University of Minnesota.

JOHN H. RANDALL III was educated at Columbia University and the Universities of California and Minnesota. He has taught at Northwestern University and Wellesley, has been a Fulbright Lecturer in Belgium, and teaches now at Boston College. He has received a Ford Foundation Teaching Internship award and a grant from the American Philosophical Society; his book, *The Landscape and the Looking Glass: Willa Cather's Search for Value,* won in manuscript the Houghton Mifflin-NEW ENGLAND QUARTERLY literary fellowship award. His other publications include articles in American and foreign periodicals on Poe, Ellison, Salinger, and James, the latest of which, "The Genteel Reader and *Daisy Miller,*" will be published in AMERICAN QUARTERLY.

M. K. SINGLETON took his A.B. degree from Yale University and his M.A. and Ph.D. from Duke. His book, *H. L. Mencken and the 'American Mercury' Adventure,* attracted national attention and he has taught "Mencken seminars" at the University of Wisconsin and at San Diego State College. He teaches now at the University of California (Berkeley).

ROBERT O. STEPHENS teaches at the University of North Carolina at Greensboro. His Ph.D. is from the University of Texas; he has published articles about Texas oil folklore, colonial American literature, and on Ernest Hemingway and F. Scott Fitzgerald. He is at work now on a book about Hemingway's journalistic writings and recently won a Duke-University of North Carolina Cooperative Program in the Humanities Fellowship for 1965-66.

WILLIAM E. TAYLOR took his three degrees at Vanderbilt University. He has taught at Lincoln Memorial University, Vanderbilt, and is now a Professor of English at Stetson University. His volume of poems, *Man in the Wind*, was published as IMPETUS CHAPBOOK #1, in 1960, and he was an editor (with Richard E. Langford and Guy Owen) of *Essays in Modern American Literature*, Stetson University Press, 1963; his essay, "Tennessee Williams: Academia on Broadway," appeared in that volume. With Guy Owen he edited *Southern Poetry Today*, an anthology of recent Southern poetry (IMPETUS CHAPBOOK #2, 1962) and served as co-Editor of IMPETUS, a poetry journal. His essay, "The New Poetics or Who Shot Tennyson's Eagle?" appeared in TRACE #57. He is now preparing a second volume of poems for publication and is at work on a novel of contemporary Florida.

ROBERT G. TUCKER has long been interested in e.e. cummings. In 1954-55 he was project supervisor for a series of taped radio broadcasts with New England poets, including cummings. Professor Tucker has published poetry in such places as THE MASSACHUSETTS REVIEW, NEW CAMPUS WRITING NUMBER 4, THE NEW YORK TIMES, and in other journals and periodicals. His short stories and articles have appeared in THE MASSACHUSETTS REVIEW, THE CEA CRITIC, etc. His book of poems, *A Way of Looking*, was published in *Curious Quire*, by the University of Massachusetts, in 1962. He earned his A.B. at Amherst, M.A. at Harvard, and his Ph.D. at the State University of Iowa. He has taught at Amherst, and is now at the University of Massachusetts.

WILLIAM L. VANCE took his M.A. at Oberlin College and his Ph.D. at the University of Michigan. He is an Assistant Professor in English at Boston University.

WILLIAM VAN O'CONNER published his first collection of poems in 1964 (*High Meadow*. Everett Edwards Press, Inc.) but his books, essays, articles, reviews and anthologies are widely known and used both in the United States and abroad. He has written more than a half dozen volumes of criticism, a book of short stories (*Campus on the River*), and with Allen Tate, Robert Penn Warren, and Leonard Unger he is an editor of the University of Minnesota Pamphlets on American Writers. He has contributed *William Faulkner* and *Ezra Pound* to that series. Professor O'Connor has had grants and awards from the Fulbright Commission, Rockefeller Foundation, and was Berg Professor of English and American literature at New York University. He recently returned from England, where he served as Visiting Professor of American Studies at the University of Hull, Hull, England. A Columbia University Ph.D., Mr. O'Connor is now Professor of English at the University of California (Davis).

EDWARD WAGENKNECHT has had a long and productive academic career. He has produced standard histories of both the English and the American novel; biographies of Hawthorne, Washington Irving, Poe, Harriet Beecher Stowe, and Charles Dickens; and many other books, essays, and articles of critical importance. He was educated at the University of Chicago and the University of Washington, has taught at both those universities and at the Illinois Institute of Technology, and is now at Boston University.